PLUCK

PLUCK

Resourceful courage; spirit.

**A FAITH BASED MEMOIR of Living with
Electromagnetic Hypersensitivity**

Deborah A. Hyatt

XULON PRESS

Xulon Press
2301 Lucien Way #415
Maitland, FL 32751
407.339.4217
www.xulonpress.com

The information presented in this book is in no way intended to be used as medical advice or to replace medical counseling. The contents are intended to be used in conjunction with the care and guidance of your personal physician.

Unless otherwise indicated, Scripture quotations taken from The Woman's Study Bible New King James Version (NKJV). Copyright © 1995 by Thomas Nelson, Inc. Used by permission. All rights reserved

Printed in the United States of America.
Photography credits: R. A. Bond
ISBN-13: 978-1-54564-961-9

In loving memory
of
Dr. William J. Rea
February 2, 1935 – August 16, 2018

Forward

Deborah was hoping when she visited our church building to worship with us, that she would be able to make it through our one-hour service because our little church did not have a speaker system, fluorescent lights, or an electronic band. Forms of electricity and electronics like that are especially bad for people who have Electromagnetic Hypersensitivity (EHS). But, after having to be carried out of the service completely unable to use her body, she knew she couldn't continue worshipping with us.

This book is the story of someone who can't go into a grocery store, bank, most public buildings, or anywhere else with electricity or electronics. For years she found refuge in a tent, and now lives in a house with the breakers turned off.

At first some were skeptical, but we have concluded that EHS is not made up. We've seen first-hand how Deborah has to live with its effects and limitations. We have compared it to the way that kryptonite effects Superman—painful, and strength sapping.

She has sought help for EHS from various kinds of doctors and treatments, but her greatest source of healing and strength has been her strong faith and trust in God and the support of Christian friends who love her and regularly lift her up in prayer.

Those who suffer from EHS will find understanding, encouragement, and perhaps faith from this book to help them along their difficult journey.

Bob and Linda Abel, Co-Pastors
Hayesville Presbyterian Church
Hayesville, NC

My experience of Deborah Hyatt is that she is one of those rare individuals who consciously chooses to create wisdom out of her experiences. She harbors a wealth of knowledge for addressing Electromagnetic Field (EMF) Sensitivity that changes being "disabled" to being "differently-abled." I have observed her faith as a powerful foundation that supports her in all ways, including staying creative and resilient within her journey.

Elaine Mueller, RN, HN-BC

As a society, we take for granted so many things. Just for a moment, consider a world that becomes difficult to function in, as a result of not being able to use modern conveniences. Where the simple task of heating or cooling your house brings discomfort to you. A refrigerator makes you so sick, from the motor that runs it, that you have to house it in the garage away from your living space. Imagine the simple task of communicating with loved ones by phone becoming a painful, debilitating process.

Contrary to today's technology, Deborah has shown fortitude by being able to exist under challenging and limited circumstances. She remains a strong role model to those who know her. By watching her actions, she has supplied me with a renewed strength to obtain things I never thought were possible.

Mary D.C. Marcinek, RN, CMSRN

Deborah Hyatt has managed to survive with the help of God and her own determination. All of our patients should take a lesson from her. We are extremely proud of her.

William J. Rea, M.D.
Environmental Health Center - Dallas

Contents

Pluck by Definition

The American Heritage dictionary defines:

PLUCK:
Resourceful courage and daring in the face of difficulties; spirit.

S haring my story with my friend, "The Professor," provoked him to call me "Pluck." Upon hearing that for the first time — unfamiliar with the word, I was tempted to slap him. What was I thinking?

Anyway, after looking up the definition of the word *pluck* in the American Heritage dictionary, as described above, it became apparent why this would become my newly-earned nickname. I found myself using pink nail polish (the only resource available to me at the time) to paint PLUCK on the front of my kayak as a reminder of my spunk, with each launch out to camp on the islands on Lake Chatuge; to get relief from my condition. More on that later; read on.

Although this book is a true story, some of the names have been changed to protect the privacy of the individuals. However, Dr. William Rea is the doctor who diagnosed me; he is non-fiction.

Purpose

To everything there is a season,
A time for every purpose under heaven
Ecclesiastes 3:1

The purpose of this book is to enlighten anyone who is unfamiliar with EMF (Electro Magnetic Field) sensitivities. To bring awareness of the harmful effects the signals transmit and to show how faith plays a powerful role in coping with what life deals our way.

The disease is referred to as EMF (Electro Magnetic Field) sensitivities, EHS (Electromagnetic Hypersensitivity) or ES (Electromagnetic sensitivity). All of the different names being one of the same. It is the up-and-coming environmental illness.

Cellphone radiation is a serious issue. By sharing my story and the knowledge that I have acquired along my harrowing journey, I hope to prevent other people from having to experience the same. I share resources and ways to protect yourself before you become sickly, or to share the tools to heal if you are already affected.

I went through the process of: shock upon learning my diagnosis, to giving up the lifestyle I had become accustomed to, to staying out of society for extended periods of times, to camping for relief, to making changes in a new residence to be able to tolerate the indoors through winter. I endured everything from ridicule and humiliation, being the butt of jokes when I tried to share my new reality, to total acceptance of my condition. I have learned through lots of hard work to manage my EMF illness.

This is not a God-inflicted illness. What I have is a man-made illness. Our society is upping technology faster than our bodies can adapt. Add today's exposures with a lifetime of toxins and it's no wonder I imploded.

Not everyone is susceptible to the degree of meltdown that I had, nor will they become completely disabled from the effects—which has been my reality. I learned that all EMF patients have sensitivity in common. We are more emotionally, spiritually, and physically sensitive than most. It's kind of like having a seventh sense. I can feel the electricity, or Electro Magnetic fields, that others are not aware of.

Other factors come into play. We are, after all, made of body, mind and spirit. The other factors that play into the total picture include: life experiences, body make-up, genetics, exposures, geographies, nutrition, and stress levels. These all play a role in the EMF intolerance.

Thankfully not everyone will develop the EMF disease, just like not everyone gets diabetes or develops an allergy to bee stings or peanut butter.

I recognize that technology offers many conveniences. All I'm asking is that you be made aware of the harmful effects that EMF and wireless signals have on you and your loved ones' minds and physical bodies. By taking the necessary steps to avoid and/or shield yourself, you will prevent possible toxic exposure. Be aware that too much of anything is not good; that includes overexposure to electronics.

Pregnant mothers, you may be unaware of the danger of holding your smart phone against your engorged bellies. Keeping the phone away from your unborn fetus, whose brain is not fully formed, will protect it. Wouldn't you rather be a knowledgeable mother, than find out when it is too late that you could have helped your child(ren) simply by preventing exposure to them?

It is highly recommended to entertain your children the old fashioned way, with stuffed animals and a picture book—avoiding the exposure from electronic toys.

Look around. We live in an age where people are so grossly addicted to texting that they are ignoring the people around them. Mom and Dad, if you are compulsively texting while your toddler is tugging at you for your attention, and you keep saying "not now," what do you think the outcome will be in a few years when your child is able to text by him or herself? You will be the one left out. They will be the ones saying "not now."

If you must use a cell phone, the best approach would be to reduce the time you spend on a call. You can use shielding and/or a headset when using or carrying a phone. It is highly recommended to charge, store, and use the phone away from your body.

There are many styles of phone shields on the market. Look for the one that fits your model of phone and your style of phone use.

Computers emit several kinds of EMF radiation and each computer component will have its own unique emission. Newer LED monitors tend to show lower levels, while all-in-one and laptops tend to have the highest level of emissions. This is because these styles put the entire computer right at your fingertips. Any component that is wireless will emit a radio signal in addition to the low frequency emissions from the internal electronics. This includes keyboards, printers and the Wi-Fi router.

In offices and classrooms, where there may be multiple computers in a small space, the amount of total radiation present is multiplied and can quickly exceed safe levels. It has been shown that computer and Wi-Fi radiation can obstruct the progress of learning.

You can dramatically reduce the amount of EMF exposure you and your family receive from your computer equipment. The most important way is to turn off Wi-Fi and run cables for internet connection. Replace any wireless components with wired ones. If you must use Wi-Fi, shield the router. Move all the components of the computer away from your body, except for keyboard, mouse, and monitor. Use a remote keyboard and mouse on your laptop. Use a shield on the computer screen. Check for residual emission with an EMF meter. Never, ever, use a computer in your lap if you are pregnant.

Devotion

Establish Your word to Your servant,
Who is devoted to fearing You.
(fearing means in awe of, respect.)
Psalm 119:38

To my Lord and Savior, Jesus Christ, the love of my life, for sustaining, enlightening, and empowering me. I recognize that I am in humble, unashamed, dependence on You. Without the love and divine guidance of Jesus my health would not have stabilized and this book would never have been realized. Praise Him.

Dedication

My sheep hear My voice,
And I know them,
And they follow Me.
John 10:27

Sadly, this book is dedicated to all the EMF patients who didn't make it. To the ones who died at their own hands due to hopelessness. To those whose families didn't believe in them, those who could no longer function well enough to hold jobs, and those the system failed by not honoring benefits as a means to support themselves.

This book is written with the hope of educating the public on the negative effects of EMF's (electromagnetic fields) on the human body. It is also meant to encourage EMF sufferers who are unaware of what is happening to them and offer ways to think outside the box. . .when there is no box, to get relief.

I pray this book somehow reaches the canaries, the ones out of society that no one is aware of, the silent sufferers.

Introduction

Then the Lord answered me and said:
Write the vision and make it plain on tablets,
That he may run who reads it.
For the vision is yet for an appointed time;
But at the end it will speak, and it will not lie.
Habakkuk 2:2, 3

Imagine, if you will, living in today's world (the twenty-first century), where everything around you is running more and more by the use of electronics and wireless devices. People everywhere are hooked up to cell phones, iPods, computers, and newer technology every day, as a way of life to function in their professions, social lives, and even are required in the school systems. Then, imagine that you can't be a part of the world as it has progressed. You have allergic reactions to the use of any and all electronics and even ordinary electrical objects such as a landline phone, TV, radio, computer. . .even the refrigerator makes you ill. Now you are in my world. Disturbing, yet very real. What is even more disturbing is that I am not the only person experiencing this new reality. It happens to those whose bodies become burdened by chronic electrical exposure, causing overwhelming toxicity. It feels like I'm playing a role in a science fiction film. It feels like my body no longer belongs to me.

I recognize that it is not socially acceptable to say that electronics are dangerous; electronics have become a social affair. However since exposure to electronics were the main cause of my failing health, I would be negligent to withhold such health awareness information.

Arthur Firstenbergs' book entitled The Invisible Rainbow – A History of Electricity and Life, paints a clear picture of the effects that electricity has had on our bodies. He tells it from an environmental point of view. It is written scientific in nature but easy to read. We live in an electrically polluted world.

Everybody has a story. Some stories are more believable than others. Honestly if I didn't live my story, I'm not sure I would believe it either. That is the basis of why I felt so compelled to bare all. I pray something in my journey will expand your world, if for no other reason than to instill compassion for those of us whose lives are lived differently than most. For those of us who have experienced what exposure, raw pain, and trauma is capable of inflicting on our bodies, minds, and spirits. For those of us who, despite all the forces against us, find the hidden joy in what we can't see, but believe—a passionate faith in God.

All of our lives are like a book. My book encompasses many intricate parts to make a whole; part drama, comedy, tragedy; love stories all coming together, resulting in an enlightened soul.

Life is meaningful because it is a story determined by significant moments. I want the difficulties I have endured in my life to be devoted to a greater cause, to a purpose larger than myself.

I wish I had understood many years ago that we are all the authors of our own chapters, each of our stories unfolding by the choices we make in our lives. If you want to change the direction of your path, make choices that support and substantiate the way to your new life adventure. It is called *free will*. Your life can change and it will be all your fault.

No matter what your choices and experiences are in life, you can continue to move forward as long as you incorporate love, a belief in the future, a positive attitude, and faith in God.

You may not be able to control life's circumstances but getting to be the author of your life means getting to control what you do with those circumstances. There needs to be a point to my suffering. The grief of my situation had crippled me. I needed to rise above my circumstances and do something with the knowledge of this debilitating life altering affliction.

With enlightened faith and gratitude, I expose these chapters of my life.

Eight years ago, the world renowned Doctor William Rea, founder of the Environmental Health Center in Dallas, Texas, gave me the EMF (Electro Magnetic field sensitivity) diagnosis. I learned I couldn't work where I worked, live where I lived or play where I played. In fact, my sensitivities became so hypersensitive that I could no longer function in society. I was advised to avoid all public buildings.

The one thing I was rebellious about still doing was to attend church; but it became apparent after several stubborn attempts, that I couldn't stay in the building long enough to get through a complete service. So, after multiple failed attempts I concluded it was just too disruptive to the people around me and worshiped privately at home. I recognized that I just couldn't keep doing the same thing and expect different results.

You are probably questioning what could possibly happen with exposure to these seemingly harmless devices. . .first I can't make a decision, and then my emotions go out of whack, producing episodes of tears. Something trips in my brain causing me to not be able to stand, walk, or communicate. I shut down. I know I'm in a blank stare, I can reason that. I can see and hear but I can't respond. Extreme exposure provokes me into seizure mode.

Let's examine my world as I lived it, prior to my setback. I awakened on the second floor of my condo in beautiful Asheville, North Carolina. My alarm clock sat near my head on the night stand. I already heard the TV blaring from the other side of the wall behind my head from my upstairs neighbor. Smoke from the bad habits of the couple who'd recently moved into the condo below was irritating my sinuses, the smoke sneaking through the outlets and any possible openings it could find, the dryer vent became the favorite method of freedom. The husband downstairs smoked cigars, sometimes leaving four different flavors smoldering in the ash tray at once. The wife was a chain smoker, despite the fact that she was spending most of her last days confined to a bed on the floor directly below me. I arose to get to my electric-air-freshening machine and cranked it to the highest level. The low setting during the night didn't quite do its job.

I'd jump into the shower, chlorinated because it was city water, to mistakenly freshen myself for the day ahead. No time to waste, I microwaved a cup of tea or oatmeal cereal.

My daughter, in the next bedroom, awakened to prepare herself for the day at school. She wasn't even out of bed yet, and I heard her receiving and sending text messages. This continued as she prepared herself for Early College.

Time management was not one of her strong points yet, and I was stressed, not wanting her to be late for school, or me to be late for work.

After driving my daughter to school, I arrived at work and had to circle the building several times to find a parking space. We were so overcrowded, there simply weren't enough places to park. Entering the building, all employees had to put our personal belongings on a table; pocketbook, briefcase, lunch bag, etc. After security searched through everything, it was given back to you. Then the security officer used a long electronic rod to scan you head to toe, front to back. If no metal was detected, you were allowed to enter the building.

The security check was implemented after several threats were made to management. Understanding this to be a necessary procedure, I just followed the rules. Not yet realizing its contribution to my demise.

The stress of getting to work and the unsuspected exposures left me tired and stressed before I even started my day.

I walked through the building, which consisted of approximately 125 work stations, with a computer in each one, all on one floor. The company has now become a "call center." This new position as Inside Sales Rep was not even close to the Administrative Assistant's position I was hired for eleven years ago. Each cubicle, which was now downsized to the size of a phone booth to fit in more employees, consisted of a small corner desk, computer, headset, phone, and two drawers for storages or files. More elaborate fluorescent lights were added for better clarity. I didn't learn until much later that fluorescent lights flicker and, although we don't see the flicker with the naked eye, our brain picks it up. We were told we couldn't keep things on our desk. Rolodexes. . .something I considered to be my bible, was a thing of the past. I pleaded with the head office administrator to please allow me to keep my Rolodex. She wasn't buying it. I knew at this point that I was having trouble retaining information, but I was not exactly sure why. I couldn't imagine not using a Rolodex for contact information and to find passwords to the multiple systems that were expected to be used. Despite the fact that I cleverly disguised the passwords, my request to keep a Rolodex was repeatedly denied. No, not buying it. I should be able to memorize all passwords. I was allowed a couple of weeks to adjust, but then everything went from my desk top. A spit-shined desk was the goal. The administrators' theory was that everything you need, you should be able to access from your desktop once logged in. I was thinking I need my password to access the system. We were expected to change and remember the password every thirty days for security purposes. Add that to the stress pile! The changes meant more time spent staring at the computer screen; provoking more direct exposure.

With yet another merger and new management, you had to apply for your job all over again. Since I'd been through the process four times in eleven years I knew there was no guarantee any of us would continue doing what we were trained to do. Along with our regular jobs, which were already a full plate, we were now expected to answer the 800 line. I began to refer to this phone line as the 1-800-NO-BITE-ME line. At least that is what I called it to myself, because it was almost a given that when you answered the line, someone on the other end wasn't getting what they needed. They have either been bounced around from division to division or they were so frustrated that they just wanted answers to questions that frankly no one knew the answers to. After several complaints, a concierges' line was set up to direct all calls that were unanswerable, which pretty much involved most calls. Chronic stress, downsizing, upsizing, and merging led to a major setback in my health since stress exacerbates my symptoms.

One particular customer calling in made me happy to realize it was my department that he wanted. He was frustrated. I said confidently, "You have come to the right place, sir; my job is to make your job easier—how can I help you?" What a shock to my system when his energetic reply was sarcastic to say the least. "Well, you think highly of yourself," he concluded. He was so difficult during the call that I ended up having to escalate the call to my manager. We were told to do so in these instances, so I followed protocol. The result from escalating the call was being written up for not handling it on my own. My boss wasn't much help either. Add more stress to the pile. My boss's resolution was to stare at the phone while the customer complained and give the phone the "two middle-finger salute," while *yessing* the customer to death. Real. Class. Act!

After work, I'd venture over to the YMCA to keep myself fit and attempt to alleviate stress. More exposure. The YMCA installed an electronic screen to welcome you after you walked through the electronic doors. The screen would kick on with a running message "Welcome to the YMCA." Next, you walked over to the customer service desk to the entrance to the workout areas and scanned your badge for attendance purposes. Above the desk was an electronic running board that announced new classes being offered.

I worked out on weight-lifting machines that have electronics to keep track of your repetitions. I swam laps in the Olympic-sized pool, not yet aware that the reason my legs felt like lead at the end of my swim, was because my body was reacting to the chlorinated water. Fluorescent lights were displayed abundantly throughout the building, weakening my system further. Chlorinated showers added to my overall breakdown of my health.

Was I consciously aware? NO, not in the least. Aren't these modern conveniences? Aren't we supposed to be able to tolerate them? Aren't all these luxuries supposed to make our life easier? One would like to think so.

In order to achieve the EMF status, I'm told you have to be chemically sensitive first. EMF sensitivity is the top of the food chain, so to speak.

As my body was getting weaker and weaker, I would only go to the YMCA long enough to use the sauna for detox purposes.

I found myself less and less able to make decisions. My body and mind were breaking down at a rapid pace. It was difficult just to get myself to the YMCA and back home. Sometimes I'd sit in my car, feeling physically depleted, until I could gain the strength to drive. Sometimes I'd have to put my seat back to sleep for a while, hoping I could regain enough strength to drive. That usually resulted in a two-hour nap in the car before I could function enough to get myself home. Luckily the Blue Ridge Parkway was near the YMCA and my condo was just off the parkway at the other end. It was a relaxed, tranquil, ride. . .almost totally free of overhead power lines.

Part I:

Awareness

Someone Stop This Train
from Derailing

And Jesus went about all Galilee, teaching in their synagogues,
Preaching the gospel of the Kingdom, and healing all kinds of
sickness and all kinds of disease among the people.
Mathew 4:23

Reflecting on the previous years leading up to today, I recall having nosebleeds that wouldn't quit, light headedness, muscle weakness, and overall fatigue. I would go through periods of time where I would have to walk with poles or a cane to support myself. No rhyme or reason to any of it. There were periods of time when I couldn't hear or see, which I attributed to hysteria, since these periods of time were always after a major shock or loss of a friend or family member. . .but now I'm not so sure. The wiring in my brain didn't (and still doesn't) cooperate.

After the death of my youngest brother, who was killed in a motorcycle accident back in the 1980s, my body would prove to fail me yet again. I was able to function to help my mother through the planning and orchestration of the funeral arrangements. A couple of weeks later, after the funeral, I returned to work. I was walking down the hallway and it's as if the ceiling hit the floor. Apparently I blacked out and down I went laid out on the carpeting. When I came to, I could see my boss looking over me with deep concern. Her lips were moving but I couldn't hear her. I couldn't hear or talk. My boss got me to a physician who referred me to a psychiatrist.

The psychiatrist and I spent three visits a week for six weeks writing on a blackboard to communicate to each other.

Revisiting that time, I recognize a similar pattern—high pressure job—I was in charge of the audio/video room, recent office move, chronic stress as a single parent and loads of EMFs everywhere on the fourth floor of the corporate building.

With a reprieve away from all of the stimuli, I was able to regain my hearing and ability to speak.

The most difficult part of that period was my son's response. My son would have been around two and a half years old. He looked at me with his big loving eyes and said, "Don't you love me anymore mommy? You are not talking to me." It ripped my heart out to not be able to respond. All I could do was hug him with everything within me as the tears streamed down both our faces.

Fast forward to twenty plus years later and I kept plugging along. I did all I needed to do to get through life. I worked, cared for my children, now blessed with two children (ten years apart in age), and kept up with the home front. I was physically running out of gas. I would start going to bed earlier and earlier at night. I had nothing left to give.

To this day, I question if my body's reaction to exposures was the straw that broke the camel's back, resulting in the end of my second marriage. I remember it being the end of a long day at work. I managed to get myself home and up to our second floor bedroom. The goal was to change out of my business suit. I was on the floor, laid out in our bedroom. The floor seemed to be the only place I was able to find comfort. I couldn't quite make it to the bed. I was exhausted after a long hard day at work, riddled with chronic fatigue. I heard my husband's abrupt footsteps coming up the stairs. He came into the bedroom, stepped over me, and blurted out, "I suppose you want dinner." Shocked and numb I remember thinking, "*What is wrong with me? I can't eat. I have no appetite.*" When I look in the mirror, a stranger looks back at me. I was a frail version of my former self. I looked like Olive Oil with feet (Popeye's girlfriend).

If only I could just lift myself onto the bed. . .I tried but I couldn't. The struggle was too abrupt, too hard. I passed out instead, right where I was, sprawled out on the floor.

4

Later that evening, I dragged myself into bed. Not sure if I had no energy because I can't eat or if I can't eat because I had no energy. My mind goes into overload too easily. I can't take in too much; don't want to because it is too big a task.

I laid on my side and at two a.m. I was awakened as my husband made his way to our bed. He had been spending more and more time downstairs in front of the TV and online. With our bodies back to back—a new routine that established as I continued to fade away. I look back and can feel how frustrated he must have been. He had to feel rejected. To my knowledge of recall it wasn't him I was rejecting. I just couldn't do one more thing and I didn't know why.

Exhausted, frustrated, probably hungry—but not feeling hunger pangs, I passed out, yet again. I remember the kick in the back that came suddenly and the humiliation I felt at having no strength to push back. I huddled further into my corner of the bed, laying there in stunned silence, overpowered by the force beside me. My husband was not a violent man, I can only surmise that he was so frustrated and feeling rejected that he was claiming his space. The shock to my system and the fear that that one incident instilled made the wedge between us thicker.

I awoke in the morning to the sound of the alarm and almost by instinct alone, I robotically showered, dressed, and began the daily routine once again. A smile no longer existed, just a shell of my former self going through the motions to exist in a very stressful work environment, and then to a home front that had become challenging and rejection imminent.

Instead of having the reasoning skills to heal my situation; I drifted further away. I wanted to run away. Where would I go? There's no place to run to, no place to hide.

Things that were once easy are harder now. My legs don't cooperate. There are days I walk with a pole to support myself. I'm disconnecting from all the things that once brought me joy. I question myself. Why am I here? What is my purpose? I asked this despite my multiple roles of wife, mother, daughter, sister, friend, and employee. When I could function in my entirety, I was valued and respected. I needed help but I didn't yet recognize that I needed help, mainly because my thoughts didn't process as they once did. . .and apparently no one around me recognized my need for help either.

I no longer recognized my husband of fifteen years. He had become a harsher version of himself as I continued to disconnect.

I believed my husband was so frustrated with me, since I only had enough energy to give at work but had nothing left to give at home. But I didn't know yet why I couldn't function better than I was. I didn't know that what I had chosen for a profession, as an Administrative Assistant or Sales Coordinator, and exposure to electronics at work was a huge part of my demise, complicated by the stress from the lack of support at home.

I blacked out at work on the lunch table, due to a mild concussion I received the night before when my car door cold-cocked me. I didn't realize the strap from my briefcase was caught in the door, leaving the door partially open. Since I was parked on a slight angle in the driveway the door came back to hit me in the temple of my head, causing me to fall and to briefly blackout. I was temporarily laid out on the pavement of the driveway.

As I came to, I could hear my teenage son—who was concerned with my dilemma—calling out for his father to come and help me. Even in my disoriented state I remember hearing from the inside of the house, "Oh she will be fine," my husband not offering to assist me in any way. My son, a teenager at the time, was still very concerned and took it upon himself to assist me into the house where, yet again, I had to go straight to bed.

My bosses were rather surprised when they called my husband to come to my aid, when his response was that he couldn't come because he was on his way to a client's office. I needed immediate medical attention so my boss drove me. She made it clear that she couldn't believe my husband didn't put me as a priority. I'm not sure what hurt worse. . .the blow to my head or the blow to my spirit from what felt like yet another rejection.

At that point, I felt spurned and in question of my worth. Don't get me wrong, I don't have self-esteem issues. I just could no longer keep up with the demands of life; my body was failing me. I was just *spent*.

All of my efforts then went into maintaining my career and just trying to get through the day. I felt betrayed by my husband for not scooping me up off the floor, recognizing something was terribly wrong, and getting me to a doctor that would help me once and for all. And betrayed by my body for not functioning the way it was designed to do. I walked away from my marriage. Our divorce was probably the most amicable one in history. We held hands in court and parted as friends. In the end, we both found comfort in the arms of someone else.

My spontaneity in leaving had brought sorrow to those I love. I see now looking back that it was a selfish move on my part. In my defense, I was only capable of thinking of my own survival at the time. In my quest to survive, all I could do was run. I couldn't see another way. My spirit was locked in *flight mode.* It felt safe in the office and I needed to hide behind my work to suppress my emotional pain of rejection and loss. It was easier to hide my despair behind the walls of my employment. It was all so consuming and very confusing. My biggest regret is that we didn't try harder to save the marriage. We were both so eager to just give up on each other.

I have prayed on several occasions that my children and ex-husband would forgive me for the changes I made. But some things, it seems, are just not forgivable; especially if they don't know the love of Jesus.

I was able to work another eleven years, full time. Within that time period, I accepted the job relocation from Connecticut to Asheville, North Carolina. The timing of the offer seemed perfect having been newly divorced and needing a change. With any change comes additional stress. I viewed the relocation as a fresh start and new beginning.

Still having occasional complete collapses, all I managed to do was work. I still came home and collapsed in bed, early every night, so I could equip myself with the sleep I needed to get up and do it again. I kept doing the same thing expecting different results. For the most part I could function during the day, and still function well, until I no longer could at all.

Apparently the exposure from 125 computers, fluorescent lights, and telephones, cramming the space at work did me in. We were all housed in phone-booth sized spaces and expected to function. I couldn't understand why I felt worse after taking my break. It wouldn't be until I learned about my electrical sensitivities that

7

I would understand that the industrial style coffee pot/tea maker, two vending machines, refrigerator, fluorescent lights, and two microwave ovens that were housed in a relatively small breakroom bombarded me with electromagnetic fields, further diminishing my health.

The company's goal was to become a billion dollar operation instead of a million dollar one, as currently realized. Corporate greed set in. The stresses of the company's new demands were overwhelming. Add to that the new boss from hell and the stress meter broke. That, along with the exposure, was the completion of my downfall.

Sometimes, I recall those days as if they were yesterday. My mind and body were functioning in slow motion.

I've Fallen and I Can't Get Up

Therefore let him who thinks he stands take heed lest he fall.
1 Corinthians 10:12

What is happening to me? I'm disconnecting again. When I look back its been coming for a while. At first it's subtle. Over time, it became more pronounced. I remember waking up getting out of bed and falling to the floor. It was as if my legs were severed from beneath me. I'd fallen and I couldn't get up. My brain couldn't connect to the thought of using my legs. Then after a brief period, my legs felt connected again. I could use them again. That was fifteen years ago.

Fast forward to the date of January 2, 2010. To my knowledge I had never had a seizure before, but this day all that was about to change. I wasn't feeling well, yet again, so I put on my long johns to keep warm under my workout suit and decided to walk the neighborhood in an attempt to feel better. My teenage daughter lived with me at the time but wasn't home from work yet. Normally I would leave a note for her, but today I just didn't feel well enough to even make the effort. Besides I figured I'd be back before dark—no worries. Was I wrong! I headed out on my usual side of the road's path, around all of the loops and over all the hills of the condo complex. I began to feel disoriented, but was able to stay on task. As I finished climbing the last very steep hill arriving at the top, I felt as though I would collapse but held my ground—thanks to my Leki hiking poles. Looking back down the hill seemed like too far a distance to return. It never felt that way before. I cautiously started my descent. Halfway down the hill, my arms gave out. I felt like a rag doll with no muscle mass. I recall dragging my poles behind me since they were Velcroed around my hands. My fingers and arms lay limp, dangling at my side, my legs felt like lead but still moved forward. My eyes fought against me as I tried to stay focused on the road ahead. If I could only get myself home. I needed to lie down. Just as I approached the corner, now almost dark, I couldn't go a foot further. I had to lay down now. No choice in the matter. My legs lost all muscle and I was down. I passed out. Several hours later I woke, feeling frozen, disoriented, and my hands still Velcroed into my Leki poles. I managed to sit up from my fetal position. I found my way home, still surprised that no one saw me laid out on the side of the road all that time. I would hope if they did see me, someone would have stopped to investigate.

It took everything within me to make my way home. I managed to scoot myself up the stairs, sitting down backwards leaning on the outside steps. This is the one time I wished I didn't live on the second floor—it felt out of reach to get there. I managed to walk into my condo, still somewhat disoriented.

My daughter was home and sitting at the desk in front of the computer. She was engrossed in what she was doing and barely acknowledged me as she continued typing. She was concentrating on her project. When she did turn to see me standing in the foyer, she looked and said, "Mom, you are blue, wasn't that a stupid thing to do, staying outside in this weather until you turned blue." Just what I needed tonight—a rebellious teenager. I tried to explain that I didn't feel well so I lay down outside until I could feel better. I left out the gory details of collapsing alongside the road.

How is it that teenagers have a way of making you feel incredibly stupid? I tried not to give the comments energy, since energy was something I had little left of.

The closest spot to me to sit down was the stool at the kitchen counter, just inside the door to the right of the foyer. The half-wall serving as a snack bar was open through to the living room, so I could still see my daughter. I was just sitting and staring, everything became jumbled, scrambled. My daughter left the living room for a minute or two. Upon her return (she told me later) I was no longer sitting on the stool. She walked into the kitchen thinking I went back outside for air, it was then that she witnessed me bouncing around the kitchen floor. Apparently I was even bluer. She contacted 911.

The only thing I remember is the ambulance worker who was kneeling down next to me on the floor saying to another worker. "I hope she makes it, this doesn't look good." I couldn't respond but I could still hear bits and pieces of the commotion around me.

Upon arrival by ambulance at the hospital, I was left on the gurney in the hall. It was a busy night. My daughter got a ride to the hospital, refusing to be in the ambulance with me, sure that she would witness my demise. It freaked her out when she arrived at the hospital to find out that no one was attending me. The doctor finally checked on me after my daughter raised a fuss. She tried to tell the doctor how horrifying it was to see me in the kitchen, sprawled out on the kitchen floor. The doctor, young and cocky, said in response to her, "Well she is fine now." They released me. My daughter was irate that they basically did nothing for me; I didn't even rate the privacy of a room. The look of fear on her face was scary in itself. I could only imagine what she witnessed when I had a seizure and what that must have felt like to her. It couldn't have been a pretty sight.

I was exhausted and just wanted to be home in bed. So, home in bed I went. To this day I don't know how I arrived home. It's all a blur.

Not long after that my daughter moved out. Life is scary enough. She definitely wasn't going stick around for a repeat performance. I wasn't going to die on her time. The realization of what happened to me, combined with her hormones kicking in, were just two more reasons to blow me off. Nobody promised life would be easy.

Too many things just didn't make sense. Every time I had to go to my daughter's school for a visit or meeting, I would be reduced to tears. I wasn't sad. *What is wrong with me?* I would ask myself. I've usually got it together. It would be months before I would learn that the tears were a reaction to the fluorescent lights in the school. I thought maybe I was just overstressed having to visit the principal's office. Sometimes things aren't always as they appear.

Thankfully, my daughter came full circle and displayed regret for her teen years. Anyone who knows a thing about psychology knows that for a daughter to stand on her own two feet—to be independent of her mother, she has to sometimes be mean and rebellious; acting out as to not feel guilty for seeking her own life. Thankfully the stress of that period has been removed. She is now the daughter I prayed for and has created a flourishing life for herself.

When my daughter learned of my diagnosis, and that at times the condition can make you act as if you are wasted, even though I don't drink, she responded with a typical smartass but very keen observation, "That explains your behavior all these years. You've been wasted!" Oh, the joys of parenthood. She was alluding to the fact that I was always happy and very expressive. She called it over-the-top. I called it just happy to see her.

*****

On a Friday night, it was the twelfth of March, 2010. I went to meet some friends after work for pizza. I walked into the restaurant where, seated at the table across the room, were five of my friends who had arrived before me. I was escorted by waitstaff to the booth. I sat in the outside corner of the booth. I was the last one to arrive. We ordered. I didn't have much of an appetite, but ordered anyway. I looked up and, as I searched around the table to look at my friends, I was very aware they were all talking but I had no idea what they were saying. They rattled off a stream of nonsense that filled my ears but did not gain entrance to my brain. It sounded more like the Charlie Brown version of blah, blah, blah, blah, blah. I felt confused, disoriented, and unsure. A few minutes later, I said I must be tired, made an excuse and left. Thankfully I only lived a short way from there but, to this day, I am unclear how I made it home to bed.

The weekend was a blur, but I managed to get myself to work that Monday, March 15, 2010. I don't know it yet but this day would prove to be D-Day for me. It would be my last and final day in corporate America.

I arrived at work, got scanned at the entryway by a security guard. The device used was some kind of electronic wand. I remember my legs felt weaker but didn't associate it with the scanning. I made my way to my desk. I got through my morning routine of logging in, checking voicemails and emails. By midafternoon it happened: the very headset that was introduced about one year and a half prior was causing severe ear pain and I found myself becoming more compromised. I found myself becoming more and more detached. I wasn't absorbing my emails; comprehension had slowed down almost to a halt. I couldn't make sense out of the requests from customers or decipher my emails. I usually excelled at my job. I decided a long time ago, if you have to work eight to ten hours a day, you might as well do the very best job you are capable of doing. Make it worth the effort. I did not understand what was happening to me. I physically felt weak but managed to stay seated in my chair in the telephone-booth sized cubicle. I'd been having a chronic, left earache since the headset was introduced. Multiple visits to an ear doctor proved nothing. While sitting in front of my computer with my headset on, the phone rang. Out of nowhere, an electrical storm occupied my brain, presumably coming through my headset. The jolt filled my brain like a giant beehive. When I closed my eyes, it looked like a fireworks display but with only white, extremely-bright lights. The lights were ricocheting everywhere within my skull, bouncing all over out of control. It's as if there was a light show taking place in my brain. It hurt, it hurt real bad. The pain was unbearable. My eyes were flipping backwards. I was disoriented, confused, in intense pain. The pain shot through my head and down my left arm. Panicked, I tore my headset off. I felt like I was about to pass out. I said to my closest friend and co-worker in the next cubical, "I need to leave now. I need to go home. Please shut down my phone and computer, I'm not well, I need to leave." I was thinking, *if this is it, if I'm going to die, I want to be home in my own bed.* Morbid, I know. My life was flashing before my eyes. I was desperate, disoriented, and fearful. I never looked back. It would be four more long months before I would learn from a world-renowned doctor that what I experienced was an allergic reaction to the headset. Incredulous!

I made it out to my car, but was very aware that I couldn't drive. Then I remembered that I needed to call my Team Leader—that's the rule when you leave early. The stress of being a model employee had taken its toll on me. So I dialed from my cell phone and left a voice message for her. The pain worsened with the call but I was still not aware that electronics are part of my problem. I don't know what I surmised except I needed to get to my bed, I needed to lay down, but I couldn't. I couldn't process what to do next. I put my car seat back and tried to rest. When I closed my eyes, the bright lights recreated themselves. They were still there, but on a lesser scale, however still very intense. Then I passed out. After a brief nap, I managed to drive myself home. . .but in slow motion. I was aware of cars passing and honking but I continued toward home and finally made it. In hindsight, I recognize that might not have been a smart choice to drive. I did what I thought I needed to do at the time. It was all so confusing. I had no logic, no coping skills.

Once home, I took a two hour nap. When I awakened, I managed to make an appointment to meet with my neurologist and primary care doctor, yet again, for the next day. I remember holding my head all night long, thinking I wouldn't live to see morning. At the appointment with the neurologist, he scheduled an EEG, which showed inconclusive despite the light show and spasms I was still experiencing in my head. It wouldn't be until I arrived in Texas that Dr. Rea would explain that it's the wrong test for my condition. Since EMF was a fairly new disease, most neurologists weren't up on it yet.

During my visit to the neurologist, one of many prior appointments; the doctor offered a note to keep me off the phones for a while at work. I declined the note, recognizing that I couldn't put my other team members out by not functioning. My job was 80% phone work. I didn't think it was fair to the others and feared being fired if I couldn't function. I also didn't know the phone would do me in. I was always mindful of everyone else—not realizing it would have such an adverse effect on me as it did.

My primary doctor was frustrated to see me, yet again. This time she gave me information to get a natural antidepressant, telling me more kindly this time to call if I needed anything further. I went to the health store and got the over-the-counter antidepressant. I took it just before bed. I woke up with the sensation of my throat closing and feeling raw. Upon consulting my sister, since the doctor's office wasn't open yet, she told me to go back to the doctor, that I was having an allergic reaction.

I called the doctor first thing the next morning and was taken right in. After examining me she told me, "It is impossible for you to have that reaction—there is nothing new I can offer you." Now of course I'm frustrated, scared, and I am crying.

"Don't give up on me," I pleaded with her.

"I feel like I'm going to die and no one will ever know why," I reasoned.

"If something happens to me, promise me you will have an autopsy done. If I can't be helped, maybe it will help the next person with my symptoms."

My doctor looked at me as if I were auditioning for a drama series. I left her office disappointed, yet again, discouraged, and went home to bed. Climbing into bed and pulling the covers over my head seemed like the only remedy for relief. So, back to bed I went.

After my visit with both my primary care doctor and the neurologist, I spent the next three days in the fetal position, nauseous, spasms with squeezing sensations in my head, while the electrical light storm continued.

I found myself in a blank stare daily for about six hours a day, sitting in silence. This went on for about two months. I clearly blew a fuse. It felt like I was repeatedly hit with a stun gun. It felt like my brains were fried. My once orderly life felt unfamiliar and completely out of control.

My neighbor commented that she thought I had a nervous breakdown. At this point I was beginning to wonder the same thing. My life continued to spin out of control.

You would have to know me to know that I don't drink, smoke, or do recreational drugs. But if I were on a psychedelic trip, I'm quite sure this is what it would look and feel like. A Star Wars show of lights was on display each time I closed my eyes.

I felt electrified. My body changed to the point that I was blowing out watches. About every three months I'd need to replace the batteries. Someone suggested changing to the other wrist, still no relief. I finally gave up on wearing watches. It became too expensive and too frustrating to keep up with the maintenance.

Mainstream medical wasn't up on the latest information. Nor did they acknowledge its validity yet. Sweden has known about EMF for years. They even have cell phone-free towns and are Wi-Fi free in most areas. They have hospitals set up for EMF patients. The United States is behind in their knowledge of this Environmental Illness.

All I could think of was that I needed to move to Sweden, but then the reality of not being able to fly anymore or be on a cruise ship due to the heavy amount of electronics on both would leave me with the question, "How would I get there?"

Disconnecting

Some therefore cried one thing and some another,
for the assembly was confused, and most of them
did not know why they came together.
Acts 19:32

"You need a psychiatrist!" The level of frustration on my doctor's face was unnerving. "It's not possible for it to hurt when you watch TV, or while listening to the radio." My doctor was on a roll. "You've been here several times in the last two weeks. I'm referring you to a psychiatrist."

"Please listen to me Doctor—I need help, I'm going down hard and fast and don't know how to stop this train from derailing. I don't need a psychiatrist; I need you to help me."

"Look," my doctor continued adamantly. "You are depressed. See? You're crying."

"I'm crying because I'm frustrated. I'm crying because you are not hearing me. I am not depressed, something is terribly wrong, my brain keeps tripping. I feel like a beehive resides in my brain. It's painful, I'm scared." She suggested I suffered from chronic stress. I believed it was a physical ailment because the pain in my brain was so great. Reluctantly, I agreed to chill out, in case it was chronic stress. Truth be told, my life was nothing but stress. So why not chronic? Then I thought, isn't everybody's? There is the job to keep up with constant new demands, a home to run, a teenager to tend to. Trying to fit in "me time" to include an exercise routine and an occasional date night with a friend made my life certainly full. Lately, even the positive things seemed stressful. For insurance purposes, the doctor went with the chronic stress diagnosis.

"I'm giving you a prescription for an anti-depressant. Take it." The doctor dismissed me along with a note to take a couple of weeks reprieve from work to get my act together and, well, de-stress.

During the couple of weeks off, I took a break and stayed on my brother and his wife's property in West Virginia. Still not understanding what was happening to me I went to visit my mother and brothers. They all live in two separate houses on a couple of hundred acres of woods. Although still affected by household appliances, I found I got relief from most of my symptoms. During my three-week stay I avoided the use of TV, phones, computer, headsets or music. There was a profound difference in my coping skills. I shared this with my primary doctor upon my return. All of my symptoms returned when I returned to my condo and life in Asheville and tried to function again.

She concluded once again, "You need a psychiatrist."

My symptoms have been building in intensity for several years. I did, in fact, see a psychiatrist at the doctor's request about two years earlier. The only conclusion was that I was severely depressed. Funny, I didn't feel sad. I just couldn't stop crying. It wouldn't be until I could reflect back that I would understand that the fluorescent lighting in the building caused me to have a meltdown and cry. Not sad, not depressed, I was having an allergic reaction to my surroundings!

I question how many other people are out there sick, frustrated, misdiagnosed, misunderstood, and desperate for answers.

Doubting myself, I filled the prescription, just in case on that slim chance the doctor was right. . .all the time wondering if I've gone mad. I mean I've become light sensitive, sound sensitive, and any type of motion messes with me. It scrambled my brain. I could look at the TV for brief periods but instantly became nauseous. If more than one person is in a conversation, I couldn't articulate what they were saying. I couldn't keep pace with the conversation. Things were starting to be in slow motion. It hurt to listen to a radio or to use a phone. I had brain spasms that were painful, and scary. I suffered silently from a chronic earache for the past year and a half at work. It was my left ear, the side my headset was on. I had shooting pain up the back of my neck and skull. I had a beehive sensation that hovered over my brain area. My nose and parts of my face would fall asleep randomly. My brain felt dried out. There was tightness down the left side of my neck and pain down my left arm. I lived on peppermint for one and a half years, a natural remedy to combat nausea. Three of my toenails turned yellow and popped off, to include both big toenails. They just died and popped off. My hair yellowed, especially my bangs. It felt like I'd blown a fuse in my brain. I felt like I was derailing, coming unglued, at times going further and further inward, disconnecting emotionally, imploding physically. My cell phone made me sick to my stomach and weakened every muscle in my body. I couldn't sit in front of my computer more than a couple minutes without complete collapse of muscle and left ear pain. The left side of my body proved weaker than the right when using any type of electrical item. I had to wear sunglasses continuously for the first year, while inside the house, as well as outside to guard against any type of lighting. Fluorescent lighting made me so weak I ended up on the floor in Wal-Mart. Over the loud speaker a special code was announced followed by, "*Spill on aisle 9.*" That spill was me. What Gives?

Maybe the doctor was right. Maybe I do need a psychiatrist. But we have been down that road before. I visited the psychiatrist and stopped going, when each time I entered the building I had a meltdown. Again tears uncontrollable but I was not sad or in pain just a strong need to cry. I'll try it her way and at least take the prescription for anti-depressant pills. By the second day of using the pills I couldn't walk, my legs wouldn't cooperate. I felt like *lead legs* from the waist down. I got driven back to see the doctor. She made it very clear that she was done with me. Giving me contact information for a local psychiatrist, she was passing the buck. It was outside of her realm of expertise. It was clear she was not wasting any more time on me.

Thankfully, my sister is a nurse.

My sister advised me to stop taking the anti-depressant.

"You are having a reaction to the drug," she said firmly but in a concerned voice. "The doctor is mainstream, she handled that poorly. A better way to handle it would have been to tell you she has no idea what's going on with you but will investigate to get you the help that you so clearly needed."

I thanked God yet again for my knowledgeable and loving sister.

Desperate to get answers, I prayed for a doctor who could help me; a doctor who could heal me. Knowing that my primary doctor was frustrated with me and clueless as to what was going on with me, since my symptoms weren't the norm. I took matters into my own hands and picked up the phone book. I could use a landline telephone for brief periods without too much distress yet. I left messages for eight different types of doctors. Five out of the eight returned my call saying they were sorry but had no idea what was wrong with me and wished me luck. One called back and offered to see me but wasn't sure he could help. At least they had the courtesy and compassion to respond. One never called back.

The eighth doctor, a holistic doctor, called me later that night. He knew *exactly* what was wrong with me. In fact he said, "Not only do I know what is wrong with you, but I know exactly where you need to go to seek help."

Hallelujah! Someone gets it! I felt validated.

"You have an environmental illness. You need to contact Dr. William Rea. He is world renown and a specialist in the treatment of EMF sensitivities. He is also the founder of The Environmental Health Center in Dallas, Texas. Call the center and make an appointment."

I'm thinking do I do anything easy? I mean I'm in Asheville, North Carolina and I need to, somehow, get myself to Dallas, Texas. At the moment I'm having trouble walking a straight line. Well, I did pray for a doctor to heal me—I never did specify a location.

"But what does this mean. . .what's wrong with me?" I inquired further.

"You are suffering from EMF," the doctor said, as if I should know what that means.

"I have what?" I questioned dumbfounded.

"You have E M F." He repeated and spelled out, drawing out each letter for emphasis.

"What the heck is EMF? I blurted out.

"It's sensitivity to Electro Magnetic fields, otherwise referred to as ES electrical sensitivity."

20

I was still thinking what the heck is EMF? A sensitivity? My whole life I've been told I'm too sensitive. It was meant emotionally but now my body is reacting to my surroundings as well? How did I get this compromised? What do I do now?

So, what the heck is EMF? I repeated again to myself.

"Damned if I know," I thought out loud. But what I do know is what it feels like, what the symptoms are, and what limitations it puts on our bodies and how socially restricting it is. For years, I'd suffered from symptoms that mimicked MS (multiple sclerosis) to include full-body, left-side weakness. At least somebody now understands what I have been trying to tell my primary doctor all along.

Upon my call to the Environmental Health Center in Dallas, I learned that I would be expected to be there at least two full weeks for a jump start on detoxification. Up to that point in my life I'd never heard of detox except for people who drink excessively. My worst offense is that I'm a milkoholic, can't drink enough it seems. I was about to enter a whole new world of ridding toxins from my body.

"Dr. Rea can help stabilize you. He is extremely knowledgeable. I've met him recently and was very impressed," the holistic doctor concluded.

He was so matter of fact in his confidence in Dr. Rea that I knew clearly what I needed to do next. I prayed for the courage and strength to get myself to Texas. I stepped out in faith after making the necessary appointment and found my way there.

Faith Drive to the Environmental Health Center – Texas

But Jesus looked at them and said to them,
"With men this is impossible, but
With God all things are possible."
Matthew 19:26

My resources were limited, so I prayed for Him (Jesus, my Lord and Savior) to make a way so that I could get the help that I so desperately needed. I put a sleeping bag and a pillow in my car, made arrangements to be an outpatient at the Environmental Health Clinic in Dallas. I allowed three days to get there and started my journey—praying every step of the way. Using my car radio was not an option for me; it was too painful to listen to. The radio waves affected my ears and nervous system. I didn't let that hamper my joy. I became my own source of entertainment by praising and worshipping without ceasing. I sang hymns out loud, which being that I consider myself the joyful noise, provoked a different method of pain.

It would not be until I got there that I would realize that sleeping in my car was not an option. It felt like 110 degrees in the shade.

I had two hundred and fifty dollars cash, two gas charge cards, and continuous prayer. My regular charge card was not an option for me to use, because I needed that for the clinic, they were self-pay and do not deal with insurance companies. I'm telling you this for an important reason. Listen closely to how God works when we are completely focused on Him.

The night before, as I was getting ready to leave home, a new friend of mine stopped by to see me. She was excited about getting married in the next week. I knew she didn't have the resources for shoes for her wedding. I took $40.00 dollars (the amount laid on my heart) and told her it was a wedding gift. "Go buy a pair of shoes." I knew this would make finances even tighter, but it's what God laid on my heart to do.

I was given four coupons from a friend to use for four nights stay at a hotel; I was counting on that for financial means. I called to reserve the night before leaving. During that call, I learned that the coupons earned were nontransferable and it would not be an option for me to use them. *Bummer.*

Another dear friend, and neighbor lady, approached me before I left and gave me a lunch box. She asked me not to open it until I arrive at a rest stop at lunch time. Upon opening the lunch box I found all kinds of snacks and goodies, along with a card. In the card was $200.00. These two hundred dollars paid for my hotel rooms two nights out and two of the three nights back. To say that she were generous would be an understatement.

At a rest stop in Arkansas, a man approached my window and knocked, asking me for money. He explained that he and his sister were stranded, and needed a part for their car. Startled I said, "Sorry, I can't help you." But after going into the rest room to pray about this it was laid on my heart that, "If a man asks for your shirt, give him your coat too." I went out to my car, took $10.00 dollars, walked it over to the man, repeated my thoughts and said "this is my coat." Was he a con-artist? Maybe. Was I obedient, yes!

Later that evening I stopped at a Motel 8. . .the cheapest hotel I could find in the area. I asked the gentleman behind the counter for his best price; he gave me the price but it was $10.00 more than I could afford and I had just given that away. Discouraged, I asked if I could just sit for a few minutes in the lobby, knowing that I couldn't stay. I prayed silently to myself for a few minutes; and to my surprise; the man said, "Well I guess I could knock $10.00 off the price. Done — I booked the room.

The next morning, I was driving down the highway. As a rule I waited until my tank was ¾ of the way down before I would refill. This seemed logical to me. I came across a busy intersection with lots of gas stations, but was too tired to deal with getting off the highway; my logic was I'll wait until the next exit. Well, unbeknownst to me, there would not be another exit for a very long time. My car was reading empty; there were two truckers in traffic with me but no cars, nothing around me, no exits, no gas stations, no nothing. Desolate. Scary, but I wasn't scared. My spirit knew it would work out, and eventually it did.

At this point, I started praying out loud, Father God, I need a gas station, I'm on empty and I know that you are capable of miracles. Off to my far right I was approaching one exit with what looks like a gas station sign, but it's faded. Am I delusional since I have been on the road too long? I got off the exit; only to find an old, boarded-up Exxon station. At this point I was reduced to tears. I'm off the highway, my gas tank read empty. I hate to admit it, but I was starting to panic.

I began praying out loud. Actually. it was more like screaming out to the Lord. "Okay, I get it, you have a sense of humor. I should have been more explicit. I need a gas station with gas!"

I got back on the highway and began down the road; no exits in sight. I'm still praying, and screaming out, and crying out for a miracle, when off in the far distance I see a sign up on the hill that reads Exxon. Now the needle read under empty and I'm not there yet. I got off the exit and literally coasted into the gas station on fumes. I envisioned kissing the ground I walked on. I filled up my gas tank, sat in the parking lot for quite a while until I could calm my nervous system down, all the while thanking and worshipping Him in total awe.

I got back on the highway. I know He (my Lord and Savior) was with me, but I was starting to doubt what I set out to do. With tears flowing down my face once again, I looked up to see a billboard that said "With God All Things are Possible." That was the jumpstart I needed to continue on. The drive was becoming more challenging. I found I was only able to drive forty miles an hour because the motion was starting to scramble my thought process again. The only solution was to keep stopping to rest my eyes.

It's 10:30 a.m. Sunday morning; I have made it to my destination. I was sitting in my car outside of the Environmental Health Center – Dallas. I was excited to have made it – thinking. . .*great, I made it,*

I'll just sit here in my car until tomorrow morning for my appointment. Then it occurred to me, I can't, it's scorching hot, sleeping in my car is no longer an option. I wasn't totally unprepared; I printed out a list of Convents, Monasteries, YWCAs, and Hostels should the car idea not work out. I knew that the convents were ruled out because I called ahead of time and all of the nuns were traveling to a music convention and were away this week. That still makes me smile at the thought of hundreds of nuns at a convention. I so wanted to be a nun growing up, but that is a story for another time.

I started to pray out loud, "Father God, Lord Jesus, I don't know where I am laying my head tonight, but you do! Open the way". At that moment, a remarkable peace came over me, you know the one that surpasses all understanding.

I started my car, proceeded to drive down the road. It was laid on my heart, "It's Father's Day, and I need to attend a church service somewhere." I pulled into the very first church parking lot and prayed. It didn't feel right, so I drove to the second parking lot, pulled in, this time it felt right in my spirit. It was a Presbyterian Church and I had been a member of that denomination for ten years, long ago in Connecticut.

I went inside. I was in awe of the church's beauty. I sat down to enjoy the service, the whole time totally composed and in perfect peace. Normally, Father's Day is a very emotional day for me, due to the devastating loss of my Dad when I was just a teenager, but today was different. I was at peace. The Holy Spirit was embracing and comforting me.

There were couples to my right and to my left. The couple to my right was elderly, in their eighties, I guessed. The wife said, "I've never seen you here before dear, are you new?" I replied, "I just arrived in town." She asked, "Where are you staying?" "I'm not quite sure yet but it's being worked on," I responded timidly. "Why don't you stay with us?" she offered enthusiastically. Thinking this was the answer to my prayers, I put on a big smile. *Surely it couldn't be that easy*, I was thinking. Just after that, I glanced over at her to see her husband giving her a rather powerful nudge with his elbow and I could see how displeased his reaction was to her generosity. He doesn't know me. So I said very lovingly to her, "that is a really generous offer, but I'm okay, thank you."

25

The couple to my left asked about my situation and offered to introduce me to the church coordinator after the service. I thanked them.

When the service was finished, I was brought to a lady named Fran. I introduced myself and explained my dilemma. "Hello, my name is Deborah Hyatt. I just arrived here from Asheville, North Carolina. I have come to see a doctor just down the street from here. I'll be here for two weeks as an out-patient. I have references. Do you have any resources?"

At that moment Fran took a good look at me, paused, and said, follow me. She led me to the church office and asked me to wait ten minutes. The very caring couple that sat to my left stayed with me through the whole process.

Fran came out and said "I think we just may have a spot for you. It may take a little while, possibly a couple of hours, to get approvals, since it's Father's Day and all of our board members are out celebrating with their families. Would that be okay? Betsy will call you. Here is her number, should you need it."

Okay? That would be fabulous! I thanked her, went out to my car, but realized after a couple of minutes, I can't stay in my car. . .it's too hot. I did not want to drive anywhere for fear of not finding my way back. So I approached the church doors, but by this time they were locked and all of the parishioners had gone. So, I walked to a side door, peeked in to see a maintenance man. I asked if it would be okay if I stayed in his lobby to get out of the heat and wait for a call. He let me in with no further questions.

For the next three hours, still not knowing if this was going to pan out, I trusted God to take control. For three hours I praised and worshipped him. At one point I went into the sanctuary and knelt before the alter and completely surrendered to him and asked that His will be done.

Three hours came and went—still no call. I was not discouraged, just concerned that I may have been forgotten. It was laid on my heart to call Betsy, let her know I was still in the church, and ask if it was okay to stay there, out of the heat. So I called, not only did she say it was okay to stay in the church, but she had just finished her Father's Day celebration with her family and had one more call to make on my behalf. She said she would call me back as soon as she gets a response. This gave me hope that I was still being considered.

Not ten minutes later, the phone rang. Betsy asked me if I had a pencil and paper. She had an address for me. She went on to say that the caretaker will greet me when I arrived and gave me his number to call when I got there.

I hung up the phone relieved. At that very moment the maintenance man approached me with concern and said, "You must be thirsty and hungry. You've been here a long time. Come with me. The church has a kitchen and I can feed you." Hungry and thirsty and not sure when I would get to a grocery store, I jumped at the chance. He provided me with a chicken pasta dish with Gatorade. What a blessing. This gave me the energy I needed to drive to my sleeping quarters.

The place was a well-hidden camp and pastors retreat near Dallas, Texas. It is by invitation only. The campers that were supposed to be there for the next two weeks cancelled two and a half days before I arrived. The exact time I started praying, "Jesus take the Wheel, pave the way!"

To my awe and amazement, I stayed on approximately fifty acres of fields, paths, ponds, pastors' lodge, there were twelve air-conditioned apartments, and as if that weren't enough. . .there was a chapel – so on Sunday, the church came to me. I didn't have to drive anywhere. After being horrified all week driving in Dallas to the clinic and back, He knew I needed the break from driving.

This was fifty acres to myself with only the caretaker at the very back of the property. Most nights, the caretaker had to leave to attend to his mom, so I had the place to myself.

There was an outdoor church consisting of a large wooden cross and four rows of benches overlooking one of the ponds. That was my favorite place of worship on the estate. It also planted the seed for a future outdoor chapel of my own. When I could no longer stay in a building long enough to worship I created an outdoor sacred sanctuary.

The caretaker, painfully shy in demeanor, greeted me and gave me keys to my room, along with a key to the main meeting hall, so I could have access to the kitchen. He provided me access to the washer and dryer to wash clothes later that week.

Upon entering my room, the first thing I noticed was the cross on the far wall and a prayer closet. It consisted of a wooden bench with attached shelf for supporting a Bible. It was a place for me to kneel and pray. . .which I did daily, sometimes twice.

The one item I didn't bargain for was a large box in the corner of my room. It looked like a large shoe box. Something in my spirit told me not to touch it and good thing I didn't. Later I asked the caretaker what the box was for. "Oh, that, it's just a spider trap. I noticed a tarantula earlier when I was cleaning your room and didn't want you to have to deal with that." "What. A what?" Okay, so maybe I'd better use the prayer closet to pray that that thing doesn't come near me." From that moment forward, I kept all my things up high off the ground. Thinking back, I must have been a sight. Good thing I was alone. I proceeded to stand on the bed to change my clothes. A pitiful sight, since my balance was off. I checked my shoes, my clothes, the shower, I was petrified but then gave in to the fear and realized I have a lot more to be concerned with right now than a well, you know. . .a large, black, hairy, jumping, biting, SPIDER! It's hard to even say the word without getting the creeps.

Stepping outside the door of my assigned apartment was like walking out into paradise. I felt like Dorothy in the Wizard of Oz when she stepped out into Munchkin Land. It was beautiful, amazing, and magical. There was a pond. I would stand at the shore of the pond and be still. One morning I stood there for one hour, silently praying to myself, praising and worshipping Him. After several minutes, the creatures starting coming, one by one, as if on demand. . .the mother duck followed by her babies, the turtles, turtles, turtles, everywhere turtles, a squirrel, a rabbit, dragonfly, birds of all sorts, a large long-legged bird, and a large beaver swam by.

I mentioned my pond experience to a Christian brother. He said that was God's intent for our entertainment before man invented TV. At first I thought he was just trying to make me feel better since it was too physically painful for me to watch TV. But after thinking about it I realized it was so much better than TV, it was spiritual, magical, and most definitely entertaining.

One night I came home from the clinic to find a large raccoon outside my door. We startled each other but I was pleased to see him; I'm not so sure he felt the same way. The turtles kept coming on land to lay their eggs. One turtle came right up to the sidewalk outside of my doorstep and laid its eggs right there. I continued to be fascinated and in awe of the creatures in God's Kingdom.

Two Thursday nights in a row, charismatic, formally-Pentecostal preachers (husband and wife team) came to the center to deliver a sermon on healing. They heard about me and invited me to attend in the fellowship hall.

Not only did I get blessed by those teachings but they were the same two preachers preaching at the chapel on the property for the two Sundays I would be there. They invited me to both services.

After our first encounter, the male preacher came to me with encouragement. He said he saw me at the outdoor church worshipping and wanted me to remember, "When man couldn't do it, God sent Deborah!" He seemed intrigued that I followed the spirit all the way to Texas to get the help I needed. His statement left me speechless but it somehow confirmed my being there.

The first Sunday after enjoying the church service, a couple quietly approached me and asked to speak to me in the back of the church. They gave me a message and said God laid it on their hearts to give me this. . . they held out some folded money bills. I said, "Oh no, I couldn't accept that. I'm usually the giver." They insisted, as the wife shoved the money down into my bible, stating, "Don't deny us the blessing of giving." I was deeply touched and as I walked back to my room, sobbing with emotion I was in awe that someone who never met me before would offer this to me. It could only be a nudging from God.

I little later I looked at the money provided and it was $40.00. It didn't occur to me until I arrived home but that was the $40.00 that I was obedient in giving my friend for her shoes. It was also the exact amount I needed to finish my journey home, as I was unable to find a BP or Exxon station while in Dallas, on the designated route to and from the clinic. So I could not charge gas once I arrived there. I was too afraid to alter from my route for fear of getting lost. I had to use the only cash I had on me.

I was horrified to drive in Dallas. The roads were five lanes wide, bumper to bumper traffic, no helmet laws, so motorcyclists would weave in and out of traffic with no helmets, roads crisscrossing over top of each other, sometimes five roads high. As if that weren't bad enough, every day I saw roadkill. Roadkill where I come from might be a deer or a squirrel. But I'm not at home. In Dallas roadkill is mostly armadillos. How scary is that. They have a hard shell like a tortoise – God help the motorcyclists. But what were my options? I had to drive to and from the clinic each day, so I began to pray, pray over me, my car, the road, the people next to me, I was frantic. Most mornings I woke up early to pray for a hedge of protection. That is exactly what I got! If you were a helicopter looking down at the highway, you would see my car with a couple of hundred feet ahead of me, to the sides of me, and to the back with no cars around me. Now there could be another reason for that. I was driving down the highway praising and worshipping him, with one hand on the wheel and the other lifted towards him. The people there probably saw the North Carolina license plate, witnessed my behavior and thought, "This woman is nuts, we are not going near her!"

****

I never knew when the onslaught of exposures was going to manifest itself into a physical reaction; still not getting the severity of my ailment, I paced along just trying to get through the day.

Returning back to the apartment at the pastors' retreat, realizing food was scarce, I decided to walk to a local pizza joint that I'd passed while trying to find this place. It was probably a twenty-minute walk and I felt confident with the use of my Leki poles that it would be easier to walk since driving the car would produce more exposure.

Most of the walk was through the grassy pastors' estate and one dirt road so it was comfortable. Once I approached the sidewalk the place would be only mere minutes away. I felt confident and somewhat strong in body.

Opening the door to the pizza shop introduced a bombardment of over stimulation. New smells, noise from the pots and pans in the bustling kitchen, people's voices. I surveyed the scene; it was only maybe fifteen feet straight ahead to the counter to order my meal. Although feeling overwhelmed, I thought surely I could make it to there. I noticed a rather large big screen TV on the wall to my left once I walked in a little further. It was on.

Moving skeptically forward, cautiously putting one foot in front of the other, I started to lose momentum. My muscles weakened and I walked with the appearance of a drunkard.

The gentleman behind the counter witnessed the abrupt change in my demeanor. "Are you okay?" he offered in a concerned voice. "I thought I was but I'm sensitive to electronics. Your TV might be affecting me." I replied in a voice filled with embarrassment. "We can fix that, I'll turn it off," he commanded.

Within the minute my body righted itself. I was able to bounce back. My muscle strength returned. The gentleman said he never saw anything like it. The transformation was astounding. I placed my order. He suggested I find a seat where I'd be comfortable. He even offered to assist me there.

I made my way to a table. I barely settled in when three of four teenagers approached me from another table across the room. "What just happened? they inquired. "We have never seen anybody do that before. How did you do that?" they asked in amazement as if I were some kind of a magician.

Apparently, I must look worse than I envisioned because they were blown away by my change in overall appearance. I tried to explain my predicament as best that I could, but even I found what I was stating as hard to believe.

The fourth teenage was a skeptic, he wasn't buying any of this. He was really hard on me. He felt it was some kind of trickery, treating me as if I were a master at deception.

"It's not possible," he blurted out at me from across the room. He held a cocky confident manner.

I had only arrived in Texas a few days before. Since I was having a difficult time processing what was happening to me, I had no defense. I listened as he ridiculed me. The other three teens were still intrigued and remained in awe of my predicament.

As I sat in stunned silence, they wished me well.

Part II:

Diagnosis

Assessment: Have I Gone Mad and No One Has Told Me?

Therefore we do not lose heart.
Even though our outward man is perishing,
yet the inward man is being renewed day by day.
2 Corinthians 4:16

I was totally unprepared for Dr. Rea's initial intake assessment of me.

"Are those real?" Dr. Rea asked point blank as he looked at my chest. Looking at me as if I sat there butt naked, but I was fully dressed.

"Dr. Rea in my wildest, wildest, and I do mean wildest dreams, it didn't occur to me that you would care. After all I'm here for my brains. It's my brain that is causing the problem."

Okay, so if I knew, or if I could think more clearly, I wouldn't have carried on so. It seemed unbelievable to me that I'd driven half way across the United States only to be asked, "Are those real?"

In hindsight, I recognize the doctor was just doing his job. After all, thousands of women had implants that later proved toxic. Many woman suffered, or worse, *died* from breast implants that leaked. He was just trying to determine the origin of my toxic brain. Also, if I figured out I was being charged by the minute I'd have just answered the question and not carried on so. That, and the fact that I consider myself tiny breasted so it never occurred to me that anyone would ask if they (the ta-tas) were real.

We moved our focus of conversation up to my mouth. "Doctor, I had all of my fillings removed, since they were amalgam—the silver looking ones—now they are all the white fillings. I knew a co-worker many years ago, when I worked at GTE, who almost died from the severe reaction to his dental fillings. He dropped down to seventy pounds. After having the fillings removed, he was able to regain his weight and return to a normal life. So, just in case this was causing my chronic nausea, I wanted to be proactive in their removal. The only thing I have left in my mouth is one root canal."

Dr. Rea looked into my mouth and replied, "You should be okay with that but, just in case, I'm going to give you the name of a holistic dentist in Texas." Of course, I realized going to yet another doctor while I was in Texas wasn't an option at this time. For one, I could barely get myself here to the clinic every day. It was stressful and confusing to drive in Dallas. And, two, I couldn't have surgery now. I'd have no way to get myself home to North Carolina. I would need time to recover. I would investigate that at a later date. And three, it just wasn't affordable at this time. I dismissed the thought and focused on all the other things I needed to do to get well. After all, I'd had an x-ray taken of the root canal, and visited an endodontist—a dentist specializing in root canals—and she concluded nothing was wrong. Since I wasn't in pain at the time of my appointment, it was concluded, why touch it? It flared up from time to time but wasn't in distress at the time of my appointment which is, of course, Murphy's Law—anything that can happen *will*.

With all the other chronic symptoms I figured since the tooth was inconsistent with flare-ups, it would be ok to leave it alone. I still wasn't getting the exposure concept. It hurts upon exposure.

"Dr. Rea, I don't understand what's happening to me. My primary doctor prescribed an antidepressant and believe it or not, I couldn't walk with one brand prescription and my throat closed up with the over-the-counter natural brand from the health food store." I shared hesitantly. "That's because you are allergic to your own serotonin." The doctor shared emphatically. "If you continued taking the antidepressant you wouldn't be here right now."

"I'll bet your regular doctor told you that you need a psychiatrist," Dr. Rea went on to say, "You are NOT crazy." In 2010, three percent of the population has already been diagnosed with EMF, also referred to as ES (electrical sensitivity). It is the up and coming environmental illness.

"Dr. Rea my toenails turned yellow and popped off and my hair turned yellow," I said, embarrassed by so many strange body behaviors. "Did somebody poison you?" the doctor inquired gingerly. "Things like this only happen to chemo patients or poison victims and you are not on chemo!" Having been in a toxic relationship that I recently ended, it probably shouldn't surprise me that poisoning me would be an option. It certainly didn't help my health any – but being poisoned, I mean REALLY! That was so outside of the realm of how I think or could process, but certainly a possibility given the situation. "Have her bangs cut off her forehead and sent for analysis," he commanded his assistant. Later that day, I was sent across the hall to the lab for the removal of my bangs which were symmetrically angled around my eyebrows. The lab technician spoke broken English and appeared to be of an oriental descent. She was beautiful in appearance and heart. "I can no cut bangs – so pretty." She replied panicked and in broken English. I said "Oh go for it. We will start a new trend, a sort of reverse Mohawk. All of the kids will want this haircut." I was trying to help her feel less intimidated. She looked at me, stunned and laughed nervously. "Oh, but they look so perfect." "Dr's orders," I said. She looked under the nape of my hair at the neckline to take a sample but was advised that for accurate assessment it had to be the bangs. So painfully she took the scissors to my bangs and proceeded with *chop, chop*. I couldn't lose my sense of humor now. I was determined to get answers no matter what was required. Her facial expressions were priceless. It caused her great grief to follow orders. As it turns out I was just that toxic that it caused the damage to my hair and nails. Amazing!

"What do you do for a living?" Dr. Rea asked. "I work in a call center with one hundred and twenty five computers on my floor." Both Dr. Rea and his assistant looked at each other with great concern. Later the assistant would share with me his take on the situation. "You don't know it, but your job did you in."

During our next consultation, I shared my take on my employer. "I certainly don't blame my employer for my setback. They couldn't have known the debilitating effects 125 computers in a small proximity would have on me." I blurted out in my employer's defense.

The assistant raised his eyebrows. "After all," I continued, "why was I the only one affected? Were other people having symptoms but somehow better equipped to cope?"

Dr. Rea explained that sensitivity is the one thing all EMF sufferers have in common. Some are more sensitive than others. I happen to be hypersensitive.

I've always known, but never verbalized, that I was different than most people I've met. As a child and into my adulthood I was extremely sensitive to my surroundings. I could feel profound empathy for others. I was in-tune to things I wished I weren't. An example would be, when I walked into the kitchen with all three of my brothers standing around talking. I could feel the blanket of death, a profound heaviness in the room. I knew on some level that one of my brothers was going to die. I didn't know when or how or which one. I felt sickened and left the room. That weekend my youngest brother, nineteen at the time, was killed in a motorcycle accident. That was the year the drinking law in Connecticut changed from twenty-one to nineteen years old. So many teens died as a result that the law was changed back to twenty-one years old. There were so many unnecessary losses as a result of the age-change permitting youngsters to drink.

When I first had my setback, my body felt like all the nerve endings were raw. If you touched my hands, I would jump. Trying to hold hands with a boyfriend sent electrical charges through me that if I had been younger would have mistaken for cupid's arrow of love.

I would get brain fog on and off with regular periods of not comprehending conversations around me and then I'd slowly bounce back.

As I understand it, our bodies simply are not adapting to the rate that we, as a nation, are growing electronically. The exposure is causing havoc in our cells our muscles and tissues.

My visit to the Environmental Health Center would be a two-week process as an outpatient. Most days I was the first one in and the last one out. I was determined to do everything it took to beat this thing. I tried to learn everything I could to heal my body. I took notes, not trusting my memory, which was severely compromised since this setback. In fact, I have been writing daily to-do notes for years, just for basic daily routine things, things as simple as taking my vitamins. I was worried my daily tasks would be forgotten. My short term memory was screaming! (It was just not working for me).

The Environmental Health Center holds a wealth of information. I was like a dry sponge trying to take it all in.

At the beginning of my two-week stay, I was given a schedule to follow. My days were packed with skin testing, blood work, vital signs checkup, balance tests, sauna treatments, vitamin mineral IV treatments, and oxygen therapy. I met with Dr. Rea and his assistant on a daily basis. Much of the conversation high points I tried to capture in this summary.

The skin testing was intense. I would spend, sometimes, four hours a day in the lab. The room was impeccably clean—no fluorescent lights, clean fresh air, no scents allowed, no noise, it was quite calming. We weren't even allowed to bring in any personal stuff, due to possibly contaminating the environment. Lockers were provided just outside the area to leave our belongings. You were not allowed in the room if you wore anything that wasn't unscented—absolutely no perfumes allowed. Someone else could have a fatal reaction to any of those toxins. Chairs were lined against two walls. We were called from our waiting area chair to sit in a chair near the technician one at a time. Sometimes there would be two technicians present, if there were more than a couple of us in the waiting room. Then two of us would go up at a time for skin testing. The process entailed being pricked with the antigen for testing. You would go back to your chair and sit waiting for a reaction, or ten minutes, whichever came first, for results. Then back to the technician to have your skin reaction measured and documented, and then pricked again with a different antigen. . .repeating the process.

My arms looked like a junkie's with track marks up and down them. They tested me for reactions to metals, chemicals, foods, and environmental reactions from things like mold and grass. It was a little unnerving to sit in a lab with, sometimes, ten other people. We all took turns. We had to record our own reactions, on a pre-printed paper provided to us by the lab. Along with that, the technician recorded the size of injection site. Did the substance cause itching, hives, throat closing, tears? All reactions were to be documented on our sheet by us. One test in the lab involved placing a drop of concentrated chlorine under my tongue. Within seconds, I was bawling out loud. The technician told me to make sure Dr. Rea was aware of this. Apparently it is a severe reaction to chlorine. That explains why I always felt like lead legs coming out of a chlorine pool. No more indoor swimming or chlorine pools for me. It's time to find a clean swimmable lake. Not to mention I had city water for showers, tainted with chlorine. No more drinking from the tap for me either.

I am still amazed by how many ways our body can react to present allergic reaction symptoms. Take a look at the Allergic Reaction Symptoms Chart that I entered at the end of this chapter to see if any of these reactions are relevant to you. I found this extremely helpful. I was learning a lot about toxicity and didn't want to forget what I came so far to learn.

The next test involved a balance test, which I failed miserably. "You do realize you would not be able to pass a DWI test?" It was explained to me with the results of the test. "But I don't drink." I blurted out defensively. "It doesn't matter, when your body can't rid toxins, it spills over in the form of alcohol in your body."

This was all very confusing to me. Just when I thought I couldn't be more surprised by the things taking place in my body, this gets laid on me. I mean *REALLY*!

I entered a room for what I will call the warming test. A woman technician entered the room. She seemed startled to see that I still had my clothes on. I was startled that she expected me to know to take off my clothes. I had no idea what a warming test was or what it involved and needed an explanation. I was asked to take off all my clothes from the waist up. This was another woman technician, I'm guessing from China.

"Take off blouse," She exclaimed.

"Okay."

So, naked from the waist up I stood, feeling very vulnerable, as she took the test with some kind of machinery. The warming test took a photo of my body showing warmed areas of possible concern. "What else don't I know?" I ask myself.

It was time to go on to the next test.

I was warned by the technician administering the immune test that it would be the most painful test. Okay, so I braced myself for the torture and told her to proceed. The thing is I couldn't feel it. "What pain?" I asked. Then I realized that I was so traumatized that

40

I couldn't feel much of anything. Needless to say, they took a block with eight needles in it and had it down on my forearm against my wrist for ten seconds. Not surprisingly, I failed that test as well. My immune system was not cooperating.

We discovered through testing that I was allergic to my own serotonin. That's why I had reacted to the over the counter antidepressant called SAM-E when prescribed by my regular doctor. You know, my primary doctor, the one who said it wasn't possible to have a reaction to an antidepressant. It makes me recall the verse in the Bible: *My people are destroyed for lack of knowledge. Hosea 4:6*

"Don't tell me you drove here?" The doctor was less than pleased that I drove myself to get to him, especially in the condition I was in. My balance was off, I was in physical pain. He just shook his head in disbelief.

"When you realize you are going down hard and fast, you do whatever it takes to fight your way back." I said rather proudly. "Besides, I like being on this side of the grass and was hoping to be here a little longer."

I saw no way around it. None of my family lives near me and besides, they all have full-time jobs. I'm it, I'm all I've got. Besides, my faith is strong, I'm never alone. I have me and my faith in Jesus. This is stated beautifully in the Bible under Hebrews 13:5, *I will never leave you nor forsake you.*

"Unbelievable," Dr. Rea stated as he rolled his eyes. But, deep down, I knew he admired my spunk and realized if there was any way to beat this thing, I would be the one to do it.

"Not to worry, doctor. I was prayed up and so was my car. My faith is what has sustained me this far and hasn't failed me yet. That's how I found you. I prayed for a doctor that could heal me. Oh, I know what you are thinking, if my God is all that powerful, why I didn't just pray to be healed? I'll tell you why, it's because I believe that God put doctors in the world as a means to get the help and healing we need. After all, God didn't do this to me, this is a manmade illness."

After hearing me talk of my journey to get there, and praying all the way, Dr. Rea offered, "You have no idea how sick you are, but it's your faith that is going to heal you!" The doctor looked at me with compassion. I had to think about that statement. Does it mean that I'm causing this to myself? Hardly—I want to be well. I have everything to live for: a good job, family that loves me, two amazing children, and a strong faith. So I handed it over to God, praying reverently. I prayed morning, noon, and night. I prayed while I dressed, I prayed while I ate, I prayed when I walked, I prayed until I became exhausted from praying and then I prayed some more. I needed a miracle healing.

I would never put anyone else in jeopardy. I knew driving forty miles an hour was all I could tolerate. I couldn't take the motion of the road coming at me while driving. It took me two and a half days to get here, but the point is I did it. I made it. I'm determined to beat this thing, whatever the heck it is.

"How much time do I have?" The doctor inquired. "Two weeks," I stated abruptly. I believe in direct honesty. "That's a tall order to fit into two weeks." He was looking at me with grave concern. "Dr. Rea, I wasn't born with a silver spoon in my mouth. Two weeks is all I can afford." He is looking at me like *it's not possible to achieve all that needs to be done.* "I need you here at least six weeks, maybe longer." He stated. "That isn't going to happen. What do you say, will you work with me on this? Can you give me the tools for healing that I need in two weeks?" Hesitantly, he stated, "Let's get started, I'll order the tests. Pick up your itinerary at the front window first thing in the morning." I could tell by the twinkle in his eyes that he liked my determination and my quirky sense of humor. I'm thinking we ought to work well together.

"Doctor, one more thing; I just want you to know how happy I am to be here. I knew you were the person who could change my life. Thank you, I appreciate you."

The doctor was already one foot out the door as I concluded my comments. He's a busy man. In my opinion, the man is a genius. He has credentials a mile long. He was a thoracic, cardiovascular and general surgeon, has written numerous books to include text books, has won multiple awards in the medical field, he has compassion, and best of all he knows his stuff. Dr. Rea founded the Environmental Health Center – Dallas (EHC-D) in 1974. I might have acquired a crush on him during our two weeks working together. I love powerful men. They say it's not uncommon to fall for your doctor. I wished I was well. I would have loved to work with him and his staff. He has hired all top employees. Prior to my setback, I took pride in always doing my best at work.

I've always had a strong desire to learn from people who are much wiser than me. I gravitated to anyone with a formal education and hard-earned credentials, always secretly wondering what I could have become if I were able to seek a higher education. My health and high stress had always crippled me from taking that risk. Everything I learned, I learned the hard way, but I did learn.

Most of his employees were doctors from other countries but couldn't practice medicine in the states without further certification. So he hired them on as technicians and paid them well. He had a brilliant, compassionate staff. His right hand man, Trep, his assistant, was another brilliant man who took care of the details behind the scenes. They were relentless in their pursuit to help patients with the most unusual disorders. Not that I am brilliant, although my favorite saying has been, "I'm practically a genius." This status acquired by a high school diploma, various college courses, intense corporate training, and a strong compassion and deep concern for people. I've never met a stranger. I have a profound love for people of all walks of life. That would shine through, as it has in the past, if ever given the opportunity to be well enough to reenter the workplace.

If I was going to learn anything on my visit to this clinic I needed to get organized. I was given my schedule but it was all overwhelming. What I needed was someone to coordinate my moves. Oh sure, I could read the schedule, but was having trouble keeping up with what to do and where to go next. It was a full day with various testing, detoxing, oxygen treatments and IV therapy.

For the next two weeks we buckled down.

Every day, I would check in with the doctor for my daily consultation, armed with a notebook and pen in hand. Frankly, I wasn't really sure what to ask. However, my sister and I were able to touch base most evenings by phone. Although it was painful for me to use a phone, she was my lifeline. My sister suggested using a notepad and offered various questions to ask. What would I do without the love and ongoing support of family? Thank you Lord!

What relief I got when Dr. Rea administered the much-needed oxygen therapy and an IV of vitamins/minerals mixture. Up to that point my brain was starving for oxygen. Just the simple process of putting a ceramic face-covering over my nose and mouth and inhaling pure oxygen gave me such comfort and relief. The IV gave me unbelievable relief from the dryness I felt in my brain after only three treatments. I had one treatment on Monday, one on Wednesday, and one on Friday. Prior to that, my brain felt like the inside of a nose feels with chronic dryness when trying to clear the nostril a piece of skin accidentally rips off causing a burning sensation, relieved by Vaseline. You can't however put Vaseline on your brain. There was no relief prior to the vitamin/mineral IV treatments.

EHC-D Environmental Health Center – Dallas, is known as one of the oldest and most innovative clinics for the treatment of chronic diseases. What an amazing clinic.

The diagnostic tools they used included but not limited to:
- SPECT Scan for the Brain
- Laboratory evaluation, blood, urine, hair and stool samples
- Sauna and detox regime
- Immunotherapy—a specialized type of vaccine treatment
- Patient education—to learn about their sensitivities and actively becoming involved in carrying out the prescribed treatment plans
- Nutritional supplements

The majority of patients were considered "chemically sensitive." I had been diagnosed chemically sensitive and a step up from that. My diagnosis was Electromagnetic Field Sensitive also known as EMF (Electro Magnetic field sensitivity) or ES (electrical sensitivity). Being EMF means basically to avoid electromagnetic fields. I had no clue yet what a challenge that would present in today's ever electronic world.

There were two male massage technicians. It is best to have a massage after your sauna so that your muscles are relaxed. A good massage is pretty much the next best thing to heaven in body form. Oh, but I felt relaxed for the first time in a very long while. I could definitely get used to this feeling of letting go of chronic stress.

"How long have you had symptoms?" Dr. Rea inquired. I went on to explain that I have been seeing different neurologists for over twenty years but was still able to function and hold a job. I even had a spinal tap to rule out MS (Multiple Sclerosis) and thankfully it was clean. MS was not the cause of my unexplained symptoms. A spinal tap is an excruciatingly painful test that I wouldn't recommend to anyone unless all other options are ruled out. A rather long needle is inserted into your spine to extract fluid for lab testing. I felt like I had been shot point blank in my back.

More recently, I saw a neurologist in Asheville on a quarterly basis, baffling the doctor with unexplained symptoms of left side weakness, chronic fatigue, and disorientation.

I got brave enough to ask him the much dreaded question, "Dr. Rea level with me. . .do I have brain cancer?" I was petrified of what his answer would be. I figured I had less than a year the way my brain was afflicted.

"We don't use the "C" word! Just be sure to use your oxygen as prescribed. Cancer can't live in an oxygenated environment."

Later, I revisited that conversation with my sister, the nurse. She said if I had brain cancer I never would have made it this long. That gave me the confidence to fight this with everything within me.

Dr. Rea was confident, just by all I shared of my symptoms, without testing me that I was a clear cut case of EMF. . .but I needed and wanted proof. I needed the proof to gain disability benefits from my employer. Since I couldn't stay in a building long enough to do my job, I needed the disability income to be able to feed myself. The proof displayed itself in the nuclear brain scan. My brain showed moderate toxicity. During preparation of this test, the technician asked me to envision my feet in the sand and the waves washing up against me. I tried as hard as I could, but as I was led into the machine for the test, with that thought in mind, all I could see were footprints in the sand. I knew then that He, my Lord and Savior, was carrying me through this. I had never heard of anyone reacting to effects of Electro Magnetic fields. I never heard of the term Electro Magnetic fields.

Despite the grueling process of getting myself to Texas to a world-renowned doctor and obtaining the proof I needed to realize my disability benefits from work, I still was repeatedly denied any corporate benefits. Thankfully, the best pension I received was the time to heal and worship my Lord and Savior Jesus Christ. Praise God! No monetary compensation can compete with that.

Toxins

Total Load Cumulative Factors
of Body Burden

B elow is a chart I acquired at the Environmental Health Center. It describes all of the ways our bodies can become burdened.

Chemical		Physical
Pesticides		Heat
Petroleum		Cold
Alcohols		Electromagnetic Fields
Formaldehyde	CHEMICAL	Radon
Heavy Metals	PHYSICAL	
ie Lead	BIOLOGICAL	Biological
Silver fillings	PSYCHOLOGICAL	Molds
Barium (enema)		Dust
		Pollen
Psychological		Bacteria
Relationships		Viruses
Life Events		Parasites
i.e. deaths, births		

The next page will give a summary of all of the allergic reactions that a body can realize. Our bodies are so complex. This chart, also from the Center, helped me to justify all I was experiencing.

46

Allergic Reaction Symptoms

(my symptoms when first seeking help are italicized in chart below)

VISION	HEAD PAIN	LUNG, HEART
blurring, spots, flashes	headache, mild, moderate, *migraine*	coughing
Acuity decreased	Ache, pressure, tight, explode	Sneezing
Darker, *vision loss*	Throbbing, *stabbing*	*Reduced air flow*
Photophobia, brighter	*Fainting*	Retracting, sob
Diplopia, double vision	*Depression, mood swings*, hallucinations	*Heavy, tight*
Dyslexia, difficulty reading	*Hyperactivity*	*Hyperventilation*
GU	*Irritability*	Hyperventilation
Frequency, urgency, pressure	*Fatigue, apathy*, lethargy	*Chest pain*
Painful or difficult urination	Somnolence	Tachycardia, rapid pulse
Dysuria, general itch	*Confusion*	Palpitations, rapid, violent or throbbing pulses
Yeast infection	*Blackouts*	**MUSCLES**

GI - ABDOMEN	Insomnia	*Tight, stiff*
Nausea, vomiting	**SKIN**	*Ache, sore, pain*
Belching, full, *bloated*	Itching, local, general	Neck, trapezius
Pressure, pain, cramps	*Moist, sweating*	*Upper, lower, back*
Flatus, rumbling	Flushing, *hives*, with contrast	Upper, lower extremities
BM, Diarrhea	Pallor, white or ghostly	
Gall bladder symptoms		
Hunger, thirst	**JOINTS**	**EYES**
Hyperacidity	*Aches, pain*	Itch, burn, pain
THROAT, MOUTH	*Stiff*	*Lacrimation, tearing*
Itching	Swelling	Infected,
Sore, tight, swollen	Erythema, warmth, redness	Allergic shiners
Dysphagia, difficulty in swallowing, choking	**EARS**	*Feel heavy*
Weak voice, hoarse	*Itching*	**NASAL**
Salivation, mucous	*Full, blocked*	Sneezing, urge to
Bad metallic taste	Erythema of pinna (reddening)	Itching, rubbing
	Tinnitus, ringing in ears	Obstruction
	Earache (for 1 ½ years left ear)	Discharge
	Hearing loss	*Post nasal drip*
	Hyperacuisis, abnormal sensitivity to sound	*Sinus discomfort*

I n addition to what is considered the "normal" allergic reactions as noted above, I experienced the following:

- Electrical storm in my head, blinding me for one and a half minutes.
- Painful spasms on my brain (continuing for over one month straight, then reoccurring periodically.
- Intense ear pain in left ear.
- Shooting pain up the back of my neck
- A beehive sensation that hovered in my brain area for almost two months (reoccurring periodically).
- Loud noises in my ears, nose and facial parts falling asleep
- Dryness in head
- Tightness down left side of neck
- Nausea for one and a half years (I lived on peppermint, a natural nausea reliever, during that time period.)
- Hair, my bangs turned yellow
- Toenails, three nails, two big toenails and the next toenail in from those died and popped off (not uncommon in chemo patients, but not the norm for the average person, and I wasn't on chemo!)

Nutritionist

So continuing daily with one accord in the temple,
and breaking bread from house to house,
they ate their food with gladness and simplicity of heart.
Acts 2:46

It's time for my first visit to the nutritionist at the Environmental Health Center – Dallas. I arrived at a rather small room, consisting of only a desk facing the back wall, the nutritionist's chair and a chair he pulled up to the desk for me to sit in, in front of his computer. I felt confined. Before I could even tell him I was an EMF patient he reached across to hand me a magazine in front of the computer screen and we both heard a loud z-z-z-zit sound and the screen was staticky. The nutritionist seemed startled and he apologized for having the computer on. With so many patients, he had not remembered my EMF status as there are many types of allergies. He immediately turned the computer off. My thoughts since I wasn't convinced yet of my status, was, *what kind of scam are they running here?* Somehow, my sitting near the computer had an effect on both the computer and me. It was all very confusing. Unfortunately it is all very real. My toxic body was causing havoc with the computer and the computer causing havoc in me. After that little episode we reviewed printed hand-out sheets instead of the overview that was prepared on the computer that I could no longer view.

I became aware of how much I didn't know about nutrition. I learned that wheat was a major reactor in me, causing inflammation. So this was the hardest thing to give up since I am a lover of breads. I recall saying to the nutritionist that it's okay if I have to give up wheat—I like mostly white bread." He looked at me with concern. "White bread *is wheat*." Dahhhh. Okay, so I spent most of my life in a cubicle at work. How was I to know that white bread was actually processed wheat? Talk about feeling stupid. No genius here. Removing wheat from my diet was no easy task. Wheat seemed to be in everything, pasta, breads, and even some soups. It was a challenge to follow. Thankfully gluten free products became a big thing shortly after this so more food choices became available to me through those products. It was explained that it's not the gluten I can't have but my sensitivity was to wheat. However gluten free products don't have wheat so go with those.

One of the most important health issues I learned about from the nutritionist was that becoming regular with bowel movements should be my goal. I was the queen of constipation. Always living my life at such a fast pace. I never stopped to think about drinking more water or eating better foods. Forget about relaxing long enough to use the potty to rid all of the toxic waste. It never crossed my mind how unhealthy it was to NOT be able to go to the bathroom. Oh sure I peed like most, but the other function, the one I'm blushing about as I write of, being able to poop was not something I've ever been good at. Sometimes it would be a week or two for me to pass a stool. BINGO. Major Toxin! It's critical for our wellness to get ourselves regular, empty our bowels. So now I needed to add pooping to my list of wellness to-dos. By following a good organic diet with bulk, oils, and lots of fluid, not to mention strong doses of magnesium, I was able to achieve my goal. . .and what a difference it made. The sluggishness I've felt for so long was lifting, moving along and out. At least one area of my body felt relief and can only benefit the rest of me long term. A dear friend of mine said, "Don't be embarrassed to discuss this subject—even the Queen has to poop."

Based on results from my skin and blood testing, the nutritionist was able to arm me with the tools I needed to replenish myself. I came away from my sessions with the nutritionist with information on a rotation diet, a list of nutritional supplements based specifically on my body's deficiencies. He provided me with a list of vitamins and minerals, along with information on elimination and rotation diets. The emphasis was put on using the most-pure brands as possible. Use brands like Pure Encapsulations, Allergy Research Group and Biotech.

I learned that there is no such thing as a universally safe food. Any "health" food, "organic" food or "non-organic" food could be harmful if you are sensitive to it. It makes sense. I just never thought about it before now.

The rotation diet mainly consists of four-day increments where you don't repeat what you have eaten, the theory being that it takes four days to process what you've eaten and you have a greater chance of reacting to a food by putting more of the same in your system before it's eliminated. I had a long way to go to get up to par on the four-day elimination theory.

I cannot emphasize the importance of nutrition to keep your mind and body well. That may seem simple but there are a lot of people who do what I use to do—eat fast food, not checking labels on store-bought foods, eating just to fill the void. Years of my life were spent just eating when hungry. It didn't matter what was eaten, just fill my empty stomach. Life was going so fast around me that there seemed like no time to plan or think about what was for breakfast, lunch or dinner.

I remember grabbing a Devil Dog (a Drakes cake) on the way out the door, as a kid, just to quiet the hunger pains. I was not taught about nutrition growing up and apparently, I wasn't smart enough to figure that out until my later adult years.

Good organic foods, clean water, and vitamin supplements are a great way to put you on a wellness path to health.

Heal your brain, and you will heal your body. No one can function well without a healthy brain, the control tower of our bodies.

The only downfall I could see to the Environmental Health Clinic is that it was self-pay, meaning you paid up front and were given forms for you to submit to your insurance company for reimbursement. That was an "ouch" financially. Luckily, the agent I was dealing with at my insurance company went above and beyond to help me get my claims processed. It was extremely tedious though, because every item, every test, had to have a code. So, for example, if I had ten skin tests that day, the insurance company expected ten different codes, and it was timely. My agent asked for several updates, most times daily. That would mean I needed to use a phone, which in turn compromised me more. Go figure.

Other Patients

To speak evil of no one,
to be peaceable, gentle,
showing all humility to all men.
Titus 3:2

I'm amazed at how we as humans are all the same, yet at the same time very different. We all want to be loved and respected. Basically we all have pretty much the same body parts but how those parts interact within themselves can be very different. Made up of body, mind and spirit; we react based on our experiences, and our exposures.

I was the only patient at the Environmental Health Clinic during my two-week stay that was being treated for EMF sensitivities that I am aware of. Another patient was being treated for severe depression. He had been depressed for twenty years to the point where he could no longer function at his job. I encountered him *one on one* in the sauna. He simply had no voice. Don't misunderstand me, he could talk, we talked. Somewhere along the way he simply gave up standing up for himself. He'd lost his voice. He gave up his fight.

In the waiting area one morning, I met a 6'2" woman who was sitting in a wheel chair. She was skeleton-like in appearance. I can't remember ever seeing any one as thin as she was. Compassionately I asked, "Can I pray for you?" To my shock and horror she verbally attacked me.

"I don't believe that stuff," she yelled at me.

"NO, NO PRAYERS HERE!" she screamed.

How naïve of me to think that just because I came to the Lord when I was thirty-eight-years old, that everyone else surely did at one point in their life as well. Years of living in the Bible belt, as a result of relocating with my job, have really reprogrammed me. I was stunned by her response to my loving request. She truly DID NOT believe and wasn't buying into my *Holy Roller* attitude.

I walked away, apologizing with each step away from her until I was out of sight in the nearest bathroom. Then I did what I seemed to do best in those days and had a total meltdown. My heart was broken for her. I started crying and praying for a woman who clearly didn't believe and had given up all hope. She said she didn't want me to pray for her. The one good thing about our God is we don't need permission to put our heart out there and pray for people whether they want us to or not. So pray for her I did, with a vengeance.

Somewhere deep inside me I still needed her to have hope, to want to pray to our maker. After all, if she'd given up, how would I, who is basically allergic to anything with electricity, going to cope? We all need each other to be strong. No negatives. I have to believe the God I serve is capable of healing us both, no matter how gloomy our situations appear.

One patient was being treated for a severe reaction to a rod he had put in his leg. It had to be removed and treated for allergic reactions to the rod.

Another lady had a severe reaction to the oil spill at the Gulf. Although she lived one hundred and fifty miles from the spill, just the inhalation from the toxins that the wind blew her way left her completely debilitated.

I thank God for Dr. Rea's wisdom and heart to want to help all those of us who can't help themselves through the regular medical profession.

Getting myself to Texas proved to take more out of me than anticipated. On my trip home, I could feel and hear the electrical currents zapping my brain as I drove under power lines. It was disturbing to hear the *zit, zit* sound and feel the motion of that sound penetrating my brain waves. I prayed harder and was ever so grateful to have acquired shots from the Environmental Health Center to self-administer for temporary relief. It is only by the grace of God that I made it home to my condo in Asheville.

Backward Slide

Be anxious for nothing, but in everything by prayer and supplication,
with thanksgiving, let your requests be made known to God;
and the peace of God which surpasses all understanding,
will guard your hearts and minds through Christ Jesus.
Philippians 4:6,7

It's taken me five years to even try to write about my condition. I was so compromised with such a diminished capacity to think that I couldn't articulate my thoughts into writing. I kept getting confused and thoughts would scramble. I had to rebuild myself after the significant decline in my health. I do recall sitting and staring into space for long periods of time, sometimes days. I no longer belonged to myself. I felt like a stranger in my own skin. Luckily I kept some notes along the way that I was able to reflect back on insulating the distance between me and the world.

In retrospect, I remember being a bit of a dynamo. I was independent, dedicated, hardworking, goal-oriented, a loving, vivacious person. That would classify me as perfect partner material. . .all that has changed. I'm spent. I have nothing to offer, nothing left to give. It's hard enough to get myself through the day, let alone think about the needs of someone else.

A close friend of mine stopped by to visit me and we would color and play with play dough—that's how far back I regressed. I had to start learning all over again. I couldn't read because it would scramble, I have not watched TV because when I tried to it hurt and didn't make sense when I looked at the screen, the sounds from a radio or CD player caused me to have a complete meltdown neurologically, making me feel like the muscles in my body were giving way. The telephone was excruciating, causing middle ear pain, inner brain pain. The cell phone was useless, making me feel like my muscles collapsed and scrambling my thought process. I remained a mess.

Attending the two weeks at the Environmental Health Center of Dallas armed me with the knowledge and tools I would need to be able to manage my EMF illness.

Upon my last consult with Dr. Rea, I still had no idea how much my world was about to change.

I knew there would be hard choices and sacrifices along the way, but once the magnitude of the lifestyle changes were realized, the knowledge became stifling at first.

What would you do if you are told, basically: you can't live where you live, can't work where you work, can't play where you play, and can't go to church where you go to church? No public buildings, period.

Once I got past the shock and the realization of what I needed to do to heal, which was not easy to act on, but very necessary for recovery, I had to access and make a game plan for my new reality. After all, I loved my work family, loved my church family, loved my condo neighbors like family, and had grown very fond of the friends at the YMCA. There was a time when I was healthy and filled with ambition. Problem is, I could no longer function in any of those places. I had to refrain from all public buildings due to exposure from electronics, wireless technology and fluorescent lighting.

I sat down and wrote a list of my new reality. The following conclusions are what I surmised: can't work where I worked, can't live where I live, need cabin with minimal electricity, no beauty parlors, no hairdryers (too painful), unscented products only, can't visit a hospital, avoid hospitals in general, can't fly in airplanes anymore, must avoid airports entirely. I can last eight minutes in Wal-Mart—but must AVOID. Can last ten minutes in Ingles grocery—AVOID. Cash registers set me off, fluorescent lights are a problem, causing me to meltdown, and I collapsed to the floor under exposure to them. It's no longer an option to drive at night, due to the oncoming lights, which are now painful. No movie theatres. No more church buildings. No more gym. I can never have a new car, due to electronics with built in GPS. No more motorcycle rides, not that the opportunity presented itself often, but when and if it did again, it would be a loss not to be able to venture out. No colognes. No jewelry (although the doctor said I could wear one ring—I had a mother's birthstone ring custom made to keep my children close to my heart), If I was giving up everything else at least I could look at my ring finger and be reminded that I still have two amazing children—now young adults. The jewelry store employee went above and beyond to accommodate me by meeting me in the parking lot outside of the store, since shopping indoors was no longer an option for me. Peeking through the store window, I could see that the jewelry store beamed with fluorescent lights to make the diamonds and precious stones sparkle. I must eat organic food. No chlorine pools. I need to use candlelight lighting—unscented and beeswax only, if I can tolerate them. I can use a landline phone, on speaker, for brief periods. I could last eight minutes by standing across the room and wearing headband protection around my ears. However, after two years off the phone I can last for longer spans. I pay a price if I choose to use the phone. But let's face it, sometimes a phone call is a necessity, not a luxury. Sometimes even I need to connect to the outside world.

The only thing I wasn't willing to give up was church on Sunday. That was my support system. But after several attempts to function in the building proved negative, I had to give in to the fact that I just wasn't able to sustain myself long enough in the building. I simply couldn't function.

After assessing my list of do's and don'ts, it's no wonder most of the people diagnosed decide to kill themselves, but I'm here to tell you that that is NOT THE ANSWER! There are ways around everything. THINK OUTSIDE THE BOX. It is my hope to share with you how I built a life around the things I could do and not focusing all that I couldn't or can't do.

So what did I do next? The only thing I could do given the odds. . .I dropped to my knees and prayed and prayed and prayed. I prayed with a vengeance. I prayed to try to understand. I prayed for courage. I prayed for hope. And then I did the only logical thing I could do, I put my condo on the market.

It would take one year and three months to sell my condo. Condos are loaded with EMF's. I could control the Wi-Fi in mine, but not the neighbors', that still seeped through.

The first year of chronic exposure I didn't think I could physically make it. The pain in my brain was unbearable at times. I knew each day was a gift.

I had no income for the first time in my life and no way to financially sustain myself for very long. Between medical bills and just plain wanting to eat dinner, I exhausted my 401K. Anyone who has ever had a health setback can relate to the fact that it only takes one medical setback to wipe you out financially. It was not very comforting to go through so much cash so quickly, but it was my new reality. I always prided myself on paying my bills, so bills are what I paid.

Thankfully, my sister made good money as a nurse and was able to front my mortgage for the year and three months that it took to sell my condo, or I would have lost everything I'd ever worked for. After winning my Social Security Benefits, thankfully it pays retro, I was able to pay her back. The love of family sustained me.

It was expensive to keep up with my injections for allergic reactions, expensive to continue on a vitamin/mineral regimen, expensive to switch to organics, but all very necessary. So I asked myself what good the money would be in the bank if I no longer have my health. So I took every dime I had and did everything I was told to do to beat this. I was determined to beat this man-made environmental illness. I had nothing left but an overwhelming sense of grief.

Self-analysis is never comfortable or easy, but it needed to be done. How was I going to reinvent my life? I once found working and planning so much easier to do than relaxation. My mind couldn't articulate all the necessary changes now that I'm in snail mode. I was alone in my stillness as the world around me continued to move forward. I sat in a rest state, but wasn't relaxed.

I wish I could be the only one to experience the pain and heartache. I wish they could just use me as the guinea pig since I already have it, but unfortunately with the degree of cell towers, smart phones and electronics upping their game, our bodies simply cannot adapt to the amount of exposure we are subjected to. Our bodies are paying a price for advanced technology.

Skeptic

And you shall know the truth,
And the truth shall make you free.
John 8:32

I n 2010, three percent of the population was already diagnosed with EMF, by 2017 ten to fifteen percent have been diagnosed. This only accounts for the people who are able to find a doctor knowledgeable about EMF. Finding a doctor who is open to and informed of EMF (or ES) is a task in itself. It is a fairly new environmental illness known mostly in the holistic field of medicine and not yet recognized in the main stream medical field. It is an unpleasant, life altering, and very disturbing environmental illness.

Since I was a skeptic on the validity of my diagnosis which is basically of being sensitive (allergic) to electricity, Dr. Rea asked me to do an experiment when I returned home to my condo. I agreed, since I had nothing left to lose.

We had previously discussed how, despite my workouts, although a struggle to continue, I still forced myself to swim at the YMCA and condo pool, and walked three times a week to try to improve my health. Despite my good intentions, I was still getting weaker and weaker. I started using Leki walking poles to give me added confidence when I walk due to weakness in my legs and body.

Dr. Rea suggested I purchase a gauss meter. "What's a gauss meter?" I asked, dumbfounded. Dr. Rea methodically explained, "It's a handheld device, a meter that accurately measures the electromagnetic fields generated by a wide variety of EMF sources." I'm thinking to myself, unbelievable—this guy is a walking encyclopedia. He went on, "Some examples but not limited to would be detecting AC power lines, office equipment, household appliances, and all types of electronic equipment for EMFs." He continued on, "It will help you determine if you are in a hot zone, so you can move away from the exposure." Really, I mean REALLY, okay this is getting weird. I was feeling like I landed on another planet. All of this information is foreign to me.

"Take the meter with you into a restaurant. If the section of the restaurant you are in is in the red zone, move to a different section." He is projecting this so matter-of-factly. "I can't walk around with that thing." I remained neutral, unconvinced, humiliated somehow of my new reality. I'm appalled that I have to detect my every move.

That conversation was seven years ago when I could still go into a restaurant on occasion. Since then I've become more hypersensitive, along with the fact that mostly all restaurants now offer free Wi-Fi. Wi-Fi is one of my worst offenses. Exposure to Wi-Fi causes extreme pain and discomfort to my inner brain. It's not a headache—it's a deep, sharp pain in the inner brain. Something I've never experienced before. Like a stabbing, cutting sensation that won't quit. Even after I remove myself from the source, it lingers on. At times I thought it was the end of life for me because I didn't think I could tolerate that level of pain much longer. The average episode after exposure lasts approximately three to four days.

The last time I was able to have a dinner date out on the town was about six years ago. I haven't seen the inside of a restaurant since then. Even if I could find a restaurant free of Wi-Fi, everywhere you look in today's world, people are hooked up to their cell phones and laptops. My toxic brain picks up the signal somehow so public places and me are not a good fit.

Getting back to using a gauss meter, Dr. Rea asked me to retrace my steps where I walked three times a week in my gated community, using the gauss meter as an experiment. So, after recovering from my trip home from Texas, I did just that, and was I surprised at the findings. I carried the gauss meter with me. I call it an idiot meter because I had to purchase the one that was easiest to read. It's the only one I could understand at the time. It reflects a green, yellow and red light to detect levels of electromagnetic fields. Green being you are free of electromagnetic fields, yellow shows you are being exposed, and red means it's a warning; remove yourself immediately from that area.

One thing I didn't think of, because prior to my visit to the doctor in Texas I had no reason to think about, is the fact that my neighborhood is all underground wiring. So I retraced my walking workout routine. What a shock to learn that I was walking in the YELLOW zone the whole time, walking right over the underground wiring. And right where the corner meets the side road, the exact place I had a seizure, I was in the RED zone. That made me a believer. I didn't need any more convincing. I was able to see for myself what I couldn't fully yet comprehend.

I tried to keep things light when conveying my condition to my mom, trying not to overly concern her to the seriousness of my condition. Truthfully, I still do not understand the magnitude of my disease. Our brief phone conversation went something like this.

"Mom, Dr. Rea just made a believer out of me," I announced somewhat triumphantly. "The bad news is I took the test with my meter while walking through the neighborhood, and I'm walking in exposure from the power lines the whole way, even though its underground wiring, alternating from both sides of the road. The good news is I can still walk the neighborhood but I have to walk in the middle of the road. The worse news is although I won't have reactions from the wires, I stand the chance of getting hit by a car!"

My mother's consistent and usual response to my making a joke out of a not-so-funny situation was, "What am I going to do with you?" At least I made her laugh.

Another reason I call my gauss meters *idiot meters* is because I am now the proud owner of three different types. Thankfully, there is a company called Less EMF. It is the EMF Safety Superstore. They have a catalog which is most helpful since I can no longer go online. Anyone able to go online can connect at www.lessemf. com. See back of book for complete contact information. The EMF Superstore is a great resource and I've used many of their products successfully. I purchased all three of the meters for different applications. I saw how effective the first meter was with just colors for zones. I wanted to delve a little deeper as to the true impact of my surroundings.

I continued to use my meters on occasion to test or retest my surroundings. I do well as long as I remain in a controlled environment. The microwave oven was the biggest surprise to me. I tried my meter near it and the readings were off the chart, meaning extreme exposure. My daughter stood in the kitchen next to the microwave oven; I stood in the hallway fifteen feet away. She turned the microwave oven on and the reading was still off the chart. I moved around the corner and down the hallway and still the microwave oven read off the chart. No contest there, we will never use another microwave oven. Since I worked full time, the microwave oven had been a major convenience. I used them both at home for a quick breakfast and dinner and at work for lunch. This would now be yet another past convenience for me. I haven't touched one since.

One of my friends very lovingly tried to lighten up my "meter" experience. She said I could use it to test any new guy friends I might meet. Red light—oh yes he's hot!

The first and least expensive meter I purchased was the OSUN Radiation Finder that I spoke of earlier in this chapter.

The second more advanced meter is an Electro smog meter by Cornet. It picks up RF/LF Fields. I needed something to help me detect Wi-Fi before I actually got to the suffering phase. Since being technical isn't my thing, I had a hard time switching back and forth from reading RF fields to reading LF fields and became even more frustrated. However any guy friends or techno people that I showed this to saw a bigger advantage to this meter and they had no trouble using it.

Finally, I needed an easy meter to read so I could use it when trying to find a safe place to live. I purchased the TriField Meter Model 100XE. I found this meter the easiest advanced meter to use and the most accurate. This was extremely helpful when assessing a new home environment.

Currently I don't need to use a meter. I'm so hypersensitive I can feel when I'm being afflicted by EMFs. It's painful, scary and unnerving. It would still be a good idea to use a meter because a lot of times it's an accumulation of EMF sources that afflicts us. But the reality is EMF's are everywhere and almost impossible to avoid in today's world.

Most people recognize me by my beige baseball cap and silver headband. What they don't know is that both the ball cap and the headband are shields. I use this hat mostly fall and winter while taking outside walks.

The baseball cap protects my brain from radio frequency pollution. It is designed to shield the head from below AM through microwave, including cell phone frequencies. It's lined with *staticot* fabric woven from poly/cotton with an ultra-thin pure stainless steel thread.

The headband blocks radiation and is two-inches wide, 93% silverized nylon, 7% lycra and stretches comfortably. It shields my ears.

The ball cap and headband have proven themselves over and over again. My brain and ears were so compromised I can actually sense the differences in the level of mind and ear noise with the use of these products. I could feel and hear a *zit* sound along my brain if near an electrical line. Of course, I try to avoid power lines, but that's not always possible. These products gave me the confidence to go out in public. I simply don't leave home without my head protection. I do notice that the effectiveness of these products wears down after continued use so I recommend replacing with a new hat and headband about once every year and a half. The hat sells for $29.95 and the headband $24.95 and worth every penny for the security and comfort they provide.

I wear a bright orange hat during outings to the lake to swim. This brightly colored hat offers a different type of protection. I wear it so that the boats see me as I swim the length of the dam or around the buoy at "The Circle" (the picnic area and boat ramp to the left of the dam). I do this despite the fact that I'm told I look like a buoy.

I've tried many products that claim to provide relief. Sometimes they were successful and sometimes not.

About a year ago, I was so desperate to go back to church that I purchased the shielding poncho with hood. It's a disposable Mylar poncho, inexpensive at $4.95 each. I figured if I wore it under my coat and my shielding baseball hat maybe just maybe, I could join my brothers and sisters in Christ.

While staying at my brothers farm in West Virginia, both of my brothers and I tried an experiment to see if the Mylar poncho would provide protection from signals. One brother wrapped his cell phone turned on inside of the Mylar material. The other brother called the wrapped cell phone number from the phone in his hand. The wrapped phone DID NOT ring. This proved the theory that the Mylar does, in fact, block the wireless signal.

Remembering our Mylar experiment, I figured it was worth a shot at wearing a Mylar poncho to be able to attend church. Sunday morning came and I put on the poncho. You could only see the foil-look around my neck and ears, the rest of the poncho was covered by my coat. But even with that goal in mind, I felt ridiculous, yet determined. I wanted to be around people, around my church family. I wanted to worship in a group. As soon as I got to church, it was obvious by others reactions that I looked more ridiculous than I thought. Oh, don't misunderstand me; the pastors and people closest to me were extremely supportive of my efforts. But I noticed one couple, a man and woman, in particular that I have seen but didn't know. They looked back at me. I always sat in the last pew closest to the door should I need to make a quick exit due to reactions to my surroundings. Anyway, I saw his face and he was ridiculing me. I could read his lips. That was an "ouch." I wanted to shrink down into myself, but instead I just prayed that he would never be afflicted as severely as I and would never experience the desperate desire to do the things everyone else takes for granted. I felt like a freak. It was an honest attempt to function. Despite the kindness of my pastors who go above and beyond by providing a safe place for me, I remained unable to function.

My pastors even display a sign on an easel in the front of the church upon entering the building that reads:

> Please TURN OFF not just mute your cell phone.
> A member of our congregation suffers allergic reactions
> to EMF frequencies.
> Thank you.

Despite all the attempts and precautions taken, I still seized.

Confused about why I still seized despite the protection of the poncho. I called Less EMF. The founder is an electro physicists, he and his staff are very knowledgeable. One of his employees explained that a signal can run along the material and find its way into the nearest opening. This resulted in being a direct hit to my brain. . .unbelievable. And, yes, I had yet another seizure. So my days of going to church until I could get a handle on my health were over, for the time being. My seizures in church were too traumatizing for the people around me, not to mention taxing on my system.

I continued my worship in the outdoor chapel that I built in the woods behind my house.

Life from This Day Forward

And the apostles said to the lord,
"Increase Our faith."
Luke 17:5

I put together an assessment of all I had learned at the clinic in Texas, recognizing how drastically my life was changing. It's interesting to look at the summary and sharing what it is like to be chemically and electromagnetically sensitive.

Chemical sensitive: avoid all chemicals: cigarette smoke, perfumes, after shave, cleaners, exhaust fumes, crowds of people, etc.

No more:
- Nails done
- Dry cleaning clothes
- Hair Salons
- Lighting candles at dinner (they release gases, unless unscented and possibly bees wax if I can tolerate.)
- Swimming in chlorine pools
- Movie theaters

Use only:
- Organics: soaps, laundry (borax) detergent, cleaners, makeup, food and organic bottled water. "Yes—its true—they make organic water"

Food sensitivities: tested some foods; no wheat, no strawberries, no chicken. YIKES!

Electromagnetic Field Sensitive: Carry Gauss Meter to detect fields (which I did in the beginning, but being hypersensitive I no longer need a meter, I can feel the impact). **AVOID: power lines, microwave ovens, cell phones, portable phones, TV, 3D movies, cell phone towers, power plants, and radios.** I can never buy a new car, due to the built in electronics and GPS. I'm sensitive to anything that has electrical currents. Even batteries give off a current. No jewelry. No watches (I blow them out every three months). I must sleep in a zero-electricity zone. It is important to walk barefoot in untreated grass to ground myself. Wear leather-soled shoes. Avoid flashing lights due to my light sensitivity.

Despite all of my newly acquired limitations, I thank God for the ability to see and hear and walk and talk and be all that I am capable of being.

It took me a lifetime to get my body into this condition, so I conclude it will take some time to restore myself. With the right tools and patience, I believe that will be possible.

To heal and restore myself I must do the following:
- Continue prayer time—read more.
- Oxygen therapy (two hours a day) or as needed for allergic reactions.
- Supplements, exercise, sauna to detox and mineral replacement.
- Antigen Injections (must carry note from doctor to carry syringes in car).
- Day 1 Histamine and serotonin injection (and as needed up to 4 x's a day for allergic reactions).
- Day 2 Chemical antigen
- Day 3 Metal antigen
- Day 4 Day off, then repeat four day cycle of injections.
- Emotions—use Tri Salts to balance emotions. 1 teaspoon in shot glass with water.
- Find a clean swim able lake to swim in (no chlorine)
- Expose bare feet in the grass to ground my body
- Picnic on a blanket, use exercises to balance my body's energy. Yoga.

All of this is merely a wake-up call. Although these restrictions may appear extreme, it is the only logical way to stop my body from getting sicker. The goal being less is more. Hopefully by avoidance I could restore healing to my toxic body. I was desperate to heal my body, mind, and spirit. I was forced to leave the rat race of daily living and just sit still. It is in this stillness that I know without a shadow of a doubt that God exists. His spirit and presence is what has sustained me.

The goal now is to find complete serenity, a simpler life. I need complete restoration. I also hope to help others with the knowledge I gained so that they don't have to learn healing methods the hard way.

I am grateful for God, family, friends, and a fresh start. Initially, my diagnosis felt like the end but time has a way of healing those thoughts and feelings.

Corporate Disability
Benefits Denied

Now whom you forgive anything, I also forgive.
For if indeed I have forgiven anything,
I have forgiven that one for your sakes in the presence of Christ.
2 Corinthians 2:10

After all that I went through with testing and results, I submitted my proof to the insurance company that handled my corporate disability benefits. I thought it was cut and dried, and benefits would be realized. What a shock to my system it was to get a nasty-gram from the insurance company telling me bluntly to "get back to work—EMF's are everywhere." Like I don't know that! I can feel it. The effects are painful and debilitating, Wi-Fi being my worst offender. How disheartening.

Despite my hard work to try to get the help I needed and to get well, my disability benefits from the company where I worked for eleven years were cut off. I found out later that while I was halfway to Texas, the company stopped my short-term disability. Where's the justice in that? I was devastated when I found out. After all, I worked hard and took pride in working for a major, global corporation, but apparently I became another number at that point.

Six years after my setback, my case for corporate benefits remained on the court docket. It has been thrown out more than once and escalated to Federal Court. I try not to think of the injustice in this. No one plans anything like this. I don't blame the company for my condition, they had no way of knowing. I do hold them responsible for not paying me long-term disability when I needed it. I do expect them to honor their promise for long-term disability when one becomes unable to function and support one's self. However, that was not going to happen. My attorney was green when it came to the higher courts and the case was thrown out on a technicality. Presumably, my case was not sought out in a timely manner. Hog wash.

I had a choice to make. I could hold on to the injustice and let it manifest negatively in me. I could sue the attorney for not filing for a year after receiving all the information from me, claiming that dates were ambiguous. Or, I could let it go and release the negativity from my vibration, trusting that God would make a way for me.

End result, I let go and let God. I decided that I was so very grateful to still be alive that I let it go but not before recognizing that "ambiguous" would be my least favorite word this lifetime.

Social Security Disability Hearing

Therefore, as the elect of God, holy and beloved,
put on tender mercies, kindness, humility, meekness, longsuffering;
bearing with one another, and forgiving one another,
if anyone has a complaint against another;
even as Christ forgave you, so you also must do.
Colossians 3: 12, 13

When the realization hit me that I couldn't return to my employment, my humiliation was complete.

Confused on why I would be denied corporate benefits, I set out to apply for Social Security Disability. I needed a way to afford to feed myself.

The first two attempts to secure the Social Security benefits I made by myself. I figured it was a cut and dried case. After all, I just couldn't function to maintain employment. After being denied twice and being told by the representative at the Social Security window that "no one has ever won on the basis of EMF, so don't even bother putting in for it." I came to the hard fact that I needed an attorney to represent me. So I employed an attorney that specialized in SSD (Social Security Disability).

Being told at the Social Security office that no one ever won for EMF made me want to fight even harder. "You mean to tell me I've worked my whole life and now that I can't function I'm just to roll over and play dead?" I blurted out to the rep.

Sadly, I welcomed the thoughts of death as an alternative to the pain, humiliation and hopelessness that I found myself in.

I could face disgrace by myself, but not for my children. Ah yes, my children, I had to persevere to set an example for them not to give up, despite the hand that life deals you.

My boyfriend, at the time, drove me to the Social Security attorney's office. My attorney was no nonsense, a matter-of-fact, intelligent, attractive female who didn't waste any time. She respected my disability by making accommodations. She turned off all of the fluorescent lights throughout the building and we met in a conference room, free of electronics. Even with that I felt like a dish rag.

It didn't take long during a question and answer session that my emotions overtook me. I simply had no coping skills left. The Attorney seemed to gleam at my lack of skills. "The judge needs to see this. You have no coping skills. I want you there in Tennessee, since the only other option would be to televise you by satellite, which is probably not an option for you."

My sister flew in from New York to join my boyfriend and me to the hearing. I was praying at this point that I could function long enough to get through the hearing. The lawyer was emphatic that no hearing, no disability award. There was little regard for my not being able to function in a building.

Upon arrival, I was somewhat relieved that the building was out in the middle of nowhere. That relief was short-lived after entering the building. I was expected to sit in the waiting room area. Within minutes I went into meltdown mode. The fluorescent lights overpowered me. I couldn't stop the flow of tears. I told my attorney that I needed to leave the building and would wait outside until it was time.

My attorney came to get me because it was time for my hearing. It was overwhelming to come to the realization that after a one year and a half wait it was my turn to be heard. She escorted me back into the building.

I wasn't overly confident, I was scared. I was horrified at the thought that the judge had the power to deny me benefits and frightened of what the future held in my state of brokenness.

We walked down a long, narrow hallway. As I stood in the doorway of the court room before me and surveyed the scene, I figured I'd never get out alive. It was loaded with fluorescent lights and electronics.

His majesty sat at the other end of the room at a desk higher than the rest of us. He had a computer, my paperwork, and was intensely scanning the pages. He looked up long enough to glimpse in my direction. I can't imagine what his assessment of me was. Aside from having to hide behind dark glasses to guard me from the pain that any kind of light had on me, and the head wrap and protective ball cap, I looked relatively normal at 5'6" tall and one hundred twenty-five pounds.

The room was crowded with tables down the center, housing modems and electronic hookups. Tables lined the outside of that table in a rectangular shape. Sitting to the left was a specialty doctor with his laptop. Just inside the door to my right was my attorney with her laptop. She signaled for me to take a seat to her left. All of us had microphones displayed on the table in front of us. I suspect this was to record the hearing and for the judge to hear us clearly, although the room was small. Behind me was a full mega screen where a picture of an occupational expert was viewed via satellite from another location.

I remember thinking how intimidating the room felt and that my future was in their hands. I remember being asked to state my name, birthdate, and possibly my social security number. To myself I kept saying, "Jesus I trust you, Jesus take the wheel."

I remember the judge asking how I take care of myself, since I live alone. I remember sharing that I push the button and run if I am to use the washer and/or dryer because I couldn't be near them without reacting. I remember the judge asking how I got there and I said, my boyfriend drove me. Then, to my shock and horror, the Judge mischievously looking straight at me asked, "So, you have a boyfriend. What do you do with your boyfriend?" Stressing of what he actually wanted to know, I turned to my attorney in horror. She could sense my eyes pleading for direction. Very lovingly, she said, "He doesn't mean that. Just tell him what you are capable of doing."

"Your Honor, I can go on a picnic or a hike, I can play cards."

Whew, I really thought he was alluding to my love life. At this point holding hands was a big deal, my electrical was so far off that my boyfriend sent a jolt through me just standing next to me. Had I been sixteen, I would have mistaken the jolts as cupid's arrows.

I don't remember much after that, I knew I was retreating inward, I was losing the ability to comprehend my surroundings.

"Unbelievable! I can't believe how some people have to live." I vaguely remember the judge blurting that out. I seem to remember thinking he would welcome my comment. "I'm right there with you Your Honor, I wouldn't believe it either were I not living it." I was wrong. He bellowed back something to the effect that, "I'm not talking to you, I'll ask the questions." When he realized the effect his comment made on me, he seemed to retract and more gently replied, "I'll let you know if I have a question."

At that particular moment I felt like Dorothy, when the Wizard of Oz spouted out for her to bring back the broom from the wicked witch. I felt left without a voice, put in my place and hopeless and then everything scrambled. Next thing I knew, I was outside of the building leaning against a concrete pillar with my shoes off to ground myself. I was starting to thaw out from the numbness that set in due to the heavy exposure from the courtroom. My sister was supporting me so I wouldn't collapse and hit the pavement. My attorney went to my sister instead of me. I heard her say but couldn't compute, "She doesn't even know that she won."

Those words didn't quite register. All I could think of was I was in the building and I made it out alive. My sister shared the good news with me later on.

My boyfriend was driving down the highway with my sister in the front passenger side and me sprawled out across the back seat. As I awakened from a deep sleep, I heard myself blurt out, "I can't believe the judge believed me." The truth is I was in shock and disbelief that this was my new reality. And then I passed out.

*****

The poem on the next page was written after reflecting back on what it was like during the emotional days of my set back.

Reflection During Darkness

Imagine a world of silence where light reflects pain and sound discomfort.
A world where motion makes you disconnect
and conversation is hard to comprehend.
It hurts to feel.
It hurts to speak.
I'm alone in my suffering.
The world continues on as if I was never part of it to begin with.
Rivers flow from my eyes in solitude as if that would somehow carry away my fears.
No TV – don't miss it.
No music – drowning in silence
Sometimes the silence is deafening.
I can't participate, be part of, or feel a sense of belonging to anything.
How do I handle this handsome young man who pursues me
It doesn't matter that I want to be near him
I know inevitably it will get old when he can no longer communicate with me
Can no longer call – because the phone is becoming a convenience I once knew.
He can't text me, can't email me, can't communicate by today's standards
Oh, sure there's snail mail but how long do you think that will last in today's world?
How is it that he was interested to begin with?
Denial?
Lack of knowledge?

Oh, how I wish I could make this new reality all go away.
How I wish I could be normal and do the normal things people do.
Despite doctor's orders to refrain from public buildings
I continued to go to church, not yet understanding that I'm having
allergic reactions to my surroundings.
I'm assisted out of the building yet again in meltdown mode
I paid a price – but so did Jesus
I will not give up on my Savior
He sees a bigger picture, He knows my heart.
Discouragement is a choice. Why I've chosen that today, I don't know
I feel defeated, alone, lonely.
These feelings are foreign to me as I have always felt like the strength
to those around me.
If I were to ask why, I'd come up short.
Why the restrictions?
What's the goal?
The bigger picture?
Something is not connecting in my brain.
When I read, look at a magazine, try a phone conversation. . . . I dis-
connect, fall short, don't always comprehend, and confuse names.
I'm tired, very tired, *spent*.
PRAISE HIM for He knows best
HEAL ME, USE ME, OR TAKE ME HOME!
AMEN

Sing "HALLELUJAH" Anyhow!

The Lord will fight for you,
and you shall hold your peace.
Exodus 14:14

I heard once that life is tough, but when you can admit that to yourself, it gets easier somehow. Despite all of my losses, I find myself singing HAL-LE-LU-JAH.

When life seems out of control, I sing and say hallelujah anyhow. It would be easy to give up, but that is not what God designed us to do. Giving up is a tactic the evil one wants to lay on us, don't buy it. Don't give up, no matter how difficult things seem. Fight, fight for your life. Take a stand. Not everyone will understand or even care, but stand tall in your own right. Our God cares and He wants us whole. That's the truth.

Always remember: Do what you can do and don't worry about what you can't.

Be tenacious! Hold persistently to life. Be a *Pluck!*

As I became more and more passionate about all that I learned, my desire to help others eventually increased. Once I could articulate the horror of my circumstances I felt the need to shout out to others that are unaware that any of my symptoms are even a remote possibility.

I needed to get stronger. I needed to help others. But for now I needed to "just be."

Condo Living

The Lord is my Shepherd;
I shall not want.
Psalm 23:1

T he days at the condo proved long and void. I couldn't articulate my thoughts. My new reality paralyzed me. It was all I could do to get through the day. My mind was not yet capable of processing or taking in the severity of my situation. The one thing I did know is that my spirit was drawn to the water. The back of my condo had a small, screen-enclosed porch. Living on the second floor allowed me to overlook the stream of water that flowed by, moving swiftly at times, behind my condo and under the tunneled bridge that held the road. A waterfall graced my view. I was drawn to the ground, near the water that flowed. I spent days on a blanket near the stream, not even knowing yet that I was grounding myself to find relief. My spirit knew what I needed.

As I became more coherent, I reached for my Bible. Psalm 23 spoke loudly to me.

The Lord is my Shepherd
I shall not want

"Is this what this is all about Lord?" I prayed. "Have I wanted too much? Is this a test?"

He makes me lie down in green pastures.

I'm drawn to the earth and all I can manage is to lie on my blanket.

He leads me beside the still waters.

I'm next to the stream. . .barely moving at times.

He restores my soul.

79

He is giving me a forced break from the chaos of life.
He leads me in the paths of righteousness
For His name's sake.
Every day was soothing, providing healing for me, the stream comforting, the ground a sacred place. One day into my setback, it was cold outside, but I still continued to be drawn to the stream. I felt the urge to write what I saw and this is what came out:

The river flows swiftly as if in a hurry to get somewhere
Where will it take you?
It is crystal clear
With ice sculptures molding stray branches
911
Where is the hurry
Where will you flow?
Clear as crystal
The water roars over imbedded stone
The sparkle lures me
To swim with it were it not so cold
The rocks fit together like a puzzle on the floor below.
A waterfall cascades
Splashing, teasing, and tempting to call me home.
Dare I stay or dare I go?

*****

I arrived back to my condo after my daily nap of lying on a blanket by the stream in the neighborhood. I got so much relief by lying outside on the grass by the flowing water that I started packing my lunch daily and taking it with me. I would eat my lunch and literally pass out on the blanket. My brain was exhausted.

On this particular day I arrived home to my condo to find a handwritten card sticking out from under my door mat. One of the neighbors wanted to meet with me about the purchase of my condo. Considering that there were over seven hundred condos on the market, the likelihood of selling anytime soon were slim.

I know I should have been excited about the note but I couldn't figure out how I was going to muster up the energy to move out. I was barely functioning and needed a lot of down time. I averaged fifteen hours of sleep, deep sleep at night or else I couldn't process things like conversation or sounds outside.

I addressed the offer with my realtor. She was very aware the market was flooded with condos and this was my chance to unload it and come out from under my mortgage payments. I agreed to sell. I maintained a peace about me. The market was slow, so the buyers wanted to close in a couple of weeks. I extended that to one month to give me time to farm out my furniture to a consignment shop and box up what was left to be stored in a storage bin.

Only one problem—where was I going? I can no longer function in Asheville. I tried to inquire of other areas for a cheaper house. My income was seriously limited. So I did what I always do when I'm at a crossroad in decision making. . .I dropped to my knees and starting praying. I prayed with a vengeance. I cried out to my Lord and Savior. Lord, put me where you want me. I had planned on going further south; somewhere in a cabin by a lake, somewhere more affordable. I kept seeing a clean, swimmable lake. I just had not found it yet. I had no idea how I would muster up the strength to get myself there. And then the phone rang.

"Sis, this is your brother Chris."

"Hey Badder!" I call him Badder because, well, he's badder (tougher) than me. It's a pet name.

"Sis, I've been thinking. Why don't you come home until you decide where you want to live?" he gingerly, but very lovingly, went on to say.

"My wife and I talked about it and we have a rental on our property available and would love it if you'd come here. It could be for a week, a month, a year; you can stay until our home sells and then we will figure out from there where you need or want to be next."

"Chris, you are not going to believe this but I just finished praying about where I'm supposed to go."

I didn't hesitate, I knew in my spirit it was where I was supposed to be.

"Yes, I'll come but I don't think I can get myself there." I knew this was a God thing. The love of family continued to sustain me.

"I probably could make it as far as West Virginia because it's an easy drive with no congestion. But I know I can't drive further than that."

"No problem, sis. I'll take a flight to my farm in West Virginia. I'll drive you in your car back to my home in New York."

I couldn't believe the profound unconditional love in my brother's voice. I could hear his concern. Quite frankly, I was concerned myself. It seemed like everything I worked so hard to achieve was dissipating: my home, my health, my independence, my way of life. But still I was at total peace. God had his hand on me. Not quite grasping the magnitude of my losses, but recognizing there was a bigger picture, one I couldn't quite put my finger on yet.

I hung up the phone and worked on packing.

Consignment Shop Scam

But I say to you, love your enemies,
bless those who curse you,
do good to those who hate you,
and pray for those who spitefully use you and persecute you.
Matthew 5:44

I'm three weeks away from selling my condo. Not knowing yet where I will end up and unclear of what to do with all of my furniture, I decided it would make sense to put it in a consignment shop rather than pay the exorbitant fees to store it all.

I knew of a reputable consignment shop across town that had been in business for years, over more than thirty years, to be exact. I decided it was time to seek assistance. My neighbor drove me there, since I was having trouble driving myself, so I could find out the details of what needed to happen to expedite the removal of my furniture in person.

The owner, a bright woman, not much older than me, made me feel like she would take good care of my possessions. She even stepped outside to accommodate me to discuss my situation since I had trouble being in the building. I trusted her. She said I would receive a monthly check as the items sold. I had no reason not to believe her.

The very next day she sent her daughter and son-in-law to retrieve my furniture to include a king-sized bed, an armoire, dresser with mirror, two night stands, a TV wall unit that was a large four-piece structure, a country dining hutch, table and chairs, lamps, bedding, and a two-thousand-dollar mattress—unsoiled. Most of the pieces were bought brand new from Haverty's. They were from the Broyhill Attic Heritage line. It was difficult to watch yet another part of my life dissipate.

What I didn't know is that I looked like death warmed over when I arrived at her shop. She was a con-artist. She arranged to have my things picked up and furnished her home and daughter's home with the contents of what was taken from me. I was out of society approximately two years. I never received a dime. She never responded to my letters, despite the fact that I included a self-addressed, stamped envelope. I'd been *had*.

Upon my return to the area, I wrote to a realtor friend asking her to drive me to the consignment shop since I still couldn't drive in the city. We were two days late in our arrival. The place had been sold and the previous owner skipped town. I learned later that she reopened in her daughter's name in a nearby town, a town the local kids refer to as Swanna-no-where.

I wasn't about to play dead. I needed the money for future expenses and to get new furniture when I figured out where I will be living. The realtor called the local police for me since I couldn't stay on the phone long enough to explain my predicament.

The Asheville police department was amazing in their pursuit. They were able to track her down. They arranged a conference call with her, the officer, and me on the line, since I didn't want to be near her in person and could use a land line for brief intervals.

Thankfully my brother warned me. He told me the woman is a con-artist; don't be surprised if she cries into the phone. That is exactly what she did. I wouldn't have believed it unless I heard it for myself. Not only did she cry, but her excuse for not answering my letters for two years and not paying me was that she got bit by a spider and was in the hospital one month ago. *REALLY!*

I saw through her excuses. The police reminded her that not only did she scam someone, but she scammed a disabled person for over five-thousand dollars, which is a felony. She was told to pay or go to jail. I was only asking for what would have been mine as per the original deal. Since she breached the contract I could have asked for the entire value. We agreed to the original contract and to avoid jail time, she paid up. Thank you, Jesus. The whole incident left me feeling disappointed in her actions. How do people live with themselves when they prey on the less fortunate? I have a hard time with that concept. I find it hard to believe that someone would take advantage of you when you are at your lowest point.

I learned that there were approximately ninety-plus people ahead of me that she'd scammed. Most of them never pursued their losses, they simply didn't know how to or were so discouraged they gave up.

I thank God that I was given the strength to stand firm to recover what was rightfully mine.

It took me a long while to get past the disappointment that someone could take advantage of me when I had regressed so far. After two years, I was finally able to put the owner on my prayer list for healing of her desperate, wayward ways.

Part III:

Avoidance – Where do I go from here?

The Trip North

Since you have purified your souls in obeying the truth
Through the Spirit in sincere love of the brethren,
Love one another fervently with a pure heart.
1 Peter 1:22

My brother and I were en-route to his New York State property of fifty acres. Everything was going well. To look at me you wouldn't guess I had this peculiar ailment. However, seeing me in a reactive state is disturbing and disbelieving.

It was midday and my brother pulled into a rest stop area. We both got out of the car and walked toward the rest stop building to use the bathroom facilities. There were people ahead of us and people behind us so we were walking with the flow of the human traffic. As we walked into the rest stop building just past the front doors, my body failed me—no warning, just reaction. My muscles weakened in an instant and I became in a collapsed-like state, leaning on my brother. Actually hanging on him paints the true picture.

I appeared completely wasted and, with little muscle power left to support myself, he held me to support me. Lovingly and playfully, I say, "Hi BAA Der." Not only do I think he is badder than me but years earlier one of my children said *badder* when they couldn't pronounce brother and it stuck as a nickname.

Anyway, I was wasted even though I don't drink. It's the reaction I get to my surroundings. In this case, it was the extreme onslaught of exposure from overhead fluorescent lights, six vending machines (three on either side of the entryway), overhead fans, and who knows how many people had cell phones on, pulling in a signal.

So, it's not bad enough that my brother had the look of shock on his face and I'm all over him. We got the added bonus of the woman attendant across from the entryway yelling loud enough for everyone to hear.

"Handicapped, right this way," she was enthusiastically waving her hands to guide us in her direction.

"Bring her here," she went on to say.

"We have a separate bathroom for her." She was excited to help.

I looked around, wondering who she is talking too. Surely there was some mistake. Was she really yelling out to my brother? Wasn't I the independent business woman only the year before? Denial is a powerful emotion.

The attendant was looking at my brother as if we are lovers. She assumed from my behavior that we were a couple.

"Go ahead, bring her in there." She was suggesting for my brother to take me into the handicapped bathroom to assist me.

"We allow that here," the attendant continued on in a loud voice.

Still stunned, looking sheet white, actually grayish in color, and unable to decide what to do, my brother guided me to a nearby bench. The bench was somewhat away from the crowd but near the handicap bathroom, and we sat in stunned silence. After what seems like an eternity, that overwhelming voice from the attendant sounded out.

"If you don't take her in, I will," she shouted.

Now I'm not as disturbing looking. We were somewhat away from the intense exposure of the entryway. I am able to get a grip.

"Sis, can you go in there by yourself?" he had a look of horror still on his face.

Having enough wit left to recognize I have to relieve myself and don't want either of them to participate; I asked my brother to guide me to the bathroom door. I held the walls. I couldn't use the light because the fan comes on and both the fluorescent lights and fan would further affect me. So I did what I have learned to do. I took a quick survey of the space. I left the light switch off. I closed the door and felt my way along the wall to the toilet. In the dark I took a quick squat, flushed, washed hands, and exited quickly before I get caught with my pants down, since I needed to leave the door unlocked should I need assistance.

I was still reacting to the surroundings. Feeling the acute embarrassment and humiliation of the situation, I started crying as we left the building through a side door. I guess it was more like bawling out loud. I've always prided myself in my modest professional appearance. It was so difficult wearing my new title of *handicapped*. My brother assisted me to the car by holding onto my arm. He was still in shock, but doesn't say anything. He turned to me and sheepishly said, "This might be a good time to have lunch."

We sat in the car silently as I administered shots of histamine and serotonin into my stomach area, which I use for reactions to my surroundings. We ate, although food was the last thing on my mind.

I was still crying as he drove down the highway.

Being the loving, funny brother that he is; he quickly found a way to counter shock me. As he continued driving, he puts his right arm out with his hand pointed down and finger pointed at me and yells out,

"HANDICAPPED!!!"

"Over here, right this way, handicapped!" he continued to shout out.

I cried a little harder but then found relief in the playful love he displayed. Then he said very timidly. "Gee, I don't know why you can't drive yourself."

We had arrived at my brother and sister-in-law's fifty-acre estate. Thankfully, it was surrounded by thousands of acres of government land. Relief was in sight. I recognized that the place was for sale but due to the specialty and exclusiveness that the property offers and the fact that it had been on the market for one year already, I know I'll have enough time to get a handle on my health in the solitude. I also knew that God is in control and I'd be there as long as I needed to be. This incidentally, ended up being a little over one and a half years.

When I moved into the modest efficiency apartment above the garage. I was hypersensitive. Despite no electronics, no TV, no phones, or computers I still felt ill. Something was affecting me. The cause determined was a reaction from the refrigerator. I couldn't tolerate the motor.

My brother with his take-charge, no-nonsense attitude said, "Well, that's a simple solution." He unplugged the refrigerator, but not before exchanging concerned glances with my sister. He offered me the use of the refrigerator in the cottage next door. I felt almost instant relief when the refrigerator was unplugged. My brother purposely didn't rent out the cottage next door because all inquiries needed Wi-Fi, my worst offense. So alone I stayed on the other end of the fifty acres from my brother and his wife's main house.

The realization of my predicament hit my family hard and although they weren't quite sure what was happening to me, they supported me emotionally. They believed in me. There is major healing in that. My family spent the next year and a half just pouring their love into me with visits to cheer me up. I thought I'd only be there three months but time had no relevance to me. Just getting through the day was an effort.

As disturbing as my new reality had become, I knew I somehow had to regain my independence, but I had to be patient. Praying daily, seeking the Holy Spirit to prick my spirit, to let me know when it would be time to move on.

In the meantime, what I felt was profound loss. Loss of job and residence, loss of friends at work, condo family, church family, YMCA friends, loss of people who you thought were your friends, but were unsupportive during this setback, loss of love interest relationship, and loss of self.

The trauma of all that loss set me back emotionally. I stood before my brother, sister, sister-in-law, and daughter feeling very vulnerable, timid. It felt like I climbed deep within myself. I was mimicking my child-within, feeling like an eight year old. I felt temporarily helpless. Numb. But calm. I knew on some level that I was right where I was supposed to be at that moment in time.

God's love shined through when family members visited. They all participated in my wellness plan by helping in any way they could. They all ran errands as needed and supplied me with groceries. My sister, the RN, lived at the bottom of the mountain with her husband. She worked double-time to check on me. She spent as much time as her schedule would allow. She just poured her love and concern out for me. We played cards, mostly SkipBo, since that would help me think. I can only imagine how frustrating it must have been to play cards with me since I was operating in slow motion. We spent most of the time just catching up with all the years that we all were apart, since seven years earlier I had relocated with my job from Connecticut to Asheville, NC.

My daughter, a young adult, had recently moved back to Connecticut which placed her twenty minutes from me. That could only be a God intervention. She was able to visit on her days off from work. She blessed me with organic lunches and her love and companionship. She, too, wanted to play cards. I suppose you guessed by now that is one of the few things I could still do that doesn't involve electronics. We got to explore our mother/daughter relationship more intimately during that time and past wounds thankfully mended.

Over one year and a half had passed and I was still content just existing, just being able to function and get through the day. It was then that I realized I had to disconnect to connect with God.

The place was a paradise. The apartment I was housed in over-looked a man-made pond that my brother installed years prior. On any given day you could be privy to a fox, bear, coyote, squirrels, raccoons, abundant fish, alligator turtles, herring, bald eagles, vultures, wild turkeys, and an abundance of snakes. In fact, that whole mountain was infested with snakes. Black snakes everywhere. I would see on an average of three snakes a day. This was mostly because I had to be outdoors and would sit in a chair on the lawn and put my bare feet on the ground to get relief. A method called "Earthing" or "Grounding."

Every day after I had managed to make myself vertical and dressed, I made it my job to go fetch the mail. That was not only a chore, giving me a purpose, but served as exercise as well. It was all I could manage to do during the day. It was my big outing. The mailbox was located about one and a half miles down the mountain from the house. So I'd tie a bag to my belt loop and head down the mountain on the dirt road provided. I would only pass two cabins nestled in the woods on the way down. Once I reached the paved section, there would be six more houses on the route to the mailbox. Retrieving the mail gave me a job and helped me to feel productive, since I wasn't capable at the time to do much else. It wasn't always easy to get myself to the mailbox and back, but I persevered. On days that it took me too long to accomplish that task, my brother would conveniently just show up to drive me back up the mountain. He kept tabs on me.

Over the course of my stay, I became friends with some of the people whose houses I passed by each day. One guy in particular, Jeff, made it worth the trip down the mountain. We enjoyed each other's company, although brief, from time to time. He allowed me to enjoy his art work displayed throughout the yard. He made art out of scrap metals. Ironically, the house he lived in was a power plant station that he'd converted. What are the chances of that happening? We would visit outside on his back patio. It allowed me adult conversation and a creative outlet.

After I had been on the New York property for a couple of months, my friend Jeff, the metal sculpturer, stopped me one day as I was passing by to get the mail. In his New York/Brooklyn accent he said, "Me and the guys were talking. We don't think there is any such thing as EMF; we think you are too smart for that. We think you are a CIA Agent living undercover up at your brother's house."

He was rather convincing in his analogy of me, but really? Then he went on to say, "Whatever is bothering you, why don't you just go to the top of the mountain, scream and let it out!"

Can you see another *REALLY* here?

Wouldn't it be wonderful if life was that simple? If I could just scream and all of the symptoms would vanish. It didn't work.

A couple of times over the course of my stay I'd mentioned to my brother that I needed to go back to North Carolina; it's where my heart was. I love the mountains. God presents himself everywhere there. My brother knew how compromised I was and gave every possible reason as to why I should stay. He didn't have to work hard to convince me. I loved the time there to get reacquainted with family and deep down I knew I was too compromised to make any kind of move. I wasn't well enough to drive myself anywhere, and no one was offering to drive me back south.

I tried to put a plan of action together, but just couldn't pull it off. Using a phone for any length of time wasn't an option for me, still too physically painful, still scrambled my thoughts while trying to use one. I began writing to realtors in North Carolina. My hope was to find an affordable cottage on a clean, swimmable lake. Its vision was all-consuming. It was my hope. It was something to look forward to.

My prayers were abundant daily. One day, I thought I heard my brother and his wife drive out of the driveway. This would be a perfect opportunity to pray outside. The driveway between their main house and the apartment was a couple hundred feet long. Being the prayer warrior that I am, I began praying over the property, praying for financial relief for my brother and his wife, praying for the right and perfect person or family to come, see this place, offer full price and appreciate all of the hard work and beauty that this place displayed as a result of my brother and his wife's hard labor. Thanking Jesus and praising him in advance for a positive outcome.

What I wouldn't learn until two days later is that my brothers' wife drove away but my brother was watching me from the main house. He approached me days later and said,

"Sis, what were you doing on the driveway two days ago?" he said playfully.

"Oh, well I was praying for the sale of your property." I was stunned and a little embarrassed that I'd been caught in the act of a very private praying outburst.

He proceeded to say that he visited the neighbor down the hill and told him, "If you don't buy this place my wacky sister is going too." LOL.

Finally one day I told my brother that the reason his place hasn't sold is because I was still there. He looked at me as though I'd completely lost my mind. We were about to engage in a verbal tug-of-war. This war was one of love and concern. Like most wars it was a fight for my freedom. He began as gently as he could.

"Don't go leaving for that reason, the place will sell eventually." I could tell he was stressed.

"Sis, you can't even walk a straight line!" He pleaded with his eyes.

"But I can drive straight." I tried to sound confident.

"Sis, you can't use a rest stop," he went on.

"You gave me luggable loo the portable potty for camping," I rebutted.

"Sis, you can't use a restaurant," he persisted.

95

"I bought a case of rice and a case of beans to sustain me." I proudly offered the solution.

"Sis, you can't stay in a hotel," he argued, but tenderly realized he was fighting a losing battle.

"I mail-ordered a tent," I offered mildly.

"Sis, you don't know where you are going yet," he said incredulously.

"I've written to a realtor in Franklin, North Carolina she will look out for me," I added, with as much confidence as I could muster up.

"Sis, I can't handle it if anything were to happen to you. I'm only going to tell you this once. I need you." He looked heart broken.

"I need you too, Badder, but I can't be the family pet. I need to regain my independence." I knew everyone was spending way too much time worrying about me. They needed to regain their own lives. My leaving seemed like the only solution.

As my brother and I discussed my leaving I could read the fear on his face. We discussed every possible reason why I shouldn't go. But I knew and believed with all my heart that if I left, it would open the way for a sale. I could feel God's presence and I knew and believed with all of my heart that God knew how compromised I was. He was providing me with a shelter around family and I believe without a shadow of a doubt that I needed to find the strength to move forward so my brother and his wife could sell and move forward as well. Skeptical? Read on.

Leaving was weighing on me. I continued writing to realtors in North Carolina. My hope was still to find an affordable cottage on a clean, swimmable lake. The water was calling me. Its vision was all consuming.

As fate would have it, we had a tragic family loss in the passing of my older brother's son. The shock of the situation and the knowledge that we only pass through life once, gave me the push I needed to leave. That, and the fact that to be with my older brother, my sister would drive my car back to West Virginia. This would put me halfway back to North Carolina. Although I still wasn't able to drive myself yet, I knew the relief I would get in my tent on my brother's couple of hundred-acres farm would jump start my wellness. Soon, I could return south or make a life on the farm.

Once in West Virginia, it became apparent that I could be of no help to anyone. My only contribution was the continuous prayers I projected to them all, which I could do from anywhere. I couldn't tolerate the effects from being in the house where my Mom and older brother lived. It was inconvenient to have me around with their two TVs, telephones, wireless technology, a microwave oven, and fluorescent lighting—all affecting me adversely. Don't misunderstand me, family members were most loving, turning off anything wireless such as the outdoor barometer. They switched out light bulbs to incandescent bulbs. Mom even stopped using hairspray since I can't breathe with its contents. They waited for me to step outside to use the microwave and walked away to use the cordless or cell phones. Mom could only use the washer and dryer when I was outside. It proved exhausting to run to the farthest corner of the house each time the heat pump turned on. Remedy: I stayed in my tent.

Do I stay or do I go? Winter would soon be upon us. It was now or never. I need to regain myself back.

Something happens when you take back control of your life. You start to heal. I was on my way to recovery and a place to call home. I had happy expectations about my future home. I was finally ready to embrace the uncertainty of the future.

My brother and his wife had given me a birthday card this past June that reflected "Follow the Spirit." That is exactly what I did.

What does following the spirit mean? It means praying for direction. It means being open to your spirit being nudged when it's time to make a move in a new direction. It means knowing, without a shadow of a doubt, that God is with you and that he is leading, guiding, and directing you. If it's true spirit, you will have a calm, confident demeanor about you. You will know on some level that you are exactly where you are supposed to be and doing exactly what you are supposed to be doing. I followed the spirit to my new home, praying every step of the way.

Social Security Disability – 2nd Go Round

Then He said to the disciples,
"It is impossible that no offenses should come,
but woe to him through whom they do come!
Luke 17:1

Once you go through the grueling process of winning the award for favorable Social Security benefits, you are reintroduced to the system about one to two years later. Once again you get put through the process of proving you are disabled. This second go-round could have proved fatal to me, had my sister not acted quickly on my behalf while in the designated doctor's office building.

I received a notice to report to two doctors' appointments while living in New York State, since I was now residing on my brother and his wife's property. There was still no regard for the fact that my diagnosis included refraining from all public buildings.

The first appointment I was grateful that my sister-in-law was available to drive me. The appointment was brief, but I found myself crying through the entire interview. I didn't cry because I was sad but because it was a reaction to my surroundings.

The second appointment, in the same building, at a later date lasted much longer. This was to be a physical exam. My sister, a nurse, was available to drive me that day. We climbed the stairs to avoid the electrical exposure from the elevator. Quickly I was reminded of the public building's bombardment of electronics as I was greeted in the waiting room, once again, with a big flat-screen

TV, the receptionist hooked up to her computer and headset, the waiting room sporting people texting other people.

Lord, I pray you get me through this nightmare.

I waited in the hallway part of the time, knowing that if my body failed me yet again, I won't get through the appointment. No appointment, no disability income. Where is the justice in that?

It was my turn; I was already compromised from being in the building. My sister escorted me to the designated room. A nurse arrived to input my information. She was in disbelief of my predicament as I answered her questions.

We were moved to another room across the hall. This is where I would be put through a physical exam. The exam would have gone well, had it not been for the fact that, unknowingly, we were put in a room next to a room housing x-ray and technical equipment emitting a bombardment of EMFs.

As the doctor proceeded to do the exam, my sister was emphatic that he needed to examine me as quickly as possible so she could get me out of the building. My nose was already twitching, not a good sign. I was becoming emotional, another warning sign.

The doctor displayed zero personality, he worked robot style. He showed little concern for my predicament and went through the motions of checking me out. Despite my sister asking if there was someone with him that could help him remove me from the building if need be, he seemed to ignore the question and, to my sister's surprise, he left for lunch.

Seconds after he walked out of the exam room, I went into seize mode. My sister now set in *fight and flight mode,* ran down the hall to get help. The doctor had already left the building. Hard to believe the place was set up to help the disabled. There wasn't a wheel chair existing on the premises. My sister borrowed a desk chair on wheels while asking for assistance to get me out of the building, knowing that the only remedy was to remove me from the exposures.

I can only imagine how difficult it was to get my naked butt dressed while coming out of seizure mode. I was dead weight. With assistance from two other office personnel, they rolled me on the desk chair. Although I have no memory of this, my sister told me later that I was like a rag doll, my arms flailing at my sides. Since there were no arms on the desk chair itself I was just prompted in the seat, legs dragging, feet pigeon-toed, as my sister frantically cleared the way for my exit. I don't think we even checked out at the front desk. The goal was to get me to safety.

Once in the hall, it became clear to everyone that going down the stairs was not an option. So my sister helped get me into the elevator, giving orders to the two people holding me onto the chair to stay with me while she ran down the two flights of stairs to get to the car.

I began thawing out by the time we left the building, but still couldn't comprehend the magnitude of what just happened.

Somehow the three of them managed to get me into the car. My sister sped away from the building driving until she could find a clearing. I remember being driven out into an open field. My sister left the car to gain distance away from me to turn on her cell phone and call my brother to meet her at the property. She needed help to get me inside.

After arriving back to the property, I am told that I slept for three days to ward off the effects of the visit to the doctor's office. My sister explained that I had a grand mal seizure.

She was still in disbelief that not only did I have a total meltdown in the disability hearing, but now I had been asked to go into yet another building, which resulted in an even worse reaction.

My new reality of not functioning in public buildings was more than either of us could absorb at the time.

Going South – Six Weeks in the Elements

"I can do all things through Christ who strengthens me".
Philippians 4:13

With nothing left to lose, I started praying "Heal me, use me, or take me home." Little did I know that He, our Lord and Savior, would honor all three requests.

First He equipped me with a vision of where home should be. In my mind's eye, I saw a small, rural town sheltered from the effects of a big city with a clean, swimmable lake nearby. North Carolina had been tugging at my heart and wouldn't release. It was like an internal GPS calling me home. I needed to return, having once worked and lived in the state.

When I was praying to take me home I meant Heaven — to take me to Him out of my afflicted body. Instead He knew my time here wasn't up yet even though to me it felt that way. He gave me heaven on earth instead.

I left West Virginia on September 29, 2013, to find a place to call home before winter. After being out of society for nearly two years, it was a surprise to pull into a BP station to find a TV screen attached to the pumps. Now you can pump gas and watch TV. Does the technology ever slow down? I knew I was going to be in trouble from the effects of the electronics, but needed gas, so I prayed with all my might, covered my nose to guard from the gas smell which makes me sick, looked away from the TV screen so the motion wouldn't topple me and got out of there as fast as was humanly possible.

By the grace of God, I arrived in Asheville, miraculously without incident, the same day. I unloaded most of the contents of my car into the storage unit that I previously secured prior to leaving almost two years earlier. After checking to see that whatever worldly goods I still had left were still held safely in the rented storage bin, I went in search of a campsite. I returned to the storage bin the next day to discuss with the manager the possibility of using the unit a little longer. I told him I was close to finding a place to call home. He recommended a mover and advised that there was no need to give notice in writing; he flagged my account as a possible move. All this, but I still had no earthly idea where I was going to end up. But there was a peace about me every step of the way. I was prayed up daily, all day, and every day. I wouldn't know until another month that I'd accidentally left the storage bin unlocked. I hadn't clamped the safety lock all the way shut. The garage-type door was left partially open unbeknownst to me. They had to use their own lock to secure it. However, they had no way to reach me at this point. My cell phone was no longer an option and although they had my brother's phone number as an emergency backup, I wouldn't be talking with him anytime soon. The slip up on my part of not locking the unit completely would later prove to be to my advantage.

I stayed at Powatan Lake Campground Sunday night September 29th and Monday Sept 30th next to the Campsite Host Terry and his wife's camper. He said he remembered me coming to swim there a couple of years prior. He was very helpful.

On September 30th, I approached the guard station and the woman attendant suggested I get an Access Card. It is a card for discounts while camping for disabled people. Finally, there was a benefit. There was something positive for being in my condition. It was a chore to purchase the Access Card. The attendant said, just drive on the Blue Ridge Parkway to the end. I thought it was nearby. Over an hour later, I was still driving, exhausted, and I still had no idea how much further I needed to go. When at last, *voila*, there was the Ranger Station. Thankfully, they were all very nice, although I got the once over. I don't really look disabled until I'm in a reactive mode and then I'm really scary looking, or so I'm told by anyone who has witnessed my meltdowns.

The Access Card is a lifetime benefit. Thankfully, I have a way to afford the campsites that I so desperately needed to survive, since hotels were no longer an option. Even private campsites are no longer an option, since all the ones I investigated had Wi-Fi.

On my way back from the ranger station I came upon the Pisquah Inn at Mount Mitchel. I was extremely hungry. I parked my car, walked up to the glass entry doors and peeked inside. I knew from the surroundings that I couldn't function in the building. I asked someone to please ask the manager to come out. Moments later a young man named Ian Drobka who was just promoted to the Food and Beverage Manager came to my aid. I explained that I was hungry and had not been able to get any real nutritious food. I was afraid if I ordered a meal and ate outside I would attract one of the bears that area is known for. I asked if he had any suggestions, otherwise I would be quite happy to take the meal to my car.

Ian Drobka was unbelievable in his new role of hospitality manager. He didn't make me feel like a freak. In fact, he asked me to wait a couple of minutes. I said I would. When he returned, he asked me to follow him, leading me away from the crowded dining room and to a private dining area reserved for parties. It was empty of people but filled with linen covered tables. He sat me at the farthest point away from stimuli. He proceeded to bring me a menu, at which point I was able to splurge with a meal of scrumptious porterhouse steak, mashed potatoes, red cabbage with onions, salad, and sweet tea. As an added bonus, he brought me a dessert made of a scoop of vanilla ice cream that I was craving. He cheered me up by using whipped cream and a strawberry cut to make a happy face on it. All the while he personally waited on me and engaged in conversation. Although he had never heard of EMF, he respected my status. He must have seen the need in me. I was still at peace in my spirit but my physical body was hungry, very hungry, living on rice and beans had taken its toll on me. When I left the restaurant, I just kept praising and worshipping the God that I serve and projecting prayers towards Ian. He definitely is in the right business and has perfect mannerism for the job.

It's October 1, 2013 and I drove to Franklin, North Carolina. I had an appointment to meet a realtor by the name of Christy. We had been corresponding regularly for the past several months by snail mail. What a shock to my system when I arrived in Franklin, only to find that it was the hub of all electrical systems. This definitely wasn't working for me. I kept the appointment anyway and we explored areas outside of the Franklin area.

Christy was very protective of me. She was thrilled that I'd made it safely to her office. She had a look of disbelief on her face when she saw how compromised I was.

During my search with Christy, there was one house that stood out. It was a doll house which sat on the top of a rather steep hill. It was in a neighborhood of only about six houses. Everyone would be gone for the winter, since these were summer homes. The positive about the place is that the woman who owned it certainly knew how to market the house and bring out its good features. She put in a fire pit which basically took up the entire side yard (and only yard). She decorated the house with a very appealing vintage flair. Thousands of forest acres surrounded the place which would protect me from Wi-Fi. I noticed most of the street names surrounding the place were names like Panther Drive. "Why are they calling everything Panther around here?" I asked innocently. "Well you might get panthers crossing through your yard, but they won't hurt you," she stated nonchalantly. "What? I don't think so. So, you're telling me I would be here alone. It snows and I would not be able to get out. The nearest grocery store is off of a four-lane highway, and now I have panthers in my yard!"

As an added bonus, the only other thing that would be a negative is that a biker's convention comes to town once a year and approximately 1000 or more bikes would be circling around the hill below me. Being that I am sound sensitive, living there would be ludicrous. Do I hear an AMEN! Needless to say, despite my being extremely compromised I could still do the math. I recognized it was a seasonal, not year round home and got the heck out of there.

At night fall, she suggested camping at a campsite called "Outside Inn Camping." I drove what seemed like forever to get there only to find that it was closed and barricaded. I returned to her office. This time she called ahead to the Nantahala National Park campgrounds called Standing Indian. I could use my Access Card, so thankfully instead of $16.00 per night it turned out to be $8.00. Although $8.00 sounds inexpensive, it adds up quickly when you are several weeks outdoors. I needed every bit of the money I had saved to purchase a home.

So off I went to find Standing Indian. I settled in at dark by setting up my tent and starting a campfire. Unless I grounded every night (putting bare feet on the ground to discharge electricity from my body), I couldn't get enough relief to drive the next day. So barefoot by the campfire became a nightly ritual. I finally passed out by 11 p.m. At 3:30 a.m. I was awakened by a yelping noise. I wouldn't know until the next morning upon visiting the camp store that it was a mother bear and two cubs. Yikes! That explains the voices I heard walking past my tent at night saying, "Doesn't she know she is only in a tent? That thing could rip right through that." It seemed that everywhere I camped I was the only one in a tent. Everyone else had fancy recreational vehicles. Thankfully, every place I went cleared out shortly after my arrival. I would have had to leave due to the satellites and generators that all these fancy RV's had installed on them if they had stayed put. God continued to lead me and have my back!

The Standing Indian Campsite is run by the U. S. government. I was only there a short while when, at midnight, one night they decided to shut down all of the Blue Ridge Parkway, all government camp sites. It was some kind of political statement. The timing couldn't have been worse for me. I was hooked up to my oxygen machine when the Camp Director came to apologize to me and let me know I had to be out by Saturday at 2 p.m.. This was Thursday and I had no idea where I was headed next. So I guess you could say I was evicted from Standing Indian Camp Grounds, which brought me further south.

I was able to stay at Pines RV just long enough to regroup, take a shower and do my laundry in a tiny room that opened to the out-side housing the washer and dryer. Although they had Wi-Fi, I was desperate for a place to set up my tent so the manager/owner let me set up in the furthest part back on the property away from everyone and everything. I could still feel some residual but passed out as soon as I set up the tent. It was a messy site since I had to set up and take down my gear in the rain. Oh the joys of camping. A hot shower relieved me of some of my discomfort. The bathrooms had fluorescent lights so I had to time my shower after everyone else was finished so I could leave the lights off. I was used to taking my flash light into the shower with me and setting it down somewhere which provided minimal lighting.

Recognizing that the realtor in Franklin couldn't help me I headed further south. I was running out of camping weather. Winter was sneaking up on me. Unfortunately Christy wasn't licensed to be my rep in the area I ended up in. I would have loved to have kept working with her. She really showed care and concern for her clients and for me. Despite the fact that she couldn't assist me in the area I ended up in, we kept in touch for a while after I settled into my new home.

I drove further southwest, praying all the way. I tried eight different camp sites (both on the North Carolina and Georgia sides of the states) and couldn't tolerate the Wi-Fi. I was so desperately in need of sleep that I stopped at a hotel. What was I thinking? At this point I wanted to try to be indoors, maybe I can tolerate it and I didn't care what it cost. I just wanted to be indoors for at least one night to refresh myself. I pulled into the hotel and asked the attendant if I could just stand in one of the rooms to see if I could tolerate the surroundings before booking the room. She complied and walked me to the furthest room away from the center point where most of the electrical was housed. I lasted exactly one and a half minutes and I knew I had to get out of there. I felt so sick. I knew if I didn't drive away right then and there that I wouldn't be able to drive. So off I went on a mission to find a place to set up camp for the night.

I found a camping village called something that sounded like Pond or River Side. I pulled in, but the place looked abandoned. The attendant came out of the trailer at the end of the row closest to the creek, a fast running stream/river going by. The man was in his early forties, sporting dark eyeglasses that he never removed, despite the overcast. He had a grin from ear to ear, which seemed glued there and quite cartoony. Our conversation went something like this:

"Hey, I'm looking to set up camp somewhere affordable. Do you allow tents here?" I asked somewhat skeptically.

"Normally we just do RV campers, but most campers are gone for the season," he grinned even wider after using his Georgia boy drawl.

"I can't be around Wi-Fi and all that nonsense," I explained, exhausted from the effort of trying to explain yet again.

"Well we ain't got no outdoor bathrooms but you can set your tent up right there by the creek, right next to my camper, you can take a bath right there in that there old creek and I'll keep an eye on you." He grinned and, if I didn't know better, I saw a drool.

Panicked inside I said, "Well that's mighty nice of you. I have a few more leads that I need to check out; if they don't pan out I'll be back." I kept speaking as I backed toward my vehicle.

"Oh. . .you'll. . .be. . .back, you. . .ain't. . .gonna. . .find. . .no. . .place for $10.00 a night like here." Georgia boy was drawing out each and every word for emphasis.

"Old Jethro over there will keep an eye on you, too." He nudged his head towards a camper across the way, where a man in his late seventies sat in front of a laptop on the deck of his camper, intense in what he was viewing. I didn't want to even guess or assume what his eyes were glaring at. Whatever he was viewing on the screen was giving him way too much pleasure.

"My daddy's gonna love you," he continued on. "He had to run an errand but he will be back. I've got an idea," he carried on. "My daddy owns some property out in the middle of nowhere on the top of one of these mountains. How about I take you there? No one will ever find you." I would say he gleamed if only I could see his eyes. "Only one thing though, you would need a weapon, you carrying a weapon?" Without pausing, he continued, "I was cooking around a campfire up there two weeks ago and a mountain lion walked through, so I wouldn't want you to be there unarmed."

I was *so* out of there. Hair on the back of my neck stood up and I didn't even know I had hair there. I made a promise to return should the next campsites not pan out, just to get the heck out of there. I don't care if it's affordable, I probably wouldn't have made it to morning.

I was driving further south now. Stunned, but relieved to be out of there.

As soon as I saw the waters of Lake Chatuge I knew I was home. I call them the healing waters of Lake Chatuge. This was the vision I've had for the past twenty or more years. It was a clean, swimmable lake with modest homes around it. At least the modest homes were the first impression. McMansions could be found once I explored the shorelines at a later date.

107

I was driving west on Route 64 and praying with a vengeance, "Lord, I have no idea where I'm laying my head tonight, but you do. I trust you!" Up ahead I saw a sign on the right hand side of the road pointing left. The sign said *Camping*. I'm thinking I missed the campgrounds because I ended up in the parking lot of the Hinton Center which was a dead end road. When I entered the parking lot, I could see a sign saying *Chapel* ahead and I knew I was where I was supposed to be. The ironic part about the sign that said "Camping" is that no matter how many times I revisited that area the sign just doesn't exist. I've asked a few locals and they never saw a camping sign there. It could only be a God thing that I saw it to begin with and was led there.

It was later in the day and most of the staff had left. One woman stayed behind and was in her car on her cell phone. She had just finished her duties in the resort kitchen. Other than her vehicle, the parking lot was empty. I waited until she hung up the phone. I approached her but kept my distance, since her phone was still on, to ask if it would be okay if I slept in my car in the parking lot for the night. She assessed me quietly to herself. I told her I was extremely tired and just needed a safe place to rest until morning. She asked me to wait while she called the after-hours manager. I thanked her. She needed to leave to get to her family, but assured me that the night manager would be along soon. Not even fifteen minutes later, in drives a pick-up truck with a big burly looking guy inside. Once I saw the truck I remembered passing that truck on the way in. I must have just missed him when he left here.

"Hello, I'm Joe."

"Hey, I've been called a lot of names but Deborah will do for today. Would it be possible for me to sleep in my car in this parking lot just until morning?" I inquired.

"Well, I don't know. What's going on?" All the while eyeing me with curiosity.

"I'm en-route to find a place to call home and I just need a safe place to stay. Is it safe here?" I asked rather boldly.

"Well, I don't know, I'm here," he remarked with cocky confidence.

"Don't make me drop you!" I blurted out. The irony in that was more than both of us could hold back and we both burst out laughing.

I mean here I was exhausted, all of 120 pounds, and here he was a rather big dude who towered over me probably weighing in at 240. I wouldn't have stood a chance should this encounter go haywire. I mean really. I can pick them.

Anyway, I knew after that we would become friends.

I explained my situation of hypersensitivity and EMF. He wasn't buying any of it. He looked at me like I had a screw loose. However, he got back to the business at hand and said, "You won't believe this, but the generator in the left side of the building is down. I wouldn't be able to rent that room out with no heat. I could let you stay there for a couple of nights at a reduced rate." Perfect. This would give me enough time to get regrouped, feel safe indoors and take a shower. I don't even remember hitting the mattress; I passed out from sheer exhaustion.

The next day I assessed my situation. I paid for the room at the office building. Thankfully the lady at the desk came out to assist me without too many questions after seeing me outside the window waving frantically to get her attention. She just accepted that I couldn't go in due to the fluorescent lighting.

I couldn't believe my luck. I'm at a beautiful Christian resort of thirty-two acres. I have a room and a hot bath. I have use of a dock to swim off of and sunbathe on. I was within walking distance to the chapel, a chapel like no other. When I walked into the small chapel early morning, I fell prostrate onto the floor. I was in such awe of this majestic place. The wall straight ahead was all glass, overlooking Lake Chatuge. The cross was centered, so you looked past the cross out over the fabulous lake. This was surreal, I must be dreaming. I don't think it could possibly get better than this.

I wasn't doing particularly well by the second day since there was Wi-Fi on the grounds. Even with my protective cap and hair band I could feel the effects. However, it was the lesser of two evils. Wi-Fi seems to be everywhere. Not a good predicament to be in. I asked the office for a recommendation for a realtor and was on my way to find a place to call home. Now that I know I want to be on or near Lake Chatuge, the next order of business was to get indoors before winter.

I opened a post office box so I could have a way to communicate with family. I would drop post cards in the mail along the way so they would have some idea of how far I had gone. They could communicate by letter to the post office box if they chose to.

I visited the real estate office that was recommended to me. When I stood out front of the office for a while, the owner finally came outside to greet me. I told her I was looking for a Christian female realtor and she openly smirked. She was rather worldly and I could see she seemed amused by my devout beliefs. Ok, so she wasn't a holy roller like me. I need to get over the fact that not everyone knows what they are missing when Jesus isn't their priority.

While we spoke one of the male realtors from her office came out. He had overheard our conversation.

He blurted out, "I'm a Christian."

"But I wanted a female realtor. I'm not well and was hesitant to be with a male realtor, I really want a Christian female that I can trust."

He looked at me with a concerned and caring look. "Please give me a chance. I'm a Christian and I came here to heal as well and I didn't even know I needed healing." Something about him was genuinely caring and I decided at that moment to give him a chance.

I was actually surprised he would want to help me since it would be a relatively small sale in comparison to the half million to million dollar homes that he was used to handling. Once we got into his truck and I saw the wooden cross on his dash where the speedometer is I knew he was to be my realtor.

House hunting didn't go well in the beginning. For one, the realtor couldn't call me since the cell phone was too painful for me to use. The realtor let me know about camping nearby. I located the Parks and Recreation Department and was able to set up my campsite there for the month of October. Wendle, the park manager went above and beyond to ensure my safety. He and his wife, Veronica, treated me with kindness and compassion. Thankfully there were few campers so I was protected from potential electronics.

My realtor's job was to go into a residence before me and turn off all of any potential electrical exposure. This would include checking on the heating unit, refrigerator, TVs, any items that may cause me to go into reactionary mode. At first he didn't get the seriousness of my dilemma until we walked into what eventually would become my home. I couldn't even walk a straight line upon entering the home. Then I found out, the realtor had his smart phone on, the refrigerator kicked on and the heating unit kicked in. These were all formulas for disaster for me. The day was done before we got started and I returned to my tent to recover. Ultimately I released him from his duties, and went with a second realtor. I didn't think he was taking me seriously.

The second realtor was prejudiced and judgmental. That relationship was even shorter lived. He would say things to me like, "Woman don't buy a house on their own. Unbelievable, she is by herself, has the money to buy a house, but she is living in a tent."

I shared with the second realtor that the first realtor had shown me a house and I owe it to him to return to him. "Do you know there is a black man in that neighborhood?" he shared with a hateful voice.

I couldn't believe my ears. Did he really just say that? It was that last comment that really got under my skin. "What year is this? Did you really speak prejudice against a black man? Is this area that backwoods that the color of someone's skin determines their character or whats in their hearts?" That was the breaking point for me. I couldn't work with this guy another minute.

As it turns out, I did buy the house in that neighborhood and that black man was the first person who cared enough to stop by and welcome me to the neighborhood. He was protective of me, knowing I was living alone and he and his wife became very good friends of mine. Although I don't see them much now, I know they have my back if needed and that goes both ways.

So, after praying about it, the home that the first realtor introduced me to kept showing itself in my mind's eye. Winter was coming and I needed to make a decision.

I returned to the office of the first realtor and suggested we try looking at the home once more but this time he needed to respect my limitations and turn everything off before I enter the home. He did. I was successful this time and said I would pray about it and see him the next day.

I returned to the office the next day to present an offer. He immediately contacted the realtor representing the sellers, who showed up at the door within minutes. I presented my offer.

To my surprise the sellers' realtor said, "We already have another offer on the table." This was news to me. The house had sat for one year and three months.

So, I very confidently said, "Then it's meant to be theirs." A little more than perturbed feeling in my spirit that it was a bluff on his part so I'd come up in price.

"Oh, well they haven't actually offered yet, they said they were interested," he fumbled.

"Okay, well this is my offer. You know where to find me." I don't like being played. I all but walked away for good.

They knew I was compromised, they knew I needed to be indoors, and they figured they could play me. Not going to happen. The God I serve had my back. The next day, I was told that the seller counter offered. I accepted. It was a done deal. I closed in two weeks, exactly one day before my motor vehicle registration was due for renewal. I needed a street address for that to happen; the DMV will not accept a P.O. Box address.

The DMV had been very good to me while I had been out of society for the two years. They allowed me to keep my North Carolina plates, knowing the goal was to get well enough to return to the state.

I had two weeks until the closing. The purchase of my new home was based upon the home inspection and insect inspection. I prayed for some kind of sign to let me know if I had made the right choice.

I met the home inspector on the site. He greeted me by calling me Dolores. I thought that was odd, although it must have been an honest mistake. It could sound something like Deborah. I let it slide and corrected him gently later, letting him know that was my mother-in-law's first name from my previous marriage.

After that I met with the insect inspector. He greeted me by calling me Patricia. Okay this is getting weird, Patricia definitely doesn't sound like Deborah and Patricia is my mother's name.

Then it hit me. This was the sign I prayed for. I was comforted, yet a little spooked by the names of both my mother and mother-in-law used to identify me. God has a sense of humor.

I was paid up through the month of October at the Park and Rec camp site. The weather had taken a turn, and it was bitter cold.

The manager of the Park and Recreation Department approached me one morning. "Deborah, my wife and I are very concerned about you. You can't stay here any longer, you're blue." he said very cautiously.

"But I paid you to the end of the month," I said mechanically. "Where will I go, I only have two weeks until my closing."

"My wife and I talked about it. We would take you inside but we have all kinds of electronics in our trailer and don't think you would do well there."

I was so touched by this kind and loving gesture; however, I wasn't looking for anyone to take me in. I needed to do this on my own.

"What about going back to the Hinton Center?" he suggested.

"I guess I could check, but I don't do well in the hotel part. Maybe they have a cabin available now. There were none without secured reservations when I was there."

So, I returned to the outside of the main office at the Hinton Center. The office manager couldn't be kinder when she saw me.

"Hi, I know this is a long shot, but is there any chance that you have an opening in your single cabins? I only need a place until my closing." I asked expecting to be turned away.

"Actually, Deborah, you won't believe this but, just two hours ago, we had a cancellation on the single occupancy cabin, the furthest one away from the center," she shared, rather surprised.

"Ha-ley-lu-yah. Praise God, He came through again for me," I praised.

The night manager prepared the cabin for me. He heated it up ahead of time since I couldn't tolerate the heating unit. He changed the fluorescent bulbs out to incandescent bulbs and turned off the refrigerator. Although after a couple of days I was able to turn the compact refrigerator on low for brief periods to store some grocery items. I drank milk, lots of milk, to make up for my milk withdrawal. Ahhh, I didn't realize how much I had craved an indoor hot shower. I'm convinced after being outside for so long that a hot shower is the next best thing to heaven itself. I was beginning to feel human again.

The closing went through without incident. I purchased the small, three-acre lot surrounded by hundreds of protected acres. The house overlooked a field with thirty rodeo horses grazing there and scenic mountain views—all this for my entertainment pleasure. This was my new TV.

The property was conveniently located to all the amenities I would need: church (although I would find out, yet again, that I couldn't maintain myself in the building), a grocery store (I was able to have a shopper assigned), and the post office (that I could get in and out quickly, given the small town atmosphere). There is a clean, swimmable lake where I could spend most of my time in or near. Although I couldn't afford the waterfront property I'd dreamed about, this was the next best thing, being only minutes from the lake. Truthfully, it was a better choice once the reality of the lake noise was realized. Jet skis and Bass speed boats definitely jolt my nervous system. I do my best to avoid noise of any kind.

It feels like He used me to set an example of what real faith means, to believe without a shadow of a doubt that He is with me at all times wherever I am, and that I am exactly where I'm supposed to be. This gave me the peace and confidence as a single woman, compromised by health issues, in my fifties, to tent my way south, led by the spirit to a new place to call home.

By taking back control of my life and venturing out to where I was meant to be, provoked healing. I found a new freedom. My new home is where the real healing continued. My place became a sanctuary. It was a place of restoration. It is a place to worship and to mend. I found profound satisfaction in realizing I was right where I belonged.

I installed an outdoor fire pit, an outdoor chapel, and a garden; all healing tools. The yard was filled with an orchestra of flowers planted by previous owners. When one flower was finished blooming the next group would surface. It was magically healing to see the beauty in the flowers, the birds and the butterflies.

The first winter at my new house I spent most of my time outdoors at my fire pit. That allowed me a way to ground while keeping warm. It also meant more time outdoors. One afternoon in January, I was barefoot-grounding near my fire pit. I would touch the cold ground with my feet, pick up one foot at a time, heating my feet over the fire to warm, touch the ground again, and repeat. The flames of the fire are healing to look at. The flames are hypnotic and have an incredible healing power. I learned to like life just the way it was.

I hadn't met any new local friends yet so I began to pray. "Lord, send me a friend, just one." I requested humbly. Not minutes later, a dog about seven months old snuck into my yard. He came creeping across my lawn crouched down on all fours. It made its way over to me. He was a mutt with tan, black, and white markings. He was handsome but very mischievous. He looked at me with loving eyes then surveyed my shoes and socks. Before I even could grasp what was happening, he grabbed my sock and ran away. I got up—stunned, laughing, and crying at the same time.

Instinctively I started running after him, not giving energy to the fact that I had no shoes or socks on and it was January and cold outside! I ran down the road after him screaming out, "This is no way to start a friendship. Get back here NOW!" My voice must have startled him because he stopped, dropped the sock, and waited for me to catch up with him. I scolded him, snatched up the sock, now blessed with holes where his teeth grabbed and slimed. I returned to my fire pit, suddenly aware that if this new friend reaches the site before me, I could be out of a shoe as well. I kept my eye on him and ran back. I got there first, since he stayed gingerly behind me. I sat on my shoes and socks to avoid further theft.

As a result of our first encounter, he not only stole my sock but he stole my heart as well. Not knowing his name or who this new four-legged critter belonged to, I named him Klepto. It only seemed appropriate since, well, he steals everything. He is a kleptomaniac.

We have been friends ever since our first encounter. His friendship keeps me on my toes. He is either stealing from me, garden tools, gloves, socks, or bringing me something he stole from someone else's yard. For example, he brought me a toy from a happy meal. It became a game for him to take something and return with something else.

Now that Klepto has become a more mature dog he seems to have given up chasing small objects and has graduated to chasing cars. He chases cars relentlessly.

This is four years after our first encounter and he now is so bold to visit for his one cookie a day. He earns that cookie by guarding my yard. Anyone who is on foot gets barked at from one edge of my property to the end until they have become far enough away to keep me in a safe zone.

115

Boldly, Klepto comes to my front gate at the deck or side door and barks once. He knows I'll hear him and reward him with a cookie (daily dog biscuit) for his hard-earned efforts.

I found out recently that Klepto's real name is Roscoe. He answers to both names so I stick with my pet name for him of Klepto. I love that dog! Thank you, Jesus for my new friend.

Indoor Living

And the Lord restored Job's losses when he prayed for his friends.
Indeed, the Lord gave Job twice as much as he had before.
Job 42:10

I had to make many changes in my new home to allow for me to be able to live inside. While I was making all of the indoor changes, I used my fire pit outdoors to cook on. I slept in my tent in my back yard when the indoor effects of electricity messed with me too much and when the weather would allow for me to tolerate the outdoor winter weather. There was a cluster of trees in my back yard that served as camouflage for my tent. It was not viewable from the road or from the horse field behind my house. I felt secure there.

The first order of business to be able to live indoors was to eliminate the most offensive areas of exposure. I had the refrigerator from the kitchen moved to the garage. I simply couldn't tolerate the motor. Ironically, the entrance to the garage was just outside my side door. A couple of steps across the deck and just inside the garage door was a platform already built with just enough room to hold the refrigerator and pass by, taking a few steps down into the garage. If my house were set up differently I could have used a remote to turn the refrigerator on and off. I learned years later that another EMF patient was able to use a remote because his kitchen was in a separate room. My kitchen and living room area are open to each other so that method wouldn't work for me.

The heat pump unit that was in the hallway closet overwhelmed me when it came on. It would leave me unable to walk a straight line. I had the entire old unit removed and had a new, more efficient unit, installed outdoors—problem solved. When the unit came on, I could still feel some effects, but nowhere near what it would be if the unit was indoors.

If I weren't so compromised when I'd first arrived here, I might have made a smarter decision where the heat was concerned and possibly converted to gas. I was so happy to have made it here and all I could think of was that the heat unit needs to be installed outside.

I had the electric stove replaced with the most basic propane gas stove available. I bought it, sight unseen, through a local appliance dealer with the recommendation from the gas company who had installed my propane tank. The most basic model still had an electronic switch to turn on the burners, but there were no clocks or other gismos attached. I could now cook again after a couple year absences from the use of the stove. The electrical panel for the house was in the hallway that you pass through from the kitchen to the garage. It was on the backside wall of the master bathroom. Two things happened to me as a result of exposure from the panel. First, I became really weak and felt like rubber when trying to pass through the hallway. Second, the first time I tried to sit on the master bath toilet, located in the area on the backside of the electric panel in the hall, I lost use of muscle mass and fell over onto the floor from the toilet. I was home alone—not a good predicament to be in. Solution: I called a local electrician to test the voltage. When everything checked out, the electrician and I put our thinking hats on. We checked out the Less EMF catalog for a possible solution. Initially, I thought I would have to put a shield on both sides of the wall. This would be to the tune of two-thousand dollars. After discussing this with the electrician, he concluded that it's not the wall that needs shielding, it's the wires in the wall. So, he suggested slitting the wall and wrapping the wires in the shielding foil that Less EMF sells. We agreed that would be a good plan with a one thousand dollar savings. My electrician discussed his plan with one of the employees at Less EMF and we all agreed it to be a go. After the job was completed, we tested the area again with the meter. This process took 80% of the hit away from the area and I was able to successfully walk down the hall with no serious ill effects and sit on the toilet to do my business. HA-LEY-LU-YAH! When I was ready to pay Steve, my loyal electrician, he asked for less than the job was worth. He said to me, "The way I see it, if you can't help someone in need, you ain't nothing but a butthead!" I like the way he thinks. None of us should act like buttheads.

I turned off as many breakers in the house as could be turned off, turning off power to the shed, the front porch outlets, and the master bedroom. As time went on, this just wasn't enough.

I had answered an ad in a magazine after my friend Margaret brought it to me. She couldn't believe someone was actually advertising to check out your house for EMF problem areas. The company owner is an EMF patient. He was formally a musician. He was able to heal to be 80% better. He used his equipment to test out my house for hot points. They had spent a fortune on specialty equipment to help with his condition, and smart enough to start a business helping others who suffer. This helped them recoup some of the hard-earned cash they had to lay out for the initial purchase of their hi-tech equipment. They benefit and the consumer benefits from their findings, without the major expense involved in the purchase the equipment for themselves.

When he and his wife first arrived, I thought they might be scamming me. He and his wife showed up driving a brand-new Lexus. Now I know that if he were for real he couldn't be in that car, not even with his wife driving. So boldly I addressed that issue before they even reached my porch. Both were exceptionally good-looking people, well dressed, professional mannerism.

"You say you are an EMF sufferer, also disabled from the effects," I said rather defiantly. "How is it that you are able to be in a new car?" The disbelief could be heard in my voice. "I was told by my doctor I could never be in a new car due to built-in GPS." He stared at my face, eye to eye, as we assessed each other.

"I'm glad you asked that question," he said smoothly. His mannerism was polished. "My wife and I had to go through a lot of hoops to get a stripped-car model. We wrote to the chairman of the board. It took three attempts to get them to agree to dismantle the GPS. You are correct—I would be unable to be in the car otherwise. My wife does the driving."

After a couple of hours of testing, he concluded that the overhead fans in the house, even with the light switch off in the room and the fan off, was bombarding me with EMFs while I slept. So now I had

---

every breaker in the main panel box turned off, with the exception of the water tank and heat pump.

I had two, eight-foot copper grounding rods, added by the electric company outside in the yard to ground my house.

It was difficult to retrieve my mail from the mailbox at the end of my driveway due to the overhead power lines. I had the power lines removed completely from the front of my property, over one hundred feet of frontage. The power lines were reattached to a power box at the far right-hand side of my property and run underground through the neighbors' property, with their permission. The removal of the power lines from the front of my property provided me with enough relief to retrieve my mail, weed the front flower box, and work in my garage without the profound negative effects that the power lines previously emitted.

When I had the sauna (used for detoxing) installed, I had it set up to turn on and off from the main electric panel. So although 240V, the breaker remained off, unless I needed to turn it on the heat up the sauna for usage. While heating the unit, I needed to stay away from the end of the house where the sauna was located.

I ordered fifty feet of tubing so I could plug in my oxygen machine at one end of the house and snake the tubing through to my bed at the other end. It was too taxing on me to be near the oxygen machine while it was on. According to the oxygen company, fifty feet is the longest tube you can use and still reap the necessary effects from the oxygen.

The previous owners left a washing machine, dryer, and dishwasher in the house. I keep the breakers off until I need to run them. After turning the designated breaker on, I'd push the button and run, when needing to use them. I needed to be out of the house when they were in use. Sometimes in my frustration, I pushed my luck and went into the back bedroom or office and closed the door. The effects still left me feeling weak.

I have a low EMF hair dryer but it's still too painful for me to use. It causes the sensation of brain spasms, so I resorted to using the sun to dry my hair on days that that was feasible or else I sometimes sat near my gas space-heater to dry my hair in winter months.

It was a creative process to invent a safe haven for me. I now have a safe place where friends and family can gather, regroup and visit.

Trying to restore my health became my new career; it took, and still takes, all of my time and energy.

Trips to the Refrigerator

. . .they ate their food with gladness and simplicity of heart,
Acts 2:46

I t is a minor inconvenience to have to go outside of the house and into the garage to get to my refrigerator, or so I thought. The physical reaction to my body that the jolt of the refrigerator provoked in me took away the luxury of having a refrigerator indoors in the kitchen. What I didn't bargain for were the challenges that nature would present in the process of going out my back side-door, across the small deck platform and into the garage where just inside that door is my refrigerator. Some of my trips proved more eye-opening than others.

In May, a beautiful time of the year, my yard came to life with an orchestra of meticulously planted flowers, carefully arranged by my home's previous owner. Every day holds a surprise, a new awakening, a new bloom, a reincarnation of the prior year's beauty. Along with the floral expression during the rebirth of nature's hibernation, came the profound joy that the beauty provoked.

In the morning, while opening the window blinds to survey the scene outdoors, I played a game I called, "Where's Waldo?" I looked around to see what doesn't belong. Find the hidden "Waldo." One day, when I opened the kitchen window blinds, I found myself witnessing the arrival of a three-foot black snake. It was investigating the bush and grass outside. I thought, *If I hurry, I can quickly go out of the side door, into the garage and back, to get milk for my breakfast cereal.* Normally, I take a glass with me and pour the milk at the refrigerator, so I don't have to return with the carton, but not today! I'm not taking the chance the snake will visit me there. I grabbed the half-gallon carton and ran back into the house.

Oh, don't get me wrong, I know black snakes are good to have around for rodent control. I just don't want one slithering curiously around me.

Whew, I made it. As I approached the kitchen again, I took a moment to survey the scene. I peeked once more out the window, only to find, in disbelief, two *more* black snakes. It was a three for one sale. Blacky had a family. The other two were only eight feet from the garage door I just left.

Ok, now I have to admit that I was a little freaked out. You would think I was a seasoned pro on snakes, after residing at my brother's estate in New York that was infested with the creatures.

Needless to say, the half-gallon of milk I brought into the house wasn't going back outside to the refrigerator any time soon. In fact, I didn't even leave the house for the rest of the day, for fear of a confrontation. Not one to waste food, I had no choice but to drink the entire half gallon of milk to avoid it spoiling.

I needed a Badder fix. I called my brother to get some input. As always, he knew just how to advise me: just use a yard stick, tap it on the deck for noise, or if they come near you just scoot them away with the edge of the stick. "They are more afraid of you than you are of them." I highly doubted that was true. My friend Stephanie, whom I lovingly refer to as "Rambo," stopped by for a visit. Together, we went out to the garage with a yardstick for protection. I needed some things from the garage. She had my back. The fact that she was with me was all I needed to overcome my "unwarranted" fear. It was Murphy's Law; with her by my side, no snakes appeared.

On another morning, I was half asleep but needed milk for cereal. I stepped out the back door, closed the house door only to find a five-foot black snake sunning himself no more than four feet from me. I froze. I know they are harmless, but I didn't really want him slithering in my direction. He coiled and stuck his head up in my direction in a curious manner. It's okay blacky, I'm outta here. I reentered my home, closed the door and skipped breakfast. Maybe I wasn't that hungry after all.

Then there was the time I stepped out the back door and was very aware in my spirit that someone or something was looking at me. I looked up to see the neighbors horse looking at me—a mere ten feet away. I knew nothing about the magnificent creature except that he was a whole lot bigger than I was. I slowly backed my way into the house. I put a call into the neighbor to advise them of their missing horse. Shortly thereafter, someone came with a harness to retrieve the horse, who seemed oblivious to the fact that it was in my yard eating my grass. Not to mention, it gave me a few more white hairs from the unexpected encounter.

It's always a hoot when Klepto, the neighbor's dog, visits. I'm usually at my refrigerator in the garage when he nuzzles his way past the door looking for his daily cookie. I get so much pleasure from his surprise visits, but only after I recover from the shock of him sticking his head around the open refrigerator door. I almost never hear him coming when he sneaks up on me.

Bees, birds, lizards, spiders, and flies, all seem to know when I'm going to the refrigerator. Sometimes it is like a convoy of critters begging to come inside the house. I have to be very careful to guard the openings, but even with the guarded movement they find their way past me.

When I have a visitor, I explain how critical it is to close the house door in between refrigerator runs. Sometimes they listen, but most times the back door gets left ajar, causing me unnecessary stress wondering what critter might make its way inside my house. I know that if a black snake, or any snake for that matter, made its way inside my house it would be nearly impossible to find it. There are just too many hiding spots in the house. I really don't want the challenge.

Every day and every trip to the refrigerator is an adventure. I may inhale the perfume of a skunk or cross paths with a vibrant colored butterfly. One just never knows what's in store behind the unopened back door.

Sauna: Some Like it Hot

He restores my soul;
He leads me in the paths of righteousness
for His name's sake.
Psalm 23:3

I love my sauna! Apparently, I like it hot. One of the most important tools to restore my health was the detoxing that occurs while using a sauna. In my case, it's not just any sauna, but a custom made sauna out of poplar wood used especially for chemically sensitive people. Poplar wood, unlike cedar, does not give off gases.

I never knew there was a right and wrong way to use a sauna. For that matter, I've had little experience with using a sauna at all. Sure, I'd jump in the sauna on occasion in the past at the YMCA to sooth my muscles after a workout, but I didn't get the concept of its true benefits.

Our bodies hold toxins, through foods we eat that have preservatives, medications—both over the counter and prescription—pollutions we ingest, even the products we intentionally use: shampoos, deodorants, perfumes have ingredients detrimental to our health, the ingredient paraben being one of the top offenders.

The best way to rid our bodies of all these extra impurities is to sweat them out. It's the bodies' natural way to keep us in balance. That is where the sauna comes in handy.

I learned the proper way to use a sauna at the Environmental Health Center – Dallas. You start by exercising for ten to twenty minutes before entering the sauna to pump up your heart rate. A stair-stepper, air-stepper works great or a stationary bike. Drinking a lot of water is essential. Not just any water, but one that pure and free from chlorine and other contaminants. A purifying system will solve that or a weekly run to an organic store that sells filtered water. You drink eight to twelve ounces before you get in the sauna to prevent dehydration.

Along with the water, I had to follow a list of detoxification medicines that I took before and after my sauna. Before the sauna I would take the following supplements:

- One tab of Niacin B3 to improve blood circulation
- One capsule of Alpha Ketogluterica acid, which crosses the blood brain barrier and aids in the removal of toxins from the brain.
- One reduced L-glutathione, a detoxicant and an antioxidant, that is an amino acid.
- Two vitamin C caps before the sauna and two caps after the sauna, this chelates heavy metals.

Thinking back, I remember being in the sauna at the Environmental Center and, *whoooo-wheeee,* did I stink. The metal smells were pouring out of me. I was so toxic from all life's exposures that I could barely stand to be near myself. It was a disgusting smell but a relief to my system to start to be rid of all the toxicity that had built up in me.

Once out of my sauna regime, which lasted about twenty-two minutes, I was instructed to shower head to toe immediately, to rinse away all the impurities that were released through my skin so they wouldn't reabsorb back in.

Once showered and dressed I had to return to the desk to take Tri Salts (a combo of sodium bicarbonate, potassium carbonate and calcium carbonate). Tri Salts aid in maintaining or restoring acid in the body. It also seems to maintain the electrolyte balance. A half teaspoon in a shot-glass sized paper cup, added with water, stirred and drank quickly. It has a chalky taste, but is not offensive.

Along with Tri Salts, I had to take psyllium as a bulking agent, a polyunsaturated oil to lubricate my bowels, and multi minerals to facilitate healing.

After returning from the Environmental Center back to Asheville I was able to use the YMCA sauna. However my sensitivities heightened as the YMCA kept upping their game with electronics. Now you had an electronic sign that tripped on when you walked past it stating "Welcome to the YMCA." Then, you get to the front desk with a trailer electronic sign above with running advertisements of classes offered. As if that was not enough of a hit, you scanned yourself in for attendance purposes. You logged yourself into the workout section, allowing you to pull up personal notes on the screen left by your trainer. Fluorescent lights dominated the dressing area in the locker rooms and chlorine smells were overpowering from the showers and cleaning agents used to maintain the area. It was another war zone for my being chemically and electronically sensitive.

I loved my time in the sauna, not only because of the physical relief it gave me, but it would soon become my only real social opportunity. I loved connecting with others in the co-ed sauna. For the most part the same people were there on the days I visited so it helped me stay connected. Along with that, it was an opportunity to share conversation regarding life's challenges and joys. There were days I'd drag myself in and drag myself out but my determination wouldn't let me quit.

My body was so compromised at that point that I would have to sleep in my car in the parking lot at the YMCA to get a grip and be strong enough to drive myself back to the condo. Luckily, I could drive on the Blue Ridge Parkway with very little traffic and no heavy exposure to power lines. There are almost no power lines on the parkway. I still had EMF exposure from the use of my car but there was really no way to get around that. The only saving grace was that I drove an older model. I drive a 2001 Kia Sportage with no bells and whistles. I could never ride in a new car due to built-in GPS. It wouldn't be just the GPS on the dash, but I understand that the new cars have a built in GPS in the motor area as a way for Uncle Sam to track the vehicle if need be. More signals that my body just can't handle.

As I became more hyper-sensitive, even the windshield wipers caused me to have adverse reactions. It was yet another restriction; no driving while it's raining outside. I found a solution in light rain. A product called Rain-X. It is a great product to use as a coating on the windshield. It lets the rain glide off the windows allowing better visibility. I couldn't believe the motion of the wipers and sound they produced scrambled my thought process. Was there no end to this madness?

As my illness got worse, I knew I'd need to get a sauna at home if I was going to beat this affliction. That would not be an option until I was settled somewhere more permanently. For one, funds were running out and it is a large unit that you don't want to have to move. Moving the unit would only add more to the cost.

So, instead, I did the lesser way to sauna. I closed the bathroom door and created virtually a steam room by running a hot shower. I got some relief, but not to the degree of relief a sauna gives with dry heat.

It took two years to be able to venture out on my own after staying in retreat on my brother and his wife's property. Now that I had my own home again I was ready to invest in my sauna. I ordered my sauna, custom made of poplar wood, from a company in Colorado named Heavenly Heat.

I managed a conference call to ask Dr. Rea how I was going to be able to use a sauna when I couldn't be around the electricity used to run it. It is a simple solution. All I needed to do was turn the sauna on for fifty minutes to heat up to the desired temperature. Turn off the unit. Set the time for twenty-two minutes and get in quickly to maintain heat. I heated to 160 degrees and get in for twenty minutes. It should be used at 145 degrees. I give it the two extra minutes due to opening the door and loss of heat. I called an electrician to put in the 240 volt needed for the sauna to run—he set it up so I could prepare the sauna (preparation included: I laid towels in the unit to sit on, closed the ceiling vent, turned the knob to setting #4, closed door) then turned on and off from the main breaker at the other end of the house. My body doesn't produce the nauseating smells like it did when I first started the detoxing process, which told me it's definitely working. I felt so much better after a sauna, I experienced major relief from muscle and joint pain.

I frequently used my sauna three times a week on Monday, Wednesday, and Friday mornings during the spring, fall, and winter. In the summer, due to the extreme heat in the south, I naturally detoxed outdoors, unless I start to smell like metals again, then I jump-started my health with an extra sauna to release the additional accumulation of toxins.

There are so many other health benefits to using a sauna: it clears up blemishes, heals your skin, takes away aches and pains, especially joint pain, and I'm told it works on cellulite, if needed. The use of the sauna makes you feel and look so much better. Swedish people have been using sauna for years. They understood its value long ago.

You can get a sauna built for chemically-sensitive people in all sizes and models. I don't like feeling enclosed and tend to feel claustrophobic in tight places. I ordered the "C Model," which is basically a long, narrow personal sauna. It looks like a large closet or a recording booth. They are custom built, so I had two sides made of tempered glass so that when I sit in it I can see down the hallway or out the window across from the room I have it set up in. I can take the middle board out of the unit and sit up or leave the center board in, lean back against the back rest and sprawl my legs out in front of me on a full-length bench, which is my preferred position.

I've stuck to the routine of ten to twenty minutes exercise, drinking water, but cut way back on the other natural meds. I still replaced mineral, vitamin C, and vitamin loss but have cut back substantially on the other recommendations. They made me feel sicker at times and I couldn't keep up with the expense.

I was lucky to be able to order my sauna with half price down, to start construction, and half due before delivery. It arrived in about six weeks from start to the finished shipped product. I had to have the unit delivered unassembled in panels to my garage. It came on a pallet, very carefully packed in sections. It required me to hire a local handyman and his son who were able to unpack and install my new sauna inside the office of my home. It was the only logical place to put it. I love my sauna and am convinced it's the component that is restoring my health, despite the detox being a lengthy process due to the severity and length of my exposures.

Public Outings

These things I have spoken to you, that in me you will have peace.
In the world you will have tribulation;
but be of good cheer, I have overcome the world."
John 16:33

I was seven years into my setback and public buildings still pre-sented a problem. I have a very limited window of opportunity to get in and out of a building. For example, I knew that when I went into the local post office, I have approximately eight minutes to get in and out before the effects from fluorescent lighting, electronics, overhead fans and cell phones grabbed ahold of me and put me into meltdown mode. So I'd quickly get in, grab my mail from my P. O. box office and get out. If I was in need of stamps or need to mail a package, I needed to time it when no one was in line or recruit someone's assistance to stand in line for me. The Post Office houses a bombardment of EMFs with fluorescent lights, overhead fans running at full speed, scanners for packages, debit card swipe machines, computerized cash registers, not to mention cell phones on the people passing through. Power lines directly outside of the building compromised me further by more exposure.

My stubbornness to want to do for myself gets the best of me at times. If I am caught in line too long my body goes into meltdown mode. I can only surmise that people view me as the town drunk (although I don't drink) as I'd stagger out of the post office, using the counters and walls for support.

My world is small. I go from my house to the post office and then landfill station every week, or every other, when I can manage it. As needed, I can get myself to the doctor's office. Thankfully, it's located in an old house off the beaten path. I go to the dam at Lake Chatuge or The Circle (a picnic spot) to walk; it is only a couple of minute's drive from my home. I have to visit when the least amount of people are present. Everyone these days is hooked up or connected to something electronic. In the summer, I camp on the islands and swim in Lake Chatuge. This is where the most healing has taken place. I feel completely relaxed in the water. Swimming relaxes me and relieves my physical pain. It's an easy way to stretch one's spine. I understand that the repetitive motion of right left movement of my arms helps to balance my brain, as does walking.

I thank God for the healing waters of Lake Chatuge.

First Holistic Doctor in Georgia

And do not be conformed to this world,
but be transformed by the renewing of your mind,
that you may prove what is that good and acceptable
and perfect will of God.
Romans 12:2

I was excited to learn that there was a holistic doctor nearby in Georgia. The doctor was just moving her office into a brand new building. Being a new building concerned me that I would not be able to tolerate the newness of it. Building supplies, carpeting, and paint—all house toxins. What a relief that the doctor was up on all of that using non-toxic paint and carpeting. Other than the effects from the exposure that the electronics posed, my chemical sensitivity did not present an issue.

I figured I would be set for a long while since she was an MD and could address normal issues like oxygen refills, estrogen scripts, regular yearly checkups as well as the need for a doctor who recognizes EMF issues.

Although the doctor had heard of EMF, I'm not quite convinced that she understood the magnitude of what I was dealing with and the restrictions as a result. She seemed guarded with me.

Upon visiting her new office, I shared with her that I needed someone who does energy work. Although I didn't really know what that entailed, Dr. Rea highly recommended finding someone who could help me with that. I knew I had come to the right place when she happily shared that she had a new person starting the following week who could help me. The new person was a nurse who deals with energy balancing. The doctor felt confident that she would be able to help me.

I was excited to keep the next appointment. Upon meeting the new nurse, Edwina, I felt an unseen confidence from her presence. She came across calm and loving. She appeared to be an old soul. As it turned out, she was a powerhouse of wisdom. Our time together was well-spent and enlightening. She was able to jumpstart my health, and arm me with more tools to put me back on the wellness path. She always displayed patience, compassion, and shared an abundance of resources — be it centering techniques or articles she came across. I learned so much from Edwina. The most important thing that I learned was that our health consists of body, mind, and spirit. To be well is to be *balanced* in all three. I learned techniques I could do at home by myself to put me back in alignment. I performed simple exercises that she shared which had a profound impact on me.

She also explained to me that EMF occurs when something so mind-blowing happens that our mind cannot absorb it, causing a short circuit of our senses. I gave that some serious thought.

Let me repeat that: "EMF occurs when something so mind-blowing happens that our mind cannot absorb it, causing a short circuit of our senses."

Wow. That makes the most sense out of any explanations about EMF that I have heard to date. I've had multiple mind-blowing experiences over the course of my lifetime. There were multiple tragedies within my family unit, the profound world tragedies of 9/11 that occurred just prior to taking a job relocation offer to Asheville, NC. I was located just one hour and fifteen minutes away from the Sandy Hook massacre, which took place while I was out of society staying at my brothers New York estate. Although Sandy Hook and the Las Vegas shootings took place after my setback, they compromised my health further from the shock and stress of hearing about such horrendous, negative, mind blowing, and frightening events.

I lived in Newtown, Connecticut for about seven years during the latter part of my second marriage. My daughter attended the after-day school in Sandy Hook at that very same school. My Girl Scout troop had some of its meetings held there. Oh, how my heart was numbed when my brother had to convey the gruesome news of the senseless killings. He wanted me to hear the guarded truth from him so it wouldn't be laid on me when I least expected it. He knows I don't handle shock well. However, nothing could prepare me for the words that came out of my brother's mouth: the words spoken that a gunman opened fire on such unsuspecting, innocent victims. These are just a few of the tragedies I've experienced this lifetime. Having experienced the news along with millions of others didn't lesson the blow.

If my body was weakened by the shock of these events, the damage that that did to my physical body made me more susceptible to the disease EMF. It makes me wonder how many others are out there suffered to the extent that I did. How many do not understand the impact this overwhelming negativity has on our bodies? It's true that we are not all built the same way—some of us are made of a tougher skin. But as the world ups its game with exposure and violence, how will we all cope?

There is only one real hope, JESUS. It is never too late to look to Him.

Just having the explanation of mind-blowing experiences, and being unable to absorb the shock of these events, helped me to process more of what was happening to me and gain healing. There is power in knowledge.

It is my hope that by passing this knowledge along, it will help others.

It continued to be a challenging journey to get myself to the doctor's office. Thankfully, it was a direct route, approximately one half-hour away. It was my new hope.

Before I would even leave the driveway, I prayed a hedge of protection around me, the car, and anyone who would be crossing my path. It was a hedge of safety. I knew how compromised I was, but felt I needed some new hope to continue to move forward with my healing.

The world kept upping it's game with electronics. Toward the end of my visits, which went on for months, I noticed electricians working in the building. I inquired about their presence. I was disheartened to learn that they were installing a wireless alarm system. After all, if my doctor claimed to know the ins and outs of EMF patients—why would she install a wireless security system? I recognized that I am not the majority; I felt defeated.

Not knowing what to do, I simply shared my thoughts with my nurse, Edwina. She didn't seem thrilled either but had no control over the doctor's choices. I felt in my spirit that Edwina was aware of something I wasn't.

Shortly thereafter, the doctor announced to her staff that she was closing the office and accepting a partnership in Asheville, North Carolina. It must have been a difficult decision to make, since she just spent a fortune setting up office here.

When I asked for my records and to be given a referral, I was stunned to learn that all this time my visits were being coded as *psychiatric*. There simply were no codes yet to get reimbursed from insurance companies for environmental illnesses; those codes would be introduced the following year.

Thankfully, I was given a referral to another holistic doctor, also located in Georgia, but closer to me and a much easier drive to get there. By the time I needed to make an appointment for my yearly checkup, the new codes were available. I shared my concern about the coding and the new doctor assured me that she would code the environmental illness code, now that it was available for use. I felt validated, relieved.

When I ran into Edwina, at a later date, walking at the Lake Chatuge dam, I expressed my concern about the coding. She seemed less than pleased as well. She explained the same way my sister the RN did, "The doctor needed to get paid." I felt betrayed by the system.

I'm not sure why the psychiatric component of EMF remained so painful to me. I think maybe it's the stigmatism behind it. It feels like a disgrace. In the era that I grew up in, you just didn't talk about it. Anyone who needed psychiatric help was whispered about. The world was not ready to validate my condition as the neurological disorder that it was.

My thoughts surfaced: code it what you will, just find a way to heal me!

If only everyone would read the well-researched book entitled, "The Invisible Rainbow." It shows clear examples of how and why we, as humans, are in this predicament of over-exposure to electricity, which has become an environmental illness. Arthur

Firstenberg has written an easy to understand book depicting the history of electricity from the beginning to date.

I lent my copy of the book to some friends at the dam. It didn't surprise me that my friend, with a scientific background, exclaimed to me, "After reading 'The Invisible Rainbow,' your EMF condition makes total sense."

Root Canal History

Beloved, I pray that you may prosper
in all things and be in health,
just as your soul prospers.
3 John 2

I had a root canal done on my upper left side, second tooth from the back (not including the wisdom tooth, previously extracted). This was about twenty-two years ago with periodic flare ups in that area, over that period of time.

Upon returning home from having the root canal procedure, I went straight to bed. I stayed there for the next two days, unable to lift my head without difficulty.

On the third day, I called the dentist and asked when I would be well enough to return to work. He seemed startled and said I should have been able to return by now. He asked me to return to his office.

Upon further examination, he apologized. He said he'd accidentally gone through to my sinus cavity. I took that to mean nothing could be done and went home back to bed for further recovery. I was too sick to question him.

I wished I'd known enough to ask to have the tooth removed. It has been twenty-two years of on and off suffering with tooth and left ear pressure and discomfort.

Fast forward to 2016. I was still dealing with on and off reactions to the tooth and left ear pressure.

I've made several attempts over the years to have the cap and tooth removed, but no dentist would touch it. My regular dentist in Asheville shared that it's not a good idea to remove a "treated" tooth.

The dentist who performed the root canal resided in Connecticut, so going back was simply not an affordable option.

I found a holistic dentist in Georgia who is an expert in root canals. She said she has never seen anything quite like it. She wouldn't be comfortable removing it without a surgeon present. After consulting with a surgeon he said he would need an ENT (ear, nose, and throat) doctor to review to be sure my sinuses are clear from a cyst or tumor.

The ENT appointment went well with the help of two of my church girlfriends. Since I could no longer drive myself any distance, two of the women from my church family offered to take me. They made it fun. They could feel my stress level and knew the trip would be taxing on me. They made it a "girl's day out." They did their best to distract me from the stress of having to take the drive and visit yet another doctor, yet another building.

The ENT said a scope wouldn't show what we needed. Disappointed, but not discouraged, I told him I couldn't have an MRI due to the magnetic fields. He suggested a CT scan. He said the CT scan would have zero magnetic fields. "Let's do it," I blurted out. I got through the procedure just fine. Result—sinuses were clear. I got the *go ahead* to remove the tooth.

Next challenge: the holistic dentist called me, upon receiving the results from the ENT. "I received the report from the ENT. Why did you tell him your tooth was acting like an antennae?" she asked incredulously. "Because that is what you and I discussed, and you agreed, and it's the truth." I responded adamantly. "Well, the doctor in Asheville will think you are crazy," she blurted out. "He even put it in his notes to me and the surgeon that you think your tooth is acting like an antenna," she commented, as if this was a bad thing. "How are we supposed to educate people on the seriousness of what a tooth is capable of doing if we don't say it the way it is and tell the truth no matter what they think?" I asked rather impatiently.

Okay, color me stupid, but what just happened here? I told the truth, my truth. If someone else doesn't believe me or doesn't think it is possible, I can't help that. I want and need to help the others out there suffering to get the much-needed relief that we all need. The only way that is going to happen is by laying it all out there.

Now the holistic dentist was telling me she was going to be exceptionally busy for the next three months and couldn't see how we could accommodate the surgeon's schedule with hers and mine. REALLY? I mean *really*. I've done all I've been asked to do, all I want is to have the tooth removed. The delay was just another obstacle on my path to wellness.

I told her she is the one I want to remove the tooth and asked if she could find another surgeon closer to her, since this one was a couple hours further south and inconvenient to her. She agreed to try and would let me know.

Upon further contact with her, she explained that the surgeon in her town does not believe in EMF. He says it's not possible. Oh, how I pray he never gets afflicted. Not only is it possible, but I live with it every single day of my life.

Currently, she still worked on finding a surgeon who will respect my illness and take the necessary precautions to ensure my safety.

Finally realizing that the holistic dentist was finding every excuse not to touch me, the perceived risk to her being too high, I sought a surgeon elsewhere. After a year of being put through multiple visits and requests for different tests and doctor visits, I found a no-nonsense young, female surgeon in Blue Ridge, Georgia. She had no problem extracting my tooth. Her exact words were "It's what I do every day, all day."

My loving sister drove from New York state to be with me when I had the surgery to remove the tooth. She suggested just getting a local anesthetic, basically just a shot to numb the area, since I don't do well with toxins. It would be hard for me to wake up if I allowed the doctor to put me out via anesthesia.

So I prayed and a local shot was what I took. The surgeon was amazing. She told me everything she was doing, every step of the way, so there would be no surprises. I felt relaxed. She said it would sound like someone was breaking my bones. That is exactly what it sounded like. It didn't freak me out like I thought it would, but it definitely got my attention. I told her she could keep talking if she wanted to, but visually I was going, in meditation, to my "happy place on Penland Island" until she was done. Most likely, I wouldn't hear her from this point on.

Because I chose having the local method, recovery was much simpler. The annoying root canal was finally freed from my system. Now I had a gap in the upper teeth that was, thankfully, beyond my smile line, the least of my problems.

The tooth removal gave me some relief to my ear and brain. Unfortunately, it wasn't the miracle cure that I was looking for. I thought this procedure was going to heal me enough to be my ticket back to church. My brain continued to react to electronic stimuli.

There was metal in the root canal. Thankfully I am freed from its negative effects to my body. Hence the "antennae effect" when combined with chronic exposure.

I'm told the new root canal procedures no longer use metal, therefore eliminating that effect.

Finding a Church Home

God is Spirit, and those who worship Him
must worship in spirit and truth.
John 4:24

It was not easy to find a church free of Wi-Fi and electronics. In fact, it was not easy to find any public building free of them. I was determined to be with a body of believers.

Not far from my Hayesville house, on the water's edge, there was a small white chapel. For three Sundays in a row, I waited until the parishioners were inside and the front doors closed. Then I would sit on the front steps, listening to the pastor delivering his sermon. I didn't hear music, so I figured this might be the place I would be able to attend.

The following Sunday I went earlier, to the same chapel, waiting on people to come. The church only had maybe fifteen to twenty people in attendance.

That week I had communications with a lady named Patty, answering questions on Medicare. We spoke briefly on the phone since I wasn't able to visit her office. What were the chances that she was the one who got out of her car and greeted me as I sat on the front steps of the church? That was no coincidence; that was a God thing.

Patty knew from our phone conversation just how compromised I was. She encouraged me to come in and meet the pastor. I was so excited to think I'd found a church home. What a blow it was to me when I walked through the front doors and one quarter of the small chapel was set up to video tape. They would be recording the sermon for the internet. Not only that, but large box-type fans were running, the pastor used a microphone for clarity, while recording—which was an over kill for the space allotted, but needed for clarity online.

I walked in, Patty asked me to sit with her. I started going into meltdown mode within minutes. I asked her to help me out of the building. My legs were not supporting me as they should. She did. I thanked her for trying, but there was too much exposure from the equipment. She asked me to wait. She went in to talk with the pastor. Upon her return she said "We want you here, we are willing to turn off the fans and the microphone to keep you here." What an act of kindness. Although they didn't understand my condition, they didn't question its validity.

I tried a second time. After getting three quarters of the way through the pastor's message, I had to be helped out a second and last time. Public buildings were (and are) still not an option for me.

I sobbed all the way home. I felt more isolated than ever. I didn't give up. I put *building an outdoor sanctuary* on my priority list for spring.

Months later, while waiting outside for my car to be serviced with an oil change, I noticed a waiting room full of people. I was frustrated, it was cold, I was outside and I still had high hopes for a church family. I said a brief prayer, opened the outside door of the auto place, stuck my head in and blurted out, "Does anyone here know of a church in Hayesville that doesn't have electronics?"

To my surprise and delight a guy spouted out "I do." He seemed quite confident. "Hayesville Presbyterian Church." He went on to give me directions. I thanked him and learned his name was Roger. "You should go, really, they don't have a microphone and they use an old-fashioned piano."

That Sunday, I drove to Hayesville Presbyterian Church. When I got out of my car, I hear a voice that said, "I see you made it." *What?* Now I'm hearing voices. I looked around the parking lot to see Roger in his car, waiting to go in. He never told me he attends this church, but I was happy to see a familiar face. He explained that he comes early because his wife plays the piano. That works. What a relief to learn it was his voice I'd heard.

I made my way into the church, sitting in the back row, just in case I need to make a quick exit. Thankfully, I was able to make it through the one-hour service. I loved that the pastors were a hus-band and wife team. The welcome I got was overwhelming from the midsized, yet modest, church group. One of the ladies, Jessica, recognized me. She had waited on me outside of the Country Cottage Deli, a local restaurant. She remembered bringing my food out during frigid, cold weather when I couldn't go inside. I now knew two faces, which added to my comfort zone.

One by one, the very loving and welcoming congregation intro-duced themselves to me. The Sunday school teacher, Neal, went above and beyond to include me. Unfortunately, I couldn't function for long. I lasted less than a couple of minutes in the basement level where classes were to be held. I was grateful to have made it through the service. That was a major accomplishment.

It was hard to drive to church even though it was mere min-utes from my house. I continued to persevere until I couldn't any longer. Little by little, my resistance to the surroundings, towers, cell phones, hearing aids, pacemakers, anything with a frequency was dismantling me.

The last episode was a doozy. I remember sitting in the back row of the church. Neal was to my right. Jessica was in the pew ahead of me. We all stood to sing a praise and worship song. I don't think we were standing but a few minutes when my body collapsed. I felt like all of my muscles gave out. I could no longer support the hymnal book and it slid to the ground with a thump. At this point, I'm told that Neal dragged me out the front door. Thankfully almost no one noticed because they were intense in song and looking forward. Being in the last row had a lot of advantages when it came to a quick escape.

The only thing Neal could do at the point was to lie me on the ground. The theory was that the ground would suck the excess acquired voltage out of me and help me to function again. Although I came to, and knew what was going on around me, I couldn't use my arms or my legs.

Someone went to get my car.

I remember Pastor Bob coming out after the church service. He prayed over me while I lay helpless on the grass. Through my blurred vision I watched as his hand came toward me landing on my forehead. It felt like my last rites were being said. I thought I'd died.

Anyway, a couple of people put me in the back seat of my car. Jessica sat in the back and held my legs still. My nervous system was acting up big time. Neal drove anxiously to my house. Although it was hard to communicate, I had enough wits about me to know that this was an accident waiting to happen. I could picture Neal, meaning well, but opening the back door of the car—on the side that I was propped up against the door. The result would be me falling out onto the stone driveway. I had no way to hold myself in the vehicle since I couldn't use my arms or legs. Somehow, I found my voice and was able to communicate to Jessica "Don't open my door." In any case, she communicated that to Neal. Frantically, he said that that is exactly what he would have done, not thinking about the ramifications of that action.

After arriving at my house a mere ten minutes away, it became apparent that Neal and Jessica would not be able to carry me. The only remedy at this point was to put me on the ground. I was too heavy to carry, so they had to drive around to the back yard. Someone got a blanket. It was a group effort to get me from the car to lay me down onto the blanket. I still had no use of my arms or legs.

The next couple of hours were spent dragging me around, ever so slightly, to keep me in the shade when the sun shifted. During that time, I could make out the concern on Neal and Jessica's face—but I had no defenses to make this nightmare end.

As I laid there, Klepto, the neighborhood watch dog came by. He was racing through the yard and came to a halt eye level with me. That dog lay across my chest, licking my face. He was heavy. I'm not sure if anyone else was nearby at the time, but no one thought to get him off of me if they were nearby. That dog didn't leave my side. I'd swear he was crying over me. We have had a solid bond since then. He's watched over me when I'm working in my yard and has never left my side.

At the end of the day, both pastors stopped by to check on me. The timing was perfect because Jessica had to leave earlier and Neal couldn't get me into the house by himself. The nerve endings in my body were starting to thaw but I was still extremely weak. Pastor Bob and Neal supported me on either side as we made our way into the house. Although my legs felt heavy—like they were filled with lead, I could support my weight long enough to make it indoors with the support of these two men. Pastor Linda helped me into pajamas and settled me into bed.

Three out of four church services resulted in my having seizures and my being bodily removed from the church building. I recognized that it was time to go back to my outdoor chapel in the woods. I worshipped daily there. Most days Neal would join me. He was mourning the recent death of his wife and I was mourning the loss of my health. We both found comfort in the outdoor sanctuary.

After witnessing what I went through, just to survive, the Professor gave me the nickname "Pluck." In my thirst for words that is one I've never come across. The sound of it mocked a curse word tempting me to act out and slap him. I really needed to clean up my act. What a relief to find that the true meaning of the word was: resourceful courage and daring in the face of difficulties; spirit.

The Professor would tell me that I was tenacious, leaving me hungry to learn more words. Much of my vocabulary, at that time, felt frozen somewhere in my brain. I had trouble articulating the right words for an application and its correct usage. Words would scramble as I worked hard to retrieve them from my tainted memory.

Neal's life was moving in a different direction. He felt led to Arizona. After his departure, I was back to worshipping alone. However, I embraced his verbal gift of my new nickname "Pluck."

The Hayesville Presbyterian Church didn't give up on me. Pastor Linda and some of the church members went out of their way to help me.

Most of the members had never even heard of my condition, but they never doubted me, and if they did privately doubt they never revealed that to me. They are all about pure unconditional love. I made several attempts to be part of the worship service on Sunday— but I just couldn't, my body wouldn't cooperate. I couldn't sustain myself in the building.

When attending church was no longer an option for me, some members of the church would visit me at home. Every Wednesday, a group of woman from the church came to teach me how to knit and have fellowship. I have a strong admiration for this group of talented woman, who I consider my mentors in crafting and life. Pastor Linda, Margaret, and Shirley always challenged me with endless projects to divert my attention from myself, from my condition—it

145

worked! I was so engrossed in learning that I forgot it was hard to do. Forgive me Margaret, for being able to knit but still cannot master pearl. That part of my brain seems to be stuck in gear. You will be the first to know when I get over that hump. Occasionally, other members would visit as well. We were a small but powerful group. We learned from each other about life, knitting, and shared pretty much everything. It was healing and motivating for me. They continuously poured love into me in the form of hugs, cards, yarn, books, supplies, bread, and food. They never came empty handed and their hearts were always full. They were all a constant blessing in my life.

Along with the Wednesday visits my two pastors went above and beyond to visit on Sundays. They even brought communion once a month. They were always there to encourage and be supportive of me.

Pastor Bob very lovingly pointed out the comparison of Superman vs. kryptonite is like me with EMF exposure. He was always finding ways to help me. He even made me a wooden bee catcher when he witnessed the damage the bees were doing to my house. Every week during their weekly visit, Pastor Bob very lovingly picked a rose from my rose bushes and brought it to me, presenting me with a priceless gift.

Pastor Linda selflessly continued with random acts of kindness. She always seems to know what I need and when I need it. She presented me with endless gifts of craft materials, books, sermons, cards, stamps, food items; the list goes on and on. She taught me the true meaning of "pay it forward."

If I searched for the rest of my life, I couldn't top the love and support that the Hayesville Presbyterian pastors and congregation displayed to me. God led me to the right and perfect church family.

Outdoor Worship

Make a joyful shout to God,
Sing out the honor of His name;
Make His praise glorious.
Psalm 66: 1-2

I wasn't going to let the fact that I couldn't be in a building long enough to worship stop me from worshipping.

When I was in Texas, I frequented the outdoor chapel on the retreat where I stayed as often as I could. It was a simple, outdoor chapel consisting of a wooden cross with a couple of rows of benches that served as pews. That planted a seed in my mind for my own outdoor chapel.

The outdoor chapel was one of the first projects I took on during the first spring that I lived in Hayesville. I cleared a patch of woods that butted up to the horse pasture behind my house. Thankfully, my professor friend was able to lend muscle and support to dig the hole, mix cement, and erect the cross. He contributed so much; he was able to use a drill and screw gun to fasten the wood benches to the tree stumps. A tool I am no longer able to use without neurological effects. He even supplied the stumps from the church property. We stood back in awe at the magical serenity the outdoor chapel provided. It is a well-hidden secret, giving me the privacy to freely worship.

The professor and I visited the sanctuary daily, sometimes twice a day. He was seeking relief for bereavement and I was trying to find healing and restoration for my body.

Those days I worshipped alone most of the time. That part wouldn't bother me so much except it is especially painful on Sunday when I was fully aware that all the other believers gathered together to worship in church. I feel left out. There is just no way around it. I loved my outdoor chapel and recognized you don't need a building to worship, but missed the fellowship and human contact with my peers.

What I learned by worshipping alone was that without excessive noise or visual stimulation you can really connect to the spirit of God. I felt oneness with Him. I received a peace and contentment that I cannot recall reaching while worshipping in the presence of a large group of people. It filled me with the spirit of God.

Occasionally, I have invited someone to worship with me and that is also loving and fulfilling. Sometimes, someone will ask me if they can join me. Those occasions are rare but very special to me. Most times when I have a visitor worship they can't believe the spiritual infilling they get from praising and worshipping outdoors. With the woods surrounding the outdoor chapel and branches hovering over top as a sort of protective blanketing, you can't help but feeling at one with God and nature.

That feeling becomes more apparent when critters decide to pay a visit. I have to cringe when I think of the time my friends from Asheville came to visit for the first time and joined me for a very brief service. We all took our seats in the sanctuary. Upon entering, Jack and Louise sat in the first pew to the right (in the last row). Pastor Bob and his wife, Carol, sat in the second pew to the left. I was excited to have a captive audience to give my sermon. I stood in the front of the outdoor chapel. As I began speaking to my small congregation, I noticed Pastor Bob in the back right pew eyeing toward Jack. Although he was trying not to alarm anyone, he interrupted the service after a couple of attempts looking in Jack's direction, eyeballing up. When Jack didn't catch the hint, Pastor Bob very calmly announced to Jack that he might want to move. When Jack resisted, Pastor Bob told him there was a snake dangling above him.

Under any other circumstances this wouldn't have been a big deal. After all, it was a small black snake. It was harmless, but obviously intimidating. I would like to think that the snake was just curious. I'm usually alone. Having four more people in attendance, that were city slickers, proved horrifying to them. I've never in my life seen people move so fast. Needless to say, my sermon was finished before it got started.

I felt really bad about that happening. My dear friend and sister in Christ, Louise is blind. So I could only imagine the horror she felt, not knowing it was a baby black snake. She wouldn't be able to detect where it was hanging or if it was moving in her direction. It broke my heart to witness the panic. It was frightening enough for the rest of them to see a snake dangling, but being blind, she was left to her own imagination as to its size and species. It had to be horrifying for her.

The snake never showed itself again to me but the damage was done. It appears the serpent won that round. I lost my congregation to the wild.

On subsequent visits to me, I felt it would be in poor taste to ask them to revisit the sanctuary. So we visited in my house or on my front porch.

Three years ago, Pastor Steve and his wife Mary from the Oakview Baptist Church brought some of the members of their church and held a full service in my outdoor sanctuary. Of course, only a few could show, due to my limitations of exposure. Anyone sporting a cell phone, hearing aids, pace maker or oxygen tank couldn't be part of the service. The price I would pay for the exposure was just too debilitating.

Despite having to share my limitations, a fair number of people came, at least eight that I can recall. They even brought a young man who played an acoustic guitar. Pastor Steve accompanied the young man by sporting his own acoustic guitar. It felt foreign to hear music after living in silence for so long. Pastor Steve presented a full sermon. We had the woods rocking. Oh, the joy that filled my spirit that day.

We sang several songs, my favorite being, "I'll Fly Away." That song proved to be very special, since my friend Mary and I sang it together when Pastor Steve gave a sermon in my sanctuary. She has passed away since then. Every Sunday I sing—actually belt out—"I'll Fly Away," in her honor. Oh how I miss her! As much as

I loved the service I had no idea how much it would wipe me out. I was exhausted. I think I slept for three days after that.

Speaking of Mary, when I met her some two years prior, we were both on a mission. We were drawn to each other's spirit with the same goal. We both came here to Hayesville to die. It may sound morbid, but it's not morbid to a believer, and we both were born-again believers.

Your spirit knows when you are spent. We were both very tired. She was tired since she was older, and I was tired due to my EMF disease process. We talked about that. After sharing our desired goal with a surprised look on both our faces; something changed. Mary learned how to "just be" and I learned how to "live again."

When you take control of your life is when you really begin to live. She was very clear in telling me God wasn't finished with me yet. We found so much comfort in each other's company. We shared heart-wrenching stories of our pasts and prayed for hope for the future.

The last memory I have of Mary is of her sitting outside of her apartment—arms raised—and although I couldn't hear her voice, I could read her lips. "Take me home," she pleaded looking upwards to Heaven. . .and Lord, please heal Deborah, it's not time for her to go yet."

Mary had a wish to be part of my healing. She contributed in many ways to my wellness. One way was her no-nonsense verbiage. She was always direct and to the point. Secondly was her *bag lady* ways of showing up with a trunk full of things we could swap, kind of like *take a penny, leave a penny.*

What an endearing surprise it was when her son and daughter-in-love (as Mary called her) came to visit me after Mary's passing. She left money in her will to assist me with the extraction of that earlier-referenced tooth that needed to be removed surgically. The generous gift of one-thousand dollars paid for the total amount of both visits and the surgery. What an unexpected blessing!

I'm always amused that God shows himself in so many unexpected ways while I am outdoors worshipping. It may be through the presence of a squirrel, a bird, or the horses that peek through the opening of the woods next door at me. Even Klepto, the dog that keeps on stealing, joined me for an occasional sermon. Sometimes he sits patiently in the aisle, or just outside of the chapel area looking in.

One dilemma that I haven't been able to control is the fact that once I finish the sermon, the curiosities of the animals seems to diminish. The moment I start singing they all run away! It says nothing in the Bible about knowing how to sing. I know I am the joyful noise, but sometimes I wish they would cut me some slack and grin and bear it. God definitely had a sense of humor when he made me.

I was made very aware of the fact that I lived in the mountains by the extravagant guest that visited my yard not twenty minutes after I finished my service one Sunday.

It was a beautiful day, the fields behind the sanctuary not only housed the rodeo horses this week but there were the rodeo steer, and an assortment of different-colored cows. What a visual treat to see so many of God's creatures so up close and personal. One creature I didn't bargain for would present itself shortly and I believe it's the new smells of the new animals that lured it in. It was a very intimidating predator!

I had just left the sanctuary and was waiting for my friend Jessica to visit after she'd finished attending church service at Hayesville Presbyterian Church. The same church I tried to frequent but miserably failed. I sat out on my deck overlooking the field on my property. The tall grass was being manipulated in a line coming towards the mowed part of my yard; the part that would give better visibility. *Oh, this will be fun, that looks like Klepto coming to visit,* I thought. I'll just go play with him until Jessica gets here. As I opened the gate on my deck to walk down the incline, I was nudged in my spirit to take another look in that direction. It's a good thing I looked. Standing before me was a full-body view of the most majestic creature I had ever had the privilege of viewing this up-close and personal. It was probably thirty feet from me, just down the hill standing with regal presence in my yard. It was a MOUNTAIN LION!

At first, I wasn't quite certain what I was seeing. Once I focused and was frozen in time for those split-twenty seconds I could see it weighed in at probably one hundred twenty pounds of pussy-cat. *Wow!*

Slowly backing onto the deck, watching its presence, it sleekly seemed to drag its huge front paws, walking with purpose and predatory attitude towards my sanctuary! This was the very same sanctuary that I was just in—not twenty minutes ago. If I were still there, my back would have been to the pussy-cat and my arms lifted in praise and worship. After reading about their behavior, especially the part where they go after easy prey, I shunned thinking of what the outcome could have been.

I called the owner of the rodeo horses to advise them of the mountain lion. They happened to be in town and came right over. Although they walked through my property, it was a lost cause. The cat had already run through the horse field and out the back side. They have since removed the calves, which I'm quite sure was the bait that brought the mountain lion this close to civilization. After all, I live not a half mile from the back of Ingles grocery store. I sure hope it's not hungry enough to pay a visit there.

I asked myself what else don't I know about this area? I called the wildlife number and was told, "There are no mountain lions around here." I was told they are in Tennessee. "Okay," I replied, "You are telling me that we border Tennessee, they have mountain lions and we don't. Do you really think that the mountain lion knows the borders?" I said incredulously. "I'm telling you what I saw," I insisted. "It was probably a bobcat," he stated. "No sir, I've seen bobcats on my brother's property, while camping there. They are much smaller with a stubby tail. This cat's tail was at least a foot and a half long. It had a cream-colored body with unusual markings on its face and ears. It was definitely not a bobcat." The agent wouldn't back down. "Do you have a photo?" he inquired. "No sir, I wasn't really thinking of taking a picture at that point, nor do I own a camera. But I can assure you I will be getting one."

Needless to say, I spent the next two months worshipping in my living room with the doors and windows closed. After I got over the shock of the predator that visited my backyard, I decided it was time to go back to my sanctuary to worship. I trusted God to have my back. However, just in case He was busy that day, I now carry a fog horn to distract any approaching predators.

I was led to call my younger brother Chris, a hunter. He would know how to handle this intruder. When I explained my dilemma of my back to the mountain lion and my arms raised toward the cross for worship, his response was, "Pray Harder!" Point taken.

I dislike admitting this, but I spent a whole lot of time looking behind me during worship the first couple of weeks after returning to my holy place. Thankfully, no more pussy cats have blessed my space. Ah, the joys and stresses of mountain living. All I could think was "What else don't I know?"

Abundant Unexpected Blessings

I will make them and the places all around My hill a blessing;
and I will cause showers to come down in their season;
there shall be showers of blessings.
Ezekiel 34:26

I t took two years of praying to be led to the right and perfect place to call home. I needed a place where healing could manifest itself.

I knew I'd made the right choice by following the nudging of God's spirit. Blessings, abundant blessings, have been poured upon me as a result of my obedience. The only blessing I sought was a place to call home and a clean, swimmable lake. The rest of the blessings are clearly gifts from God.

From the moment I set up residence in Hayesville, there has been a continuous outpouring of love and support from the most unexpected sources. I have been blessed with firewood, bread, all kinds of food items, produce, care packages, gift baskets, hand-me-down clothes, fabric, craft items, yarn, stamps, hair trims, cards for all seasons, and even toilet paper.

Some of my most cherished possessions are handmade gifts presented to me from my pastor and the support system of church ladies. My pastor made me a prayer shawl that I not only treasure, but wear often. Margaret cross-stitched a beautiful free-spirited fairy entitled, "Deborah's Spirit," regally framed. It's the first thing you see when you enter my home on the wall straight ahead. Just looking at it lifts my spirits. Most recently, she cross-stitched a pillow with a mermaid on it since I am playfully known as the mermaid on Lake Chatuge.

In 2017, I was blessed with a new neighbor, Phil, also a born-again Christian. He's a talented musician. Embarrassingly enough, he'd heard me belting out songs from my sanctuary in the woods. Although he was polite in saying I sounded good; I know I'm the joyful noise. He offered to add music to the mix by bringing over his acoustic guitar. We have practiced a couple of times and I'm so pleased with the way our voices complement each other. The music and new friendship with yet another Christian brother has enhanced my joy.

The most recent blessing is a gift I received from Kim, a very loving lady at the dam. She had no way of knowing how special her gift would prove to be, but God knew. When I unveiled the box to reveal its contents, I was pleasantly surprised to see what lay inside. It was a beautifully-crafted bracelet in the shape of an angel wing. This is the very same bracelet I saw not even two weeks ago in a magazine; at that time I prayed for a way to be able to give it to my daughter for Christmas. I knew I didn't have a Christmas budget to give it to her. God knew my heart and allowed me to give the gift forward.

I knew when I explained this to Kim she would be in awe of the God we serve and would encourage my sending the bracelet to my daughter.

The fact that I am unable to wear any kind of jewelry, with the exception of one ring, due to the metal contents made it all the more clear that this was meant to be my daughter's Christmas gift.

The gift brought me abundant joy, knowing the source in which it came and where it was going. God is always right on time.

I praise God, from whom all blessings flow!

Midnight Mass – Christmas Eve

Let us therefore come boldly to the throne of grace,
that we may obtain mercy and find grace
to help in time of need.
Hebrews 4:16

G od knows just what we need and when we need it. It was
Christmas Eve and I've been determined to go to midnight
mass. Prior to my setback, I spent every Christmas Eve at midnight
mass, for as long as I can remember. Most often I went by myself to
receive an infilling that would carry me throughout the year.

The Episcopal Church was minutes from my home and was
hosting midnight mass. It's the once-a-year outing that I cherish. If I
let the negative forces plant thoughts they would remind me of all the
reasons I shouldn't attempt to go to mass, thoughts like: I don't drive
well at night, in fact I just don't drive at night because the lights are
blinding. I can't be in the sanctuary due to all the cell phones people
would carry and the Wi-Fi in the building. The impact of electronic
devices to lock and unlock car doors in the parking lot will jolt me. I
went anyway. I have made special arrangements ahead of time to be
able to view the service through the window from the foyer.

I waited until a minute before the service and stood outside the
church entryway. I listened to the bells ring, well sort of. I covered
my ears due to the sensitivity to sound and still heard them clang. I
watched through the window of the doors to see the choir joyfully
enter the sanctuary. I already feel uplifted just being there. Once the
choir has entered the sanctuary and the main doors closed, I entered
the foyer and one of the greeters was glad to see me and offered me a

chair in front of the window separating the foyer from the sanctuary. All of the audio and lights are turned off in the foyer. I can read lips and follow the program from there. I'm left to myself as the greeters join the service. Feeling joyful, I belted out the songs, assuming no one can hear me. I couldn't be more wrong.

Out of the corner of my right eye, I spotted a person standing in the darkened hallway. I turn, startled, when I spied a young man standing there looking at me.

"Hey, I'm sorry I didn't know you were there or I probably wouldn't have belted out the songs the way I did," I said, somewhat embarrassed.

"No, really, I liked it, you sing well," the young man offered.

"I know I sing off-key but the Bible says *make a joyful noise*, it says nothing about knowing how to sing." I carry on.

"Can I join you?" he says sheepishly.

"Absolutely, it would be my best Christmas gift to have you join me," I blurted out.

For the rest of the evening, we became friends. He asked if I was married and if I had children. Startled by such bold questions, I asked how old he was. As it turned out he was fourteen years old but appeared to be sixteen. He had wisdom beyond his years. His grandmother who raised him had passed on two years prior and he was interviewing me to hook me up with his grandfather who happened to be in the sanctuary. This young man had God written all over him. All he wanted was a mother figure and apparently he saw that in me.

I did meet his grandfather and he was a delightful man. He definitely has his hands full raising his grandson and his siblings. We remained friends from a distance with mutual concern and prayers for each other.

Looking back on that evening, meeting this young man was a gift. Being acknowledged by him was even a greater gift. There was something very special about him. I believe God is going to use him in a mighty way in the future. I was missing my children; after all it was Christmas and, due to distance and timing, we just couldn't all be together. God knew what I needed and he provided. He also knew what the young man needed; we both got our Christmas wish.

Each consecutive year that I remained in Hayesville I contacted the church. One year I called the mayor who happened to be in the choir, or my friend Stephanie to clear the way for me. The church accommodated me by turning off the lights and Wi-fi in the foyer after everyone has entered the sanctuary. They provided a chair and sometimes a table in front of the fixed-glass viewing window that looks into the sanctuary. The ushers provided me with a program to follow along, a hymnal, and the white unlit candle for "Silent Night" singing. Father Bill, along with Stephanie assisting him, brought communion out to me after the congregation went forward for their sacraments.

At the part of the service where the congregation turns to greet each other, I feel a profound loss of fellowship. I feel left out because I am. I can't be in there to greet the people. I tried this year to reach out by waving to two guys who sat near the back. They looked at me, seemed embarrassed for me, and didn't acknowledge my greeting. Nervously they looked away to pretend they didn't see me.

I thought about that. They don't know me. All they see is a person outside the glass viewing window, with dark glasses on, a head wrap and a beige ball cap. They don't understand that the glasses are because I'm light sensitive, the head wrap is to protect me from signals penetrating my ears, the ball cap a protective shield to guard my brain. They can't figure out why the heck I'm out in the foyer to begin with. I'm an alien.

Maybe, just maybe, they were a bit skeptical and afraid. After all, they watch the news and hear horror stories. I can't, therefore I don't.

Easter Morning Kayak 2015

Saying, "The Lord is risen indeed,
And has appeared to Simon!"
Luke 24:34

The night before Easter, I was heartbroken with the realization that I couldn't be in a church service in the morning due to my extreme environmental sensitivities. Rather than focusing on what I couldn't do and being upset about it, I prayed about where I could be to glorify Him the most.

The vision came to me strong and clear.

I followed the nudging of my spirit and, on Easter morning, I drove my Kia Sportage, with my kayak tied down inside my vehicle, to the boat ramp at The Circle and launched at dawn. It's difficult for me to drive when it's dark outside, so I usually don't. I prayed for an opening. I didn't pass any cars en-route, so I didn't have the discomfort of oncoming lights. No one was around.

The sun was just about to rise, in all its glory. I paddled out onto the middle of the lake and sat still to watch the rising rays of light reflect upon the calm, still water. As I faced the sunrise, I became very aware of the profound silence, the stillness. Then, as if by silent demand, a fish jumped out of the water. It jumped straight up and flailed in its victory jump of glory. Various species of birds flew by. A blue heron swooped low, tracing the water's edge. Two deer peeked timidly out of the surrounding woods, making their debut at the water's edge. The sun rose, looking much larger than I'd ever recalled.

Joy, unspeakable infilling joy, penetrated my soul as I prayed out loud and exalted His holy name. "Ha-ley-lu-yah" I shouted. "He is risen, He is alive!" I didn't think it was possible to contain that kind of joy. I thought for a minute I might explode.

I'm not sure how long I floated in my kayak, but peace and serenity were all around me. Not even one boat cruised by. I had the lake to myself. Part of me felt grateful for that and part of me was removed from all traces of human life and craving contact.

After a while, I began to be aware of my numbness caused by the cold temperatures. The dampness of the water made it seem colder somehow. I paddled to Penland Island, my regular campsite, and made a small fire in the existing fire pit. I removed my boots and socks, grounded by touching my bare feet to the ground and heating my feet by the fire until I felt thawed out enough to continue on. I had packed a brunch, so I took that opportunity to enjoy eating it while comforted by the fire.

Once I was warm and fed, I decided to check out island number two. It was farther than I remembered, or maybe I was just exhausted from the chill in the fresh air and the early morning outing.

As I approached island two, I surveyed the scene. It looked uninhabited, so I paddled to shore. I pulled my kayak up onto the land. By now, Mother Nature was calling. I walked the shoreline up behind some bushes for privacy. I should be able to cop a squat without being noticed. There were hardly any boats out at this point and the nearest houses at least one mile away.

Just as I dropped my pants and squatted, without yet releasing my urine, I heard a loud swanking sound and find myself running away from there in horror. With my pants still around my knees and a huge, angry goose chasing me all the way to my kayak I must have been a sight for any one of the surrounding houses on the hilltops. I'm quite sure someone had a telescope and may have zoomed in on that farce.

I ran clumsily, while pulling up my pants and finally made it to my kayak. As I was shoving off from shore and paddling away, pants still unzipped because that goose was on my trail and not backing down any time soon. I think you can guess the rest. That would have been a good time to be wearing depends!

The wind has kicked up and it's strong. Bring me home, Lord! I held my paddle up. Kayak paddles have a paddle on both sides of the pole and, with the wind behind me, all I had to do was lift the pole and the wind used the two paddles like sails which blew me leisurely all the way back to the boat ramp a good mile and a half away.

I enjoyed the breathtaking views of the deep, rich color of the water, the tree-lined shoreline and the mountains surrounding the lake. I safety arrived back at the boat ramp. The only casualty was the chafing on the inside of my legs. When natures calling didn't have a chance to relieve itself on the island, basically, in layman terms: I'd peed my pants.

I have never been so grateful to arrive home to the warmth of a hot shower.

Part IV:
Reinventing My Life

Camping

Walk in wisdom toward those who are outside,
Redeeming the time.
Colossians 4:5

Because my new way of life involved mostly camping to get relief, I felt compelled to share the moments that stood out most in my mind.

Something profound happens when you are reduced to camping. You have your tent, minimal clothing, basic camp stuff (dish, cup, clothes line, chair, sleeping bag, hammock, bathing suit, and towel), a camp fire, air, food and water to sustain you. You suddenly realize that is all you really need. God is everywhere you look. God is in the air we breathe, the water we swim in, in the birds that soar over us in the sky, the sunrise, the sunset, the trees that surround us. Even in the fish jumping up from under the water's surface. He is alive!

Think about it. How relaxing it is with no mortgage, nothing to break down so there is almost nothing to fix. No bills. No pressure. All that matters is to exist in the breathtaking beauty of the outdoors. I simply could not handle any kind of stress. The slightest bit of stress reduced me into a meltdown mode. What I didn't bargain for were the unexpected bloopers and lack of security that a campsite offered. Some camping trips were more challenging than others. The following trips proved to be stressful with unexpected vandalism; surprises and guests I didn't even know existed.

When I looked around at my surroundings, while camping on the welcoming islands on Lake Chatuge, I questioned how my life has changed so drastically that I would end up in paradise. The greenery, the surrounding distant mountain views, the open, vast blue skies, the wildlife all adding to the amazement. I was in awe. God is all around me in visual gifts. Praising and worshipping on the island enhanced the experience, filling me with exceeding joy and comfort. Living proof that I was never alone. On any given day, you could hear the supreme joy of cheers and shouts of the youngsters and adults enjoying the lake. Praise you, Lord.

I took my baths in the lake with biodegradable soap and shampoo that I mail-ordered. I would boil water and use a touch of bleach to disinfect my dishes. I lived on mostly rice and canned beans. They were the easiest food items to sustain without refrigeration. You wanted to keep food smells to a minimum, so as not to attract wildlife. Canned beans seemed like the most effective way to get protein.

The majority of time I camped alone. It is hard to find someone willing to put the effort into camping on the island with me. The ones who have tried have very little staying power.

While camping alone, I often heard eerie sounds in the night— sounds of whisperings and movement. Was it footsteps, leaves rustling, or the wind? Could it be a small animal or a bird, or something else? If I allowed my imagination to get the best of me, I would be horrified. It was easiest to pass out to avoid dealing with what was coming. My tent held a false sense of security. The twisty-ties I used from a sandwich bag was a poor excuse for a make-shift lock.

My friend Neal asked to join me a couple of times. My body was seriously compromised the first year that I'd arrived in Hayesville and, having had episodes of not being able to use my arms and legs, I thought it would be a good idea to let him join me. It was comforting to have someone out on the island to watch my back.

We were both calm and quiet much of the time so it proved to be a healing experience. Waggie, his kid in a dog suit, joined us. The dog loved the experience and took pleasure in riding on the kayaks. He would alternate back and forth between the two kayaks. He picked inopportune times to dive off one kayak to swim to the other. The timing of his jumping overboard was exceptionally bad while we were carrying a full load of camp gear. He rocked the boat, causing unnecessary havoc. Oh, the joys of pet ownership. Waggie guarded the camp, making a great watch dog.

When Neal made the decision to leave the area, God provided new friends to come to my aid.

I arrived at the dam one day for a place to ground while viewing the serene water. When I got out of my car, I heard a bold gentleman yell from across the parking lot. "Young lady, did we meet yesterday?" he blurted out. I looked up to see a handsome older gentleman and wondered what his deal was. In response, I blurted out—without much thought first, "Well that's a new one, I haven't been called *young* in a very long time."

We struck up a conversation. He shared with me that his wife was walking the dam and he was waiting for her. Not two minutes later, a very petite, attractive woman, looking to be about my age, arrived. I loved her instantly, although she seemed skeptical of me. We spoke about sensitivities and as it turned out she has allergic reactions to new carpeting and goes into anaphylactic shock when exposed. Having this sensitivity left her more open-minded to learn about my EMF.

God sent me these two incredible people, John and Maria, as my new friends. As it turned out, we have a mutual love of the water. They would visit me during the day while I was camping on the islands. They came by pontoon boat. They seemed to really enjoy the campsite and would even bring dinner out to join me to dine and to swim.

One day, while camping on the island, I got bored and decided to kayak over to see where John and Maria lived. They told me where it was but I had no idea that to get there by kayak would take hours. As I was making my way there, a storm blew in quickly and violently. I was stuck out on the lake, paddling aggressively, while thunder and lightning was all around me. Not cool. It was a horrifying experience. I made it to the dock, tied my kayak to a cleat and was looking for a place to hide, when I saw a wooden picnic table at the shore line. I was just about to climb under the table for protection when I spotted John across the road. He invited me under their covered porch since I wouldn't do well in their house. We rode out the storm together. The day escaped us and it wouldn't be possible for me to paddle back the distance I came. It would be dark shortly.

Maria called a neighbor to ask if he could pull my kayak out of the water and drop me at the Jack Rabbit boat ramp. This would put me at the closet point to Penland Island and would allow me to get there before dark.

What I didn't expect was the blessing their neighbor would continue to be in my life. Ted proved to be a good Samaritan and a great friend. He brought furniture out to the island—a table and chairs to dine on. He provided dinners, firewood, water refills, companionship, and we shared a mutual love of swimming. He was a true southern gentleman. He always left before dark to ensure he wasn't overstepping his boundaries.

I had already concluded that I couldn't be in a relationship due to all of my restrictions but I enjoyed our long heart-to-heart talks about life and loss. He was so easy to talk to and seemed genuine. He was a true man, rugged and handsome.

During a hurricane that hit this area, his boat was blown away from his dock. After retrieving his boat, he managed to boat out to the island to check on me. He was frantic and stressed out, thinking my tent was blown off of the island. What a surprise to hear his boat come to shore in the torrential rain and high winds. I was upset with him for risking his life to come check on me. I remember telling him I'm exactly where God wants me to be. After being assured that I was okay, and the storm was subsiding, he returned to his dock.

What a guy! Most men I know won't visit in good weather, let alone check on me during a hurricane.

When my brother and his wife came to visit, Ted gave them a tour of the lake on his pontoon boat and stopped at my campsites to let them get a glimpse into my world. We even packed a dinner, compliments of my brother and his wife, and dined on Penland Island altogether. Ted supplied all of the set-ups: table, chairs, transportation, and floats to use while swimming.

Ted was still in chronic grief over the loss of his wife of thirty-eight years and I was still grieving my health. Healing, serious healing, for us both took place during his visits. I was just starting to think that maybe I was wrong. Maybe, just maybe, I could be in a relationship and actually allowed myself to fall for Ted. It happened during the outings when my brother was here. My brother and his wife, Ted and I were swimming off the beach on one of the islands.

We ended up laying on rafts. . .just floating around enjoying the hot, leisurely afternoon. Ted and I married up our floats, side by side. I felt such a strong love for him. Of course I kept those thoughts to myself, thinking he has been through enough with the loss of his wife, he doesn't need to get involved with a compromised woman. He needs the lady that can ride on the back of his Harley with him. He needs the woman who can go on the cruises that he dreams of. What could I possibly offer him? Of course I never told Ted that I felt that way, how could I? I'm so glad I never shared that because shortly thereafter, all hell broke loose. The next weekend he went to his dock only to find that his boat had sunk to the bottom. I still have no idea how he was able to retrieve it. His previous girlfriend showed up and played the jealous card, even though it had been months since they'd gone out. We weren't dating, because, well, I don't date. We were building a strong friendship, which I valued dearly.

In any case, Ted came out to see me at the island a week later. He seemed confused. He explained his dilemma of wanting to go on cruises. After all, what was he supposed to do—go on a cruise alone? I could see where this was heading, so I nipped it in the bud. I told him he has known her a lot longer than me. He owed it to her to give her a chance. They used to go on cruises together. All the while I was thinking, *I couldn't even be in the running*. Cruises are yet another thing I could never do.

It was late, getting dark. He got up from the chair to leave. I thought I was going to die, my heart felt restricted. I walked him to his boat and said, "Take care of you." We had never kissed, it wasn't that kind of relationship. But that night, he kissed me on the top of my head. That kiss proved to be the most endearing kiss I've ever received. I could feel the love behind it.

The boat motored away. At first, I couldn't even look in that direction. My world felt like it had ended. I felt defeated. *Heartsick*. John and Maria had moved to California and that was a big enough loss, but to lose Ted too, was more than I was willing to handle. Ted was returning to the only other woman he had known since his wife's passing and there wasn't a thing I could do but watch him go. I tried not to look but I couldn't help myself. As I watched him motor away I could see that he, too, was hurting. His body language gave him away. He was hunched over at the wheel of the boat. Our combined grief was all consuming, overwhelming.

I couldn't take yet another broken heart, another fracture to add to the accumulated pain that already existed there. As if I could hide my pain I climbed into my tent for coverage. The sound that escaped my mouth released in thunderous noise. I wailed out loud for what seemed like hours. I know the sound must have carried across the lake but no one came to my rescue, there was no relief in sight, and then I passed out. Another chapter closed. Yet, another profound loss.

Thankfully two years later, John and Maria moved back from California and we have spent a lot of time together. It also afforded me opportunities to cross paths with Ted. God, I loved that man! I'm thankful we could still respect and care about each other, even though our lives have gone in different directions. I simply couldn't be what he needed and I loved him way too much to restrict him. However, being his friend was a blessing I never wanted to be without. Thank you, Lord!

Unexpected Guests

Yea, though I walk through the valley of the shadow of death
I will fear no evil
For you are with me, Your rod and Your staff,
They comfort me.
Psalm 23:4

Of course, there is one thing I didn't bargain for. I had been camping on Penland Island for two summers without incident. On September 14, 2015, that all changed.

It was 5:00 p.m. Although I was sitting in my camp chair in front of my fire pit, I had not lit it yet. I was quietly reading my book. When I read I am all-engrossed in my reading, never paying much attention to what is around me.

I heard movement behind me. I didn't look, suspecting a bird or a squirrel. A few minutes later, I heard splashing in the water to my left. I still don't think to look. I'm thinking, *"Wow that must be a big fish."* It always is. A few minutes later, I heard the splashing again. I turned to look this time but couldn't quite absorb what I was looking at. It seemed surreal. I was thinking. . .this thing is cartoony. I was sure any minute now Alan Funt from "Candid Camera" was going to appear and let me in on the prank. (Okay, I'm showing my age. For those of you younger folks who don't know about the Alan Funt Show, it was a TV show with a series of practical jokes set up to catch people off guard. It was a comedy of bloopers to catch people's reactions on tape.)

I saw a large, black bear to the tune of, I would guess, 500 pounds. He was swiping his paws in the water, fishing for fish. I didn't know what to do. All rationale at that point went out the window.

All these panicked thoughts went through my head. "I've got to get out of here. Oh my gosh, that is what just walked behind me! My kayak. . .I've got to get my kayak out of the woods and onto the beach. *I can't.* There is no way out. Don't run." I'm thinking, "He will think you are prey and chase you." Panic was setting in deep within me. During these moments, it never occurred to me to pray. Fear overtook my good brain. I froze. I stood still.

After a minute or two, although it felt like forever, the bear started swimming out towards the buoy that I'd just swam back from not a half-hour prior to this. I just finished four laps, a quarter mile out around the buoy and back. I was exhausted. It's amazing how fear will prick your spirit and give you a second wind.

Panicked, I pulled my kayak out of the woods and down to the beach. The bear heard me and curiosity got the best of him. He did a U-turn and was swimming toward me. I stood on the beach, at the water's edge, and he was less than ten feet from me. I froze in time. My legs and arms wouldn't respond. I was like a statue.

As the mammoth creature came closer to me, he stood up. I cowered in his presence. The only thing between us was the kayak. Being only three feet apart, I watched in stifled terror, as he stood on his back paws, towering about one head length above me. He curiously started sniffing me. The only thing I could think in my paralyzed state was, "This is gonna hurt."

Thankfully, he wasn't interested in what he saw. It was at the end of the summer—I'm at my lightest weight of the year and had virtually no meat on me. It was conveyed to me months later by a forest ranger that black bears get a bad rap. They are basically vegetarians and have no interest in eating people. The bear circled back around and swam out and around the buoy. . .as if to mock me. Then he continued swimming across to the nature preserve, which connects to the Jack Rabbit Campgrounds.

As the bear was swimming across, I was very aware of the boats going by, pulling small children on rafts, water skiers, and fishing boats. I was waving frantically to try to signal my distress and warn of the possible danger but no one looked my way. I'm not sure I could have talked at that point to tell them about the *b-b-b-bear!*

The bear's whole body was majestic in appearance. I was amazed that you only see the top of the bears head as he swims. His whole body is so heavy it is actually impressive to watch that the bear could keep his head afloat. They do a doggie paddle. I watched until the humongous bear lifted himself up on the shoreline across the way. It was a safe distance of about one-half mile.

Had I not been so frightened, I might have been able to appreciate the awe of this once in a lifetime encounter. At least I hoped it was a one-time deal.

Still panicked, I left all of my belongings and kayaked the twenty-five minute paddle back to the original boat ramp that I'd launched my kayak from. Once I made it to shore, it became clear to me that I hadn't prayed about the situation. So pray is what I did. Lord Jesus, Father God, it's only my first of four nights out on the island. If I go back, I could be eaten by a bear. If I go home now I didn't get the four days of healing that I set out to get. I paused. It was laid on my heart *"Oh ye of little faith."* "You're not talking to me! I have big faith," I said defensively and out loud. All the while, I'm thinking it will be dark out soon and I would need to leave now if I am going to paddle back. I don't have lights on my kayak so it's a one-way trip.

I knew in that moment exactly what I had to do. I turned my kayak around and paddled all the way back to the campsite, eagerly surveying my surroundings for any possible relatives to the bear. I saw nothing.

I made it back to the campsite and immediately added to my fire pit. I built the biggest bonfire you could imagine. I don't remember sleeping at all that night. I sang loud—loud enough to chase any wildlife away. I was successful only because I remain *the joyful noise.*

Months later, I stopped at an outdoor yard sale. I was filled with hope that maybe I would be able to shop. No cars were in the driveway but I could see the tables all set up. There was a radio playing, but I was determined to shop. I asked from a distance if it would be possible to turn the radio off just long enough for me to do so. I explained for medical reasons that I couldn't be around the radio signals. They complied without a fuss. I asked the father if he had any life vests. I was hoping to get some extra ones for when my children visit. The father, in turn, called on his son. There a young man in his late twenties who was sitting with his wife and newborn baby. The young man approached and said, "Let me see what we have," and proceeded to take me to the shed. No extra vests to be had. However, he had a wealth of outdoor gear. He explained that he had taken a one-year course and lived off the land. I was impressed. As we talked further, I felt there was something very familiar about him and he felt the same way. We observed each other for a minute.

He said he camps on Penland Island.

"That's why you look familiar, so do I," I blurted out, without really thinking about it. I didn't really want people knowing I camp alone out on the island. Although, I'm prayed up and know I am not really alone. God is always with me. I still am hesitant to let the worldly men know I'm camping out there.

"Deborah, do you sing when you are on the island?" He inquired somewhat in awe.

"Well yeah. It keeps the animals away."

"Yo, dude. You are not going to believe this, but me and six of my buddies were camping out on the east side of Penland and we were tripping. We heard this angelic voice and started swimming around the island in pursuit of the sound. We thought we broke through a portal," he said, as if tripping were an everyday occurrence and something I should be aware of.

I giggled nervously, thinking, *"What do you do with that information? They must have heard me the night of the bear when I pulled an all-nighter."*

"We started swimming around the island, thinking you were an angel. However the sounds of your voice bounced off of the dam and the park and rec — we couldn't find you," he offered adventurously.

Praise God for small favors. What would I have done if I were standing by my campfire with arms raised, praising and worshipping, singing and ranting and — suddenly six young men, who are tripping, come to shore to see me? Ha-lay-freaking-lu-ya! Pardon my potty mouth. . .but I would have freaked out.

I know nothing about drugs, so I decided to ask my daughter who is in the same age group what the heck *tripping* means and would they have hurt me? She kiddingly and playfully said they probably would have come to shore and bowed down to you, thinking you really were not of this world. So there you have it.

It took the entire winter months for me to recover from the bear incident. I needed to get back to healing. I needed to camp on the island. Armed with bear spray I set out once again. On May 31, 2016, someone at the circle reported my passenger-side front window was blown out.

For appearance's sake, it looked like foul play. One of the guys who frequent the circle reported that he saw me leave with a guy in separate kayaks after arguing. And that I never returned. It was kind of like when you played telephone tag as a child. The story gets embellished along the way until it is so distorted that the facts aren't even close to what really happened.

I left by kayak, that part was true. However, the couple arguing were parked in the white car *beside* my white car before they both went off in another direction in their kayaks.

Mine became a missing person's case, however temporary that was. My car was dusted for fingerprints. The sheriff's department spent the day looking for me. They arrived at my house to find several day's mail on my porch, packages, and fresh-cut flowers left with a note from my boyfriend to welcome me home when I return. It didn't look good.

I'd notified my contact, Margaret from church, and my brother from West Virginia, as a safety net that I was out on the island but the police would have no way of knowing that. This was the first time I forgot to put a stop-mail notice out, an oversight that might have solved the dilemma sooner perhaps.

When I first started camping on Penland Island two years prior, I contacted the woman at the 911 dispatch office to let her know that I'd be doing that. Just in case something should go terribly wrong. After the humiliation of my brother telling me that "Most people don't call 911 before an emergency." I gave up that protocol. I was only trying to be proactive.

Of course, I was unaware that I was being sought after. I was safe and sound, relaxing on Penland Island.

The police officer that responded to my broken window, after thinking I was a missing person, deemed it another type of foul play. His thoughts were that it was some kids who'd accidentally broken out the window while playing *rock ball*. That would be using a stick and rock in lieu of a bat and ball. It didn't look like an accident by the number of dents in the side of my car. It looked like a deliberate act. It felt like a deliberate act.

I was camping on Penland Island when a pontoon boat approached me slowly. I figured they were looking for a camping spot and I'd beaten them to this one. At that point, I was taking a much-needed break, floating on my pink blowup raft, just off the shoreline of my camp site. I got an uneasy feeling as the boat approached. I wasn't sure what that was all about. . .but the driver of the boat was honing in on me. He was on a mission. Feeling uneasy, I got out of the water. The boat pulled up to the shoreline. There was a whole family on board, so I greeted them. The driver identified himself as an officer of the law, he was off duty, his name was Deputy Chris.

"Ma'am, do you own a white vehicle parked at the circle?"

"As a matter of fact, I do."

"I'm sorry to have to tell you this, but the passenger-side window is broken. The police have spent the day looking everywhere for you," he stated as a matter of fact. At this point it was 3:30 p.m. in the afternoon.

"Did I mention I come here to de-stress?" I stated incredulously.

"I just finished four laps around that buoy out there and don't think I have the energy to kayak to the boat ramp, it would take at least twenty-five minutes. Is it possible you could give me a lift to shore? The only problem being that I can't be around all of your smart phones." At least three people had their phones on.

"That's no problem." He asked his family to turn off their phones.

I grabbed my vest, threw a pair of pants over my bathing suit, put on my water sandals, grabbed my car keys and climbed aboard the boat, sitting as far forward as possible to avoid the engine area. By boat it was only a three-minute haul. I knew he was on his day off. I felt guilty for asking him for help to reach shore. I thanked him repeatedly.

Deputy Chris looked vaguely familiar to me, but I couldn't place him. He said we had met outside of my bedroom window. He said this so matter of fact, in front of his wife, that it confused me at first. That's not usually my style of living. I don't entertain men outside of my window. He refreshed my memory by adding that it was when I had an incident at my house last year. "Unbelievable," I said. "How many times do we have to keep meeting like this with you rescuing me?"

He was referring to a 911 call my neighbor placed last year. A young woman was walking up our road with a flashlight in hand. It appeared that she was looking for an unlocked car to sleep in. She walked by my neighbor's house first, shining the flashlight into their car window. After leaving them, she continued up the road to my house. As she approached my porch, the neighbor called 911. She had most of her belongings with her in a backpack and apparently felt safe to make a bed on my chair. Thankfully the neighbor works nights and had just arrived home around 2:30 a.m. Sadly, the young woman was drugged out of her mind on methamphetamine, but by the grace of God, the officers brought her straight to the hospital, which resulted in saving her life. I prayed for her for months. I prayed for her deliverance from drugs.

The young woman had arrived at my home weeks prior, looking for help. She claimed to have had a fight with her boyfriend. She asked to use the phone and needed monetary relief. Having no knowledge of the drug use, I gave her fifty dollars, which was all I had. I said it would be a loan. In exchange, she agreed to come back to vacuum my house, since using the vacuum compromises my nervous system. It was my emergency stash. I had hoped that this small gesture would help her in some way. I recognized now that all I did was enable her. She never returned to vacuum, leaving me without the $50.00 and a potentially un-kept house.

Back to the subject at hand. It is one thing to hear about your car having been vandalized, but it's a different feeling altogether when you actually see the damage. I couldn't help but cry from the shock of the damage and the glass splattered all over the ground and inside of my vehicle. I had bought the vehicle new in 2002. I kept it maintained and absolutely loved that vehicle. That, along with the fact that my condition would not permit me to own a new vehicle due to built-in GPS, I needed this car to last. The officer on duty, waiting for me on shore, asked me to open the vehicle and see if anything had been taken. Upon opening the door on the driver's side, I found a rock about two-inches long on the floor. Clearly, this rock was the weapon used.

Everything else was exactly how I'd left it. My license and cash, a five-dollar bill and change remained in the ash tray.

I kept the rock. Upon returning home, I wrote the date 5/31/16 on it and put it with my rock collection. After all. . .it's not the rock's fault.

The off-duty officer couldn't have been nicer. "Did you leave the seats forward?" "Yes, I leave the backseat and passenger seat forward to house my kayak for travelling." He let me know that he knew who I was. He was one of my neighbors that I'd never met. His house overlooks mine. He will be keeping a watch over my property now that he knows I camp for extended periods.

Look at the hidden blessings here. The deputy who camps on the lake now has my back, knowing that I camp alone on the island. The deputy on land has my back at the home front. Thank you, Lord!

The off-duty officer even came back for me, by boat, after the officer on duty wrote up his report and called him to let him know I was finished. He delivered me by boat back to the island. This time only he and his son were onboard the pontoon boat. He had delivered his family to the other side of Penland Island for a picnic.

My gut feeling had been correct when he'd first approached the island. He was looking for a camping spot for his family. He asked me how long I was planning on camping. At first this made me uneasy, but then I realized he was just trying to secure the spot. He asked me if they could set up their tents next to mine so they could come back and camp on the weekend. That works.

There was no way I could leave my car vulnerable with a window missing. I had no choice but to kayak back to the parking lot. First thing I did when I arrived, was sweep up all of the broken glass on the asphalt and pick up all the pieces in my vehicle. It is amazing how shattered glass goes everywhere. What a mess. I drove home after cleaning up the debris the best I could. Since using my cell phone was still extremely painful, I needed to get to a landline. The first thing I did was call my brother Chris. I called for two reasons, one because I wanted to let him know I was safe, in case the deputy called him. His number was registered at 911 as an emergency backup. But he let me know no one had called. Secondly, he is level headed. He was able to calm me down. He thinks clearly when I can't. He suggested I call my insurance company. I could hear my older brother David in the background saying that there is a service that will come to me to do the repair. I taped up the window after making arrangements through the insurance company for a service to come to my house to repair the car window. Thankfully, it was a zero deductible. The soonest they could come would be two days, unless I wanted to drive to Murphy, but I knew that I couldn't drive there. I was too compromised. Two days worked out perfectly. I didn't want to leave all of my camping gear on the island and this would give me just enough time to paddle back out, stay there the night, and return in the morning.

I called my friend Wendle and his wife at the Park and Rec and explained the situation. They allowed me to launch from their parking lot and park my car at their house for the two days that I would remain on the island. I dropped my kayak on the beach and drove to Wendle's house. He met me in the driveway. "Get in back," he said as he pointed to the back of the pickup. The cab of his truck was loaded with stuff. I chuckled as I lifted my sixty-year-old butt into the back of the pick-up truck. Oh my brothers would love seeing me in this predicament. Into the back I went, paddle and all.

Shall I mention again that I go to the islands to de-stress? It's a way to relax, de-stress, and has no challenges. This was not really going as planned. My condition exacerbates with stress. The island is supposed to serve as my time to heal. I felt provoked and out of sorts.

Wendle dropped me off at the kayak on the beach, only a couple of minutes away by truck. I thanked him and made a plan to return by noon the next day. God is good.

I had picked up a cold container of watermelon while at my house. I kayaked halfway across the lake and stopped. I was exhausted and needed the sweet pick-me-up that the watermelon would provide. "This is the life," I thought. I'm floating on the lake, slurping bite-sized pieces of watermelon, one of my favorite foods. I'm enjoying the scenic views of the mountains that surround the best-kept secret of Lake Chatuge. Thank you Lord! The watermelon served as a coolant, providing great hydration, and a break from the heated excitement from all of the running around. It took a lot of effort to expedite the replacement of the car's broken window. The heat of the extremely hot North Carolina sun was getting to me.

I wish I'd had something to give to Deputy Chris. I could leave it at the campsite since he would be occupying it this weekend. To my amazement, I saw a fishing lure floating. I take it as my responsibility to pick up anything that could be hazardous to people, boats, kids on floats being pulled by boats, and water skiers. This is a twofold win—I pick it up with the edge of my paddle, removing the hazard and planned on using it as a gift for the deputy to use with his family to fish. I'd leave a note and the lure secured in a baggy on a nail at the set-up board, the makeshift table on the island.

As I approached my campsite by kayak, I was awed by the sight revealed in front of me. Not only was my tent there but three other huge tents belonging to the deputy's family were set up. WOW, I love it! I felt safe now. It looked like a lot of people were camping there, but alas there was only me. Their tents have secured the site for the weekend after I leave. No one dared mess with the amount of people in all of those tents; at least that's the illusion. I dared anyone to mess with the deputy.

It looked like the circus came to Penland Island. There was a red tent, a blue tent, and one ultimate grey tent. The expansive sizes of their tents made mine look like child's play.

As an added bonus on this day, a rather large grey airplane flew directly over the camp, approaching from behind me. Although I couldn't see it approaching, I felt the vibration from it; it jolted my nervous system. It was around 8:30 p.m. It was a rather large and really loud aircraft. I was sitting on my camp chair enjoying the light flickering off of the camp fire, trying to calm my nerves from the day's events. Loud, scary, flying low, and breaking the sound barrier. . .you know the planes I'm speaking of. I thought it was crashing, but it was just doing a rather intimidating drive-by. I did the only thing I knew to do. I covered my ears to shield myself from the intense, deafening sound and sat tight. At that point I forgot to pray. I simply was so compromised from the day and this was one more way the world was a distraction.

The next morning, I decided to get some swim time in after breaking down camp. I swam out to the buoy. I like hanging out there. It provided me with some sense of security, knowing most boats are aware of the buoy and avoid it, therefore avoiding me.

Something changed. Boats were zooming back and forth over the water. Waves became aggressive. I found myself bobbing up and down in the rather high waves. I didn't panic, but I was starting to think I should have. I was very aware that all of a sudden it would be hard for a boat to see me. It didn't matter that I had a life vest on and a bright colored orange hat for visibility. I became simple lost in the turbulence.

Out of what seemed like nowhere, three jet skis arrived. At first I thought they didn't see me and would run me over. But they came to my rescue. All three jet skis surrounded me, asking if I needed assistance. The assumption was made that I fell off of a passing boat. I explained that I'd swam from my campsite and was heading back. When I could focus better, I noticed that one of the guys looked like a model that would be used on a Harlequin Romance cover. He could have been Tarzan himself. Now I knew I was delirious. I thanked them for checking on me. By that time the waves had settled some and I knew I could make it back without assistance. I thanked them for their concern and headed back. I was very aware that they were concerned enough to stick around long enough to be sure I was safe. Thank you, God! It's amazing how quickly the atmosphere can change on the water. The best investment I ever made was my life vest. It has gotten me out of many a jam while swimming alone.

I couldn't imagine having to explain to Tarzan that I wouldn't be able to ride on his jet ski due to the effects that the engine would have on me. I am severely affected from the effects of a motor. . .the EMFs, the noise, and the vibration. But oh, how I so wanted to be on the back of that Jet Ski. I guess I didn't picture my sixty-year-old self there. I pictured myself young, and beautiful and well, *rescued.* Sounds like a romance novel to me!

The waters calmed and I realized there was no time like the present to return to the Park and Rec. I loaded up my kayak and headed out. It would take a good forty minutes with a full load to return to my car at Wendle's place.

I spotted an opening between two camp sites on the shoreline as I approached. I paddled to shore, grateful to get there without toppling my overloaded gear. Thank God for bungee cords. What a great invention.

Two women from the next campsite saw me approach and seemed intrigued to watch me. Getting off the kayak with a full load of gear surrounding me is not a very lady-like sight. My legs were spread wide to house Luggable Lou, my outdoor potty, between them. My legs hung over the side of the kayak for balance. At this point they felt like they were asleep. I sat there waiting for my legs to wake up, to thaw out.

The two ladies came to my rescue. One offered to give me a lift to my car, when I shared that I was parked at Wendle's. The ride made my life so much easier. Thankfully, she had an old truck so I was able to ride in it without any explanations. If it had been a new truck I would have had to decline the offer of a ride. The effects are to debilitating. We talked briefly. When I asked her how she was doing, which seemed innocent enough as a conversation starter, she replied, "I'm doing good, got me a house, not in no trailer park. I've had enough," she blurted out. "I know what you mean. I come here to get away." I saw the cross on the dash. She saw me eyeing it. "I ain't no Christian." She felt compelled to share. "Sorry to hear that. It's what sustains me," I declared. Upon further assessment, I could see she was an abused woman. It appeared her most recent injury was a broken hand. She looked like she had had a stroke. Some things she mentioned sounded like both women were taking a breather from their abusers. Why Lord? I questioned to myself. There are so many people without hope.

I thanked her for the lift to my car. Without even thinking, I blurted out that I would put them both on my prayer list. She did a double take and, if I remember correctly, she thanked me back. Somewhere in her was a need to believe as well.

Bear Spray 101

Whenever I am afraid I will trust in You.
Psalm 56:3

I t's time to camp again, I need relief.

It was a Monday and, according to reliable sources, the weather report said a brief thunder storm on Tuesday and clearing the rest of the week.

I arrived at my campsite on the east side of Penland Island with my first load on my kayak. My intent was to survey the scene, set up my tent, and return to my car for firewood and my cooler.

The campsite was so trashed that it takes an additional half hour to bag all the trash. Among the trash are four large, empty hard-liquor bottles, approximately six small flasks of who knows what, endless cigarette butts, one very swollen dirty baby diaper. You know how enlarged they get once water sinks in. This one fully blessed with all the bodily functions. There were left over beer cans, food wrappings, and bait for fishing drawing multiple flies among other things. Yuck.

Yet again, I made it my job to pick up after other campers. I'd assigned myself this task since it's something I can do. It doesn't involve electricity and I feel productive, yet sad at the same time that people really do trash the paradise found on the islands of Lake Chatuge. I never want to lose the privilege of camping out here, so I do my best to maintain the grounds.

Setting up the tent was complete so I paddled back to shore and disposed of the trash in the receptacles provided by the TVA at The Circle.

A quick glimpse at the sky told me I'd need to wait it out to paddle back to the island. Darkness set in, the winds began to roar. Storms come and go so quickly around here. I waited it out in the safety of my vehicle.

One hour later, the sky cleared. I finished loading my supplies and headed back to the island. It is a relatively quick paddle to my campsite. Twenty minutes will get you there. You can actually see my campsite from the shore of The Circle now that the TVA cut down multiple trees to clear for picnic tables. Not the privacy I was hoping for. However, the hidden blessing is that I can tell before I head out whether the site is available or if someone has beaten me out there. It is first come, first serve.

Shortly after arriving back to the site, I decided to get something to eat. That didn't go well. Upon opening my camp box, which houses all of my essentials: matches, plates, cups etc., I hear a s-s-s-sound. "Surely a snake didn't get into the box," I'm thinking out loud. After all, I leave it in the garage, anything is possible. NO! Not a snake. My bear spray can released itself upon my opening the lid of the box, spraying partial contents of the right side of my camp gear box.

Logically I'm thinking "clean it up." Sounds simple doesn't it? I grabbed some paper towels from my stash and began to wipe—big mistake! I got some of the liquid from the bear spray on my hand and then, surprised on how much it burned, I instinctively moved my hands to my face in awe. Now my face burns too. OMG (oh my goodness) burn, baby, burn. My hands and face felt like they were on fire. Without hesitation, I jumped into the lake to rinse off the burning sensation on my hands and face but got no relief. It felt like it was burning worse. I accidently got some in my mouth. I kept spitting to relieve the new fire but the fire feeling kept growing. It appeared to be spreading by the second. I felt the discomfort in my mouth, my lips, around my nose, cheeks, chin, and the palms and back side of both hands. It was a *Lucy* moment.

What do I do? Be calm. I needed to be calm. I'm praying *Jesus, Jesus, Jesus*.

Once calm, I got out of the lake, found my glasses and read the hazard warning label on the bear spray. DO NOT MAKE CONTACT on skin. Rinse for ten to twenty minutes. Do not contaminate water ways. YIKE! I'm still on fire. I had no choice but to jump back in the lake. It hasn't been twenty minutes of rinsing yet. At this point, I was thinking the flesh was being eaten off of my face. I didn't have a mirror, there are no boats going by and it disabled me to use a cell phone. It says: seek medical attention. *Really?* I mean really!

I got out of the lake to retrieve the biodegradable soap and ointment to try to cool my skin.

Do I need more medical attention? I looked at my hands and, although burning like nobody's business, they remained intact. All the while I'm saying out loud, "I would never use this stuff on a bear. I would never want to inflict that kind of pain on anything." All I wanted was a safe way to deter a bear should I have another bear encounter like the one I had last fall.

So now I'll be gun-less and spray-less. I resorted back to the power of prayer; the power and protection of Jesus.

The storm was upping its game with thunder and now lightning all around me but not above me. "I can handle this," I thought to myself. I don't want to take a chance to call 911 on my emergency cell. That could cause worse problems. A responder couldn't come on the lake in this weather, too risky. I continued to pray for guidance. After about one hour the pain and burn began to cool off some. Rereading the label it says "temporary" burn. Ah, my hope is restored.

I prayed to have my skin still intact in the morning and passed out from sheer exhaustion in my tent. As the storm worsened I slept deeper. Fear forced me inward yet again.

The first thing I did when I woke up the next morning was to feel my face. It's still intact and doesn't feel pitted. Praise God! Now I see why His people perished from lack of knowledge. It's amazing I have sustained myself this long since I seemed to learn everything the hard way.

The contents of my supply box still had residue from the bear spray. It took multiple washes once I arrived home to clean up the entire residue which lingered on and, to my surprise, still burned on occasion with even a minute amount remaining. Lesson learned. I invested in an air horn should I need a future deterrent. God help me if I had to use it. I'm sound sensitive and covering my ears and pressing the button ought to be quite a challenge.

Rescue 911

O Lord my God, in You I put my trust;
Save me from all those who persecute me;
And deliver me, Lest they tear me like a lion
Rending me in pieces while there is none to deliver.
Psalm 7:1,2

I was getting ready for my next camp trip. I was tired. I needed serious relief. It took me most of the day to pack. I felt resistance in my spirit. I found myself extremely emotional during the preparations for my outing. I should have recognized this as a sign to just stay home. Thinking about why I was so out of sorts, I came to the conclusion that I was still traumatized from the last several outings. I haven't been able to find anyone willing to accompany me. So I concluded I was just tired, sick from the exposures of life, had some fear factors of camping alone and was just plain lonely. Rather than waste any more time on self-pity, I needed to buckle down to the business of wellness and continued packing. I know I got much-needed relief from my condition while on Penland Island, so off I went.

I parked at The Circle again because it is the easiest place to launch my kayak. It's the closest boat ramp to my campsites, making for an easy trip out to Penland Island. My goal, despite having had my passenger side window blown out by a stray rock during one of my last camping trips, was to launch from that same parking lot. This time I would park in the closest parking spot near the boat launch ramp instead of the furthest spot away. This should clarify whether this was an accident or a deliberate act. It would be really hard to hit my vehicle guarded by the trees and garbage cans. It would have to be deliberate.

I pushed through my fears and uncertainties and began my journey. The first trip out I paddled by the east side of the island. Not all that surprising, the camp site was trashed. Normally this would be a challenge for me and I'd take the time to clean it up first. However, these partiers really outdid themselves. The place was trashed with party stuff: beer bottles, whiskey, garbage galore. I couldn't handle it. I paddled by, looking forward to the other campsite, praying it would be available and not trashed. I could return here after I restored my energy level and clean it up, or not. If the partiers know someone is cleaning up after them, that would be enabling them. Maybe they should return to this when they are sober to get a whiff of their own disaster area.

"Holy Spirit put me where you want me," I prayed.

I surveyed the west side of Penland Island. It was available and clean. The only debris left behind remained in the fire pit. There were small pieces of paper and melted plastic bottle. I was able to clear that up easily. I picked up all branches scattered around and unloaded my kayak, set up my site and organized my gear. It is easy to get organized at this site because a prior camper hung boards between two trees for shelving in two different areas. One with a board with nails to hang pots and pans and cooking utensils. I used the other for food preparation, supplies and water storage. What a convenience. I hung my clothes line and hammock and set up my tent and camp chair.

I hung my usual disguise of men's clothes on the clothes line to create the illusion of a male present. No one needed to know I was on the island by myself. Most people wouldn't believe it anyway. Most men I know wouldn't camp on the island with someone, let alone by themselves. The point everyone is missing when I share that I camp on the islands is that I don't do it for fun. It is my survival. It is how I am healing my body. Besides that, it is hard work to continuously set up and break down camp. I try to do four-day increments, otherwise it is just not worth the amount of preparation it takes to pull off a trip. Four days is just enough time to keep supplies available. I'm limited in space on the kayak. Refrigeration in my cooler only lasts two days at best.

After returning with my second load of firewood and water reserve, I needed refreshing. This side of the island has a buoy about one-quarter mile out. I swam out to it and around it and back to shore; it helps in stretching my spine. The water was refreshing. Normally this is a safe place to swim. The buoy indicates the water is shallow. But today, for some odd reason there was a lot of boat traffic.

To my shock and horror, as I swam close to shore, maybe fifteen feet from shore. I heard a boat coming. As it came around the island, I saw that it is a pontoon boat with only one woman aboard. Surely she is not doing what I am thinking. Oh yes she is! She missed me by five feet and never even saw me. Unbelievably, she was texting. I mean really! Give me a break, people. I was so shocked that I couldn't even yell out to her. I watched as she continued along, oblivious to her surroundings. It is hard not to feel defeated. The world was becoming more and more distracted. She never saw me.

I can't let this ruin my evening. I built a huge campfire. The fire pit on this side of the island was amazing. It's huge and nicely displayed with large boulders all around it. I cooked a good dinner. I already had a cup of hot soup that I'd heated to put in my thermos. I tried to treat myself with something hot that I'd heated at home. . .soup, hot chocolate, or something to give me a pickup and it's used as my reward for making it out there.

That's enough excitement for one day, I'm worn out. I went into my tent at dark and passed out. Fresh air and swimming have a way of making you relaxed and very tired. I assumed I was dreaming when I heard howls from the other side of the island.

I was just about asleep when I heard hoofs racing by. I knew the sound. It was a couple of deer. Not far behind the hoof sounds, I heard panting, howling. . .giving the deer a thirty-second lead time. It sounded like wolves. Coyotes yip and wolves howl; this was definitely a howl. No mistake. And then they were gone. *Whew.*

Now I was awake and just lying in my tent. "I'm safe," I told myself. They have more interesting prey than me to go after, or so I thought. About ten minutes later, I heard the howling and the panting from the wolves running around my tent. No hoof sounds this time. I listened as they searched my campsite. Then, just as quickly as they'd come, they were gone. Maybe they satisfied their curiosity and would leave me alone. I needed to sleep, I tried to convince myself.

Ten minutes later, like clockwork, they all returned. I guessed from the activity outside of my tent that there were approximately five of them. Why did I pick tonight to leave the fabric on the mesh windows of my tent open? I know it's hot out, but I never do that. I never allow anything to peer in at me while I'm asleep. . .or in this case, while I'm horrified!

This was way too close for comfort. In the three years I have camped on Penland Island, I have never used my emergency cell phone, the one Dr. Rea said to have, just in case. Forget that it makes me deathly sick to use one. Now would be as good a time as any to take that chance. I dialed 911 frantically. Meanwhile I heard panting just above my head outside my tent window.

"911 what's your emergency?" I hear a calm southern male voice answer.

"My name is Deborah Hyatt, I am a female camping alone on Penland Island." I go on to say, "There is a pack of wolves surrounding my tent and I am unarmed."

"Ma'am, where are you?"

Forgetting my good manners due to my elevated stress level, I blurted out "You're kidding me right, buddy? I'm on Penland Island on Lake Chatuge."

"Oh, you must want Clay County." He dragged out the sentence for emphasis.

"Really, I mean really!" I think I was in shock.

"Please hold, I'll transfer you over to Clay County."

I forgot for at least thirty seconds that I'm supposed to be a good Christian woman. The words forming in my head were less than ladylike.

"911 what's your emergency?" I heard again.

Now panic has set in to the equation. "This is Deborah Hyatt, I'm camping on Penland Island, I'm unarmed, in my tent, and a pack of wolves are right outside my window. Listen, you can hear them panting."

The woman at the other end of the phone could hear them yelping, howling and panting. You just can't make this stuff up!

"Deborah, I know exactly who you are." It paid to register with 911 when I first arrived in town. I knew how unusual my EMF disease was, but wanted them to know who I was, since my life was is in their hands should I need them. This would be one of those times.

"Listen carefully, honey. There have been no known attacks from wolves on humans in Clay County reported to date."

"You don't know my life, I don't want to be the first. Please help me. Send someone out to get me off the island."

"Do you have a weapon?" she continued on.

"No."

"No weapon, not even a stick?" she asked incredulously.

"No. Wait, yes I have my Bible!"

At that point I could hear laughing in the background at the 911 station. Oh, God this is not the time to teach them about spiritual warfare.

"Deborah, I know you can't stay on the phone for long without it affecting you adversely. I will call you back in ten minutes." She remained calm.

"Ten minutes. . .I may not have ten minutes. Will someone be coming out to get me?"

She assured me that someone would come. In the meantime, I heard the rustling of leaves and the curious critters prancing around my campsite.

True to her word, the dispatcher called back in ten minutes. It felt like an hour.

"I'm sending a crew out, there will be a lot of them. Tell me exactly where you are."

"I'm across from the Park and Rec on the west side of Penland Island at the large campsite."

"They're on their way, Deborah. Breathe, inhale, relax. Help is on the way. I know you can't stay on the phone, I'll call you back again in ten minutes."

"Oh God, please help me. This isn't exactly how I want to meet my demise."

The cell phone rang. When I answered, I was in disbelief of what I was hearing.

"Deborah, they can't find you. They are out there by boat but they claim they can't locate you. Is your campfire lit?"

"No, the campfire burned out, but I haven't heard any boats come by yet."

"Shine your flashlight out of the window of the tent so they can see you."

"But what if it calls in the wolves again?" I'm freaking out.

Just at that moment in time, I heard the motor of a boat coming around the island from my left side. They claimed they circled the island three times. I suspect they were at Gibby Island, the smaller of the two islands. No way could they have made it around Penland Island three times within that period of time. Not only is Penland Island huge, but I would have heard them.

I shined my flashlight reluctantly out of my tent window. The wolves must have run when they heard the motor of the boat approaching, long before I heard it. I was so afraid that the light from the flashlight would summon the wolves back. But they were gone. Not just gone but extremely quiet. Go figure.

I hear the rumbling of the boat nearby and watched as it finally pulled up to the shoreline. It was like a tank. I could hear the loud vibration of the plank makes its way down and land with a loud crash on the shore. *Vrrrrrrrr Bam!*

The one officer came to shore. I could hear his walkie-talkie and he was carrying a flashlight, shining in my direction. He called out "Debbie" and this was not the time to care that my name is "Deborah, not Debbie." I answered "Yes, I'm here." It has been a lifelong process to get people to call me by my birth name—Deborah. At this point call me anything you want, but get me out of here.

I was frozen to the inside of my tent.

The officer walked closer to the outside of my tent. I thanked him for coming. It was horrifying to be surrounded by the wolves.

The male officer was abrupt. He surveyed the scene with his flashlight in hand. I could tell he was making some mental notes about my surroundings.

"Did you call in about a pack of wolves?" He was stern.

"Yes, sir I did" I said as a matter-of-fact.

"Well they are not here now, what exactly do you want us to do?"

I wanted to say, *it's not rocket science.* There are wolves on the island, get me the H-E-double-hockey-sticks out of here! But I didn't. My mind was racing and I was thinking of all kinds of not-so-nice words. I was stressed, really stressed and almost afraid to speak for fear of what I might say. I was grateful that they had come to my rescue, but losing patience on the way I was being treated. What I heard come out of my mouth instead at that time was, "Get me out of here!" Whew, I saved my dignity. This could have gone much worse, which would have provided a perfect example of how chronic stress will provoke us to do and say things we normally wouldn't.

The woman officer was rather amused and spieled out, "Well, I do see a mosquito!" She was new to the unit and was seemingly amused at my predicament. The male officer felt the need to say to me, "The next time you guys come camping out here. . ." I didn't hear the end because I was fuming. I'm here alone on the island. Hello! Then I realized he came to that conclusion when he was using his flashlight to survey the scene and saw the men's clothing I so meticulously displayed on my clothesline to create the illusion that I was not alone.

He must have made the assumption that I had a lover's quarrel and was left behind. Not really good detective work, since he didn't bother to ask where my invisible friend might have gone off to and why. I wasn't going to give him the satisfaction of knowing that I was out there alone based on the facts before him. The good news was that that tells me my masquerade of men's clothing on the clothesline works; he bought it.

"How do you expect us to get you to shore? There are EMF's on the boat!" I had a suspicion he was informed of my condition by the 911 dispatch, but he clearly didn't respect my disability. He had every type of electronic paraphernalia around his waist and made no attempt to turn anything off to minimize the effects on me. I had to take the upper hand by asking him to step away from me.

In his defense, it was not a recognized disability yet. Just like when fibromyalgia or multiple sclerosis first came into being. No one basically believed those conditions to be true.

"Let's do the math; stay here and get eaten by a pack of wolves," I stated, holding out my left hand. "Have a seizure on the boat." Holding out my right hand for emphasis, "I vote take a chance on a seizure, let's go." Thankfully, I knew it was less than a ten minute ride, on the tank that they called a boat, back to The Circle where I'd parked my car.

"You need to come out of your tent," the officer offered gruffly.

Still traumatized I offered, "I'm not ready to come out yet, what if the wolves return?"

The officer asked me to grab my essentials. I took car keys, my dry sack and a small cooler. I wasn't really thinking all that clearly, being traumatized by my unexpected four-legged visitors.

Thankfully, he suggested loading my kayak and paddle onto the rescue boat. At that point I couldn't imagine ever kayaking out there again. I was done with all of it. But I just went along with his rational. At least he was thinking that I would someday need a way back out here to retrieve my camping gear, since I was leaving it all behind. I couldn't reason that far ahead.

There was one other guy on board; he drove the vessel. They loaded my kayak, paddle and me onto the boat. After securing one of their life vests on me, I mentioned I had one of my own. They returned to shore to retrieve mine. Ironically, it was on the clothes-line — near the man's swimsuit.

He abruptly told me to go upfront and sit in the seat. I said, "I can't be near the motor, I'll sit here on the floor," and I did just that. He clearly did not want to be here and acted like I was wasting his time. I covered my ears to shield myself from the noise that the boat motor would make.

I must have looked strange, sitting on the deck of the boat, holding my ears, with my elbows clutching my knees. I'm sound sensitive, but they don't know that. The female officer came to sit with me after being nudged by the cranky officer. She offered to hold my hand and keep me company. She kept saying how lovely the stars were and how she would much rather be on the boat instead of in a squad car. She was new to this team and maintained the fact that she was amused by it all. I was losing my patience but sat quietly.

A really nice gentleman named Donnie Jones was waiting on shore. He assisted me with one arm to help me to shore. He told me he has served for forty-three years at Clay Central. He went above and beyond to help me feel comfortable.

I was off of the boat now, walking numbly toward my car. No seizure, praise God, just a numbness that will take some time to wear off. The two police officers, one man and one woman, picked up my kayak and paddle and walked it up the ramp to my car. They made carrying that thing look like child's play. They helped me, after I unlocked my vehicle, by lifting the kayak into the back of my car, sliding it over the folded-down passenger side seat, and securing it by tying it to the roof rack out the window.

It was only then that I realized in all the commotion that I was in my pajamas. Humiliated, I heard myself say to all three people, "Pretend you don't see that I'm in my pajamas!"

Not that I was totally surprised to hear the female officer blurt out, "Oh, I wish I were in my pajamas." Really! I mean really! I just want to be at home and have this entire thing over with.

On to the next dilemma; I don't drive at night. So I told the officers that if my car is here overnight it's because I can't drive home. . .thinking that this would provoke them into offering a solution, but they didn't. "Okay, as long as you are okay, we are out of here." They exclaimed as they backed out of sight and returned to the awaiting boat. Why was I thinking they would care? They had bigger fish to fry.

The nice gentleman volunteer on the shore said very kindly, "Do you need a hotel?" He was thinking I came here for a visit.

"No, I'm a local," I explained.

"Well then why aren't you driving home?" he asked innocently enough.

"I don't see well at night since my setback." I explained.

"I have an idea. How about if I follow you home?"

"That won't work, your lights will blind me." *Not out of the woods yet,* I'm thinking to myself.

"I know. What if I follow you to my house? I'll keep my eye on one of your tail lights."

We agreed that that might work. It wouldn't be until I started to follow him that I would recognize that he can't drive at night either. He left the road a couple of times with his truck ending up on the grass. We were definitely pushing our luck. He explained later that he has glaucoma and has trouble seeing.

We started out doing twenty miles an hour. I'm thinking, when I said to *go slow* I meant thirty miles an hour would do. It took us a very long time to reach my house, which should have been ten minutes away under normal driving conditions.

No sooner did we get into my driveway, than he offered to help me remove the kayak. Out of the corner of my eye, I saw for the first time that he had only one arm. With one hand, he was gentleman enough that he wanted to save me from having to dismount the kayak from my car. This touched me on such a deep level. I didn't want to minimize his manhood by refusing his offer. I skirted around his offer by saying I do this all the time. I just drop the kayak off the back of my vehicle and drag it to its place nearby in the garage. He accepted that logic and stepped out of the way.

I had just dropped the kayak off the back of the car when he got another emergency call and had to run. Before he left, he took one last moment to say, "You sure have a good demeanor for someone who was just rescued off the island." What could I say? All I could do was thank him. He had no idea what my life has been like, this is nothing in comparison to all the suffering I have had to endure. I didn't go there.

When I got home, I called my boyfriend from my landline. I woke him up from a sound sleep at 11:30 p.m. I was thinking, if I don't tell him now, I could just imagine someone at work sharing with him that, "Some idiot was stupid enough to be camping on Penland Island, alone, without a weapon, and had to be rescued." He would know that that idiot was me! I wanted to save him a step by harassing him NOW. He seemed glad I called, although he wasn't really all that awake. . .so I ended the call by saying, "This is only a dream, a figment of your imagination, you can go back to sleep now."

Word travels fast, but like the game of *Telephone*, the facts get misconstrued. One of my friends from the Hayesville Presbyterian Church, the church I tried to attend, visited after she heard about my island adventure. I couldn't believe the words that came out of her mouth. "I heard about the raccoons!" she said, rather excitedly. There is really no place to go from there. "What raccoons? They were wolves!" I said more abruptly than I meant to. "Oh dear," she stated, always the lady.

Hearing about my 911 dilemma, that concerned lady friend and her husband provided me with two very valuable resources. Two wilderness survival books were left at my doorstep. One entitled "Bush Craft 101" and the other "98.6 Degrees – The art of KEEPING YOUR ASS ALIVE!" And most likely it did.

The emphasis was on body temperature which served me well in future campouts. These were well thought out and very useful gifts.

Weeks later, I started to question myself. Should I not have used 911 for help? Did I not have the right to call them? Did I waste their time? All these thoughts kept surfacing because of the way the call was handled. I was outside of the car place getting the cars oil changed, when I spotted an officer next door. He had been there a while and I noted that he was waiting for the funeral parlor service to end so they could lead the way. I took this opportunity to ask him the questions that were weighing on me. He told me I had every right to call 911 for help. In fact, I have every right to call as many times as need be for any reason where I feel threatened. "I can't speak for the officer on duty that night, but it's possible he'd just came off of a very stressful call." This helped me to understand the officer's view point. He went on to say that, speaking of himself "Sometimes I come across arrogant or cocky when I don't know what to expect." He apologized to me that I'd had a bad experience, after seeming incredulous that I would be camping out there by myself. I don't camp out there by myself because it's fun. I do it as a way to minimize my exposure to electrical and as a way to heal my body. I also explained to him that I haven't been able to find anyone to accompany me. Most of the people I meet won't even swim in the lake, let alone camp on the island. So alone I go. Gutsy, maybe, but the way I figure it is there is only one way to go and that's up. If you are desperate enough you will do anything if you think it will heal your body.

It was the day after my encounter with the wolves. My dilemma now is that all of my camp gear is still out on Penland Island. I didn't think it would be wise to go back again by myself, even if it is daylight. The risk of crossing paths with the wolves would be too great. However I couldn't afford to replace my gear should someone else beat me to it.

I called the only person I could think of who was capable and available to assist me. I lovingly refer to her as "Rambo." She is the toughest, but most sincere and honest person I know. She wears the full armor of God spiritually, she is prayed up and loves the Lord. She follows the nudge of the spirit. The fact that she sports pink and blue hair—colorful and shocking upon first glance, could only serve us well in this instance. She is an anointed artist who believes in freedom of expression. I simply love her.

We met at the boat launch at the circle. Rambo came sporting a pistol and a bow and arrow. Okay, so I wasn't really expecting that.

What have I gotten us into? Is it too late to back out?

We kayaked out rather aggressively, arriving at the campsite prepared for battle. Rambo hit the beach first, standing ready with bow and arrow in hand. She was at full stance with the bow pulled back and arrow intact, aiming towards my abandoned campsite.

It was my turn to enter the site. We were both over-stressed at the prospect of wolves returning to greet us. I told her I would quickly breakdown camp while she had my back. Knowing Rambo was an experienced marksman gave me little confidence when I realized I was now in the center of the site where her aim was. Bringing that to her attention only riled her, evident in her next comment. "You dumbass, I'm not going to shoot you, I'm just prepared in case the wolves surprise us." Enough said.

I'm certainly not going to argue about it at that point. I just wanted out of there. All the while I was thinking, "I don't want to hurt the wolves but I don't want to be a statistic either."

I made record-breaking time dismantling my tent and loading my kayak.

Mission accomplished without incidence.

RAMBO ROCKS!

Easter Weekend 2017

Preserve me O God, for in You I put my trust.
Psalm 16:1

"Lord, the emotion and pain I'm feeling has stricken my spirit. My eyes flow endless rivers of tears. The thought comes to mind that the world was functioning and carrying on as if I were never a part of it at all. I hear about all of the wonderful things people are doing: spiritual church services, gatherings, picnics, egg hunts. I feel incredibly lonely, isolated, left behind. Then I remembered what you did for us on the cross so long ago. Those thoughts added excruciating emotional pain to think of You suffering and dying for us all."

Even my boyfriend, Robert, overbooked plans from Thursday through Sunday afternoon. He would be participating in all the events that I couldn't take part in. I don't believe he did this maliciously. I believe he is so over-the-top between work and outside commitments, he just doesn't stop to think about how it affected me. He had an opening in the afternoon on Easter Sunday to fit me in for lunch and a visit.

Knowing that it is a major Christian holiday weekend, I just can't sit here. I needed to think outside of myself and be where I can glorify You the most. My prayers revealed a vision of myself back on Penland Island; I needed to return there. I need to return to the healing waters of Lake Chatuge.

I couldn't shake the sadness. As I packed Friday morning, I mourned Your death. I saw You nailed to the cross in my mind's eye.

As I reached the boat ramp at The Circle, I was taken aback by the complete silence. No one was around. No one was at The Circle, a popular picnic area. It's around lunch time, so this is very unusual. I could see the Chatuge Dam from my launch area, but there were only a few walkers a quarter-mile away. I loaded my kayak with all of my camping gear for my first trip out. My gear made my kayak top heavy, so I prayed for a hedge of protection and safety to make it safely to my campsite.

I always took the essentials on my first trip out to the island. Upon arriving to my first campsite, I surveyed the scene for any evidence of wildlife. Then I looked for evidence of the two-legged kind. Coast was clear.

There was a bag of garbage that looked as if it had been there at least one week. The bag was discolored from the sun but fully intact. That was a very good sign. If there were a bear, coyote, or wolf nearby, the bag would have been ripped to shreds. This gave me the confidence to use this campsite.

I picked the bag up and it split open to expose the food scraps, diapers, beer cans, and whisky bottles within. At least these campers had a conscience and cleaned up the site even if they did neglect to take the garbage bag with them. I retrieved a garbage bag from my kayak, re-bagging the garbage for removal.

After unloading my kayak of its contents, I set my tent and equipment in place. I loaded the garbage onto my kayak to dispose of in the trash cans at The Circle.

It was time for the second trip out. I transported firewood and two backup jugs of water.

I wasn't scared to be on the island alone. I felt like I was in my element. I actually felt safer on the island than in the neighborhood that I live in. It would be highly unlikely that someone would scope out the island for something of value to steal. There have been so many break-ins reported in the local paper that I found myself lying in bed at night when I'm at home worrying that someone would break in. I was surprised after surveying the area and kayaking around the island that there were no other campers anywhere.

Normally May 1st is when the camping season started. It has been unseasonably warmer than in the past years, so I took the chance to camp two weeks earlier. One thing I didn't bargain for was the fact that, on Friday, the leaves weren't on the trees yet. No shade. I had to keep a baseball hat and a long sleeved shirt on at all times to protect me from the sun. The intense heat from the North Carolina sun rays would have fried me had I not kept them on.

Friday and Saturday my spirit cried out. The tears continued to flow. Normally, someone kayaks by or visits the island. No one came, adding to my loneliness.

On Saturday, I was cleaning up the campsite. A lot of branches had fallen and leaves were spread out in various piles. As I was gathering and burning leaves to tidy up the place, something odd happened. I had a gallon Ziploc bag with a lot of folded newspapers in it to use as a fire starter. Each time I turned my back, mysteriously the bag would move ten feet or so. It happened so quickly—yet there was no wind. How could this be, Lord? So I tried an experiment. I got into my tent and peeked out. Within minutes a large black raven swooped down, picked up the bag by its corner, flew ten feet and dropped it. Maybe the large bird wanted the paper to build a nest, or maybe he wanted the Daily News! In any case, it stopped my tears for a while. I recognized God is always with us. He is creative in how he gets our attention. The raven hung out at my campsite all day Saturday, hovering just above my site, curious as to what I was doing there.

I cooked a hearty meal of organic beef, squash, and tomato pieces, which I served over brown rice pasta. I made a large batch using up the one-pound package of meat, since my cooler packs would fail soon, leaving me no way to preserve the leftovers. I ate half of the meal, leaving the other half in the frying pan on a rock beside the fire pit. That would be my dinner for later. I added more logs to the fire to keep it going.

"This is a good time to bathe," I thought. No one was around, even boat traffic was sparse. As I entered the lake, I took along my blow-up float to hold my wash cloth and biodegradable soap and shampoo. I had just submerged myself to get totally wet, applied shampoo and scrubbed to make good lather, when I witnessed the raven out of the corner of my eye. He was swooping down off the tree branch and perching himself on the rock near my frying pan, helping himself to my dinner portion that I'd saved for later. I was too far from him to return, so I yelled out "Hey, that's my dinner!"

but it gave me so much joy to watch him feast and to share my bounty. It was hard not to smile after that.

The water was a cool temperature. My guess is it was about 65 degrees. It was refreshing. It helped to wake up my spirit.

Upon further assessment of my dinner, the raven had left me a hearty portion that I ate later that day to keep up my strength.

The next day was Easter Sunday. I had planned to get up to worship at sunrise. Unfortunately, I have had a great deal of trouble waking myself up these days. My brain is so very tired. I had hoped that the sunrise would wake me, but to my disappointment it was around 8:30 a.m. when my eyes finally opened to reveal the morning light. The other thing I didn't bargain for was being stuck in my mummy sleeping bag! I had the draw string pulled tight around my face with just my eyes, nose, and mouth peeking out. The zipper down the right hand side was stuck somehow in the fabric of the sleeping bag. I managed to pull and tug at the zipper but it just wouldn't budge. Yikes! I didn't panic. I looked at this as a challenge. I prayed. Lord, at least I was expecting my boyfriend later today, so if I'm stuck here hopefully he will see that I didn't make it to shore and will come to survey the scene. Please help me unzip. It was hard to maneuver my hands within the tight space of the sleeping bag, but after fifteen minutes of manipulation the latch and zipper set me free.

My boyfriend Robert and I made plans to meet at 1:30 p.m. at The Circle for Easter Sunday. I asked him to bring lunch since it would have been impossible to store perishables for what would be three days at that point.

Around noon, my spirit was pricked to leave the island now. Leave early. I don't question when I feel my spirit nudged. I just do it. So one and one half hours before we were to meet I left for The Circle, a twenty-minute paddle from the island.

Upon my arrival, there was a couple on the shoreline sitting in beach chairs. I waved and said, "Happy Easter." It felt foreign after not conversing for two days to hear myself attempt a normal conversation with someone that didn't caw back at me like the raven.

I landed at the boat dock and checked on my car. Thankfully, there were no problems with it being parked there over the period of several nights.

The couple and I resumed our interaction. I found out that they were there earlier than expected as well. They were reserving the shoreline picnic tables for their church group. They said that they, too, were surprised that no one else was around on such a beautiful day. Their peers were due there in one hour, ironically the same time my boyfriend would arrive.

We talked. We shared our faith. We prayed together. Again the dam that my eyes had built broke wide open. The flood works were back.

The husband said, "Jesus took thirty-nine stripes for us. Did you know there are thirty nine diseases?"

"But mine is a new man-made illness." I shared, scared to hear what he would say next.

"It doesn't matter, you are covered," he responded carefully but lovingly. "Believe that you ARE healed. Claim it!" he professed.

They both had a lot of knowledge and an insurmountable amount of faith. They shared their personal stories of how Jesus healed them. One was released from the hold of alcohol addiction and one from high blood pressure.

The wife couldn't have been more compassionate as a sister in Christ. We spoke privately, girl talk. She asked if she could pray for me. She held my hand and put one hand on my shoulder. I could feel the love of Christ flow through her fingers and into my spirit.

They invited me to join their church group for lunch. I thanked them and told them I had lunch being delivered. I knew I couldn't be around their guests' cell phones. I found a table away from them and waited. I used that time to thank God for always being right on time. I thank God for putting other loving Christians in my path—especially when I needed the companionship and lift to my spirit the most. Praise God!

My boyfriend arrived right on time. I watched him drive past me in his Jeep, pulling his kayak in tow. He was sporting a cooler with sandwiches, potato chips, fruit (my favorite), an organic chocolate bar and a bottle of organic wine. What a feast! It's like hitting Lotto to receive such a treat. I thanked him.

We enjoyed our meal at the picnic table first, rather than trying to paddle out to the island to eat. Afterwards, we kayaked to the island. He was able to visit for a couple of hours, then reality hit. He had work the next day, so we said good bye. When he was ready to leave, I offered to carry his chair down to his kayak, since he had the cooler. We said goodbye at his kayak. I couldn't look back this time to watch him go. I focused on organizing my camp gear to distract me. It was just too painful to be left behind again.

When I turned around, he was standing less than a foot away. His unsuspected presence scared the day light out of me.

"What are you doing?" I asked, startled.

"It's hard for me to leave you here," he confessed.

We agreed he had to go and I needed to stay to gain healing. Again, I cried. "Will these tears never subside?" I thought to myself.

He left for a second time. I got ready for bed. I laid in the tent waiting for darkness and passed out. I was emotionally and physically drained.

Reflection from the Light
(Written after swimming while on Penland Island)

Submerged beneath the surface of the lake
The water free of earth-bound ties
No longer hidden from the light
The light lures me
Invites me to emerge closer to the surface
Prayers answered
Pain lifting
Finding comfort from the all-encompassing pressure
Sight clearer
Darkness gone today
Shades removed
Wilderness relief
Nature heals
God exists everywhere
Hope restored
Portal Broken.

Do what you can do—don't worry about what you can't

Day Trip on Penland Island

Partly while you were made a spectacle
Both by reproaches and tribulations
Hebrews 10:33

Spring has finally arrived. Robert decided to surprise me by suggesting we kayak out to Penland Island for the day. He knew that the next best thing to camping on the island overnight was for me to pack a picnic lunch and enjoy a campfire, a swim, and a picnic in that very same location.

He loved paddling out to the island for a visit, although at this point he was not quite convinced about the idea of an overnight, at least not yet. So for now I wasn't going to push him. I have no choice but to be content that he is willing to, at least, visit.

We unloaded the kayaks from the trailer and the gear from his jeep. As he parked the jeep, I took the opportunity to launch my kayak and sit idle on the water until he could catch up.

As he was installing the floor-board-peddle system into his rather elaborate kayak, I headed out. He shouldn't be far behind, or so I surmised.

I was only fifty feet into the trip when I greet three people, one man and two women sitting on the shoreline in camp chairs. They all sported Cheshire cat grins. I thought to myself, "They're a happy bunch." It wasn't until one of the woman yelled out to me, "Ought to be an interesting trip," with her eyes hinting in Robert's direction, that I realized she was referring to him. Apparently, he'd put the floor board in backwards and wasn't making much headway in my direction. In fact, he was now further away from me than when we'd started. The floorboard, installed backwards, created the kayak to go in reverse. I kept my giggles to myself. The woman was correct in saying this ought to be an interesting trip. Unable to fix the floor board while he was in the kayak, he had no choice but to succumb to using the old-fashioned paddle, like me, to make his way to the island. It was that or paddle to shore and correct the installation. With the amount of effort it took him to align his six-foot-four, large stature into the kayak, that was just not going to happen.

It was an easy paddle out to the island, despite the fact that it was the beginning of the swimming and boating season, and we both felt out of shape from the effects that the winter had on our physiques.

I was in my element now, always amazed at how strong my body felt when I was away from any negative environmental exposures. I felt like superman again away from kryptonite. My spirit lifted.

In addition, lunch served as a great pick me up. I'm pumped. We lit the firepit in a joint effort of gathering tinder. I decided to go for a swim and egged Robert to the waterfront. He's a Florida boy, so the cold water wasn't calling him like it does me, being originally from the north. I gave him credit for walking in up to his knees, although secretly I snickered. He came up with the idea to wash down his already immaculate kayak. It got him into the water, still remaining knee deep, but in the general vicinity to where I was swimming so he could play lifeguard, allowing me to swim without my life vest.

Swimming without a life vest is a rarity for me since I mostly swim alone. Not to mention I have strong reactions to a power boat that might come too close, and reactions from those notorious crotch-rockets called jet skis. In reactive mode, I sometimes can't use my arms or legs, so swimming alone without a vest would put me in a precarious position.

I swam and dove playfully, the cold water provoking my spirit, egging me on to play harder.

"Deborah, do you want to try paddling my kayak?" Robert shouted from shore.

"Yes, absolutely, that is, if the floorboard sends me in the right direction," I teased and playfully replied.

"It's easy to fix near shore. I corrected it. It's a go," he said confidently.

I swam in to meet him at the kayak. He helped lift me into the kayak. It's a rarity that my independent spirit would allow him to assist me in such a manner. However, I was feeling left out from his days away and was soaking up the attention like a sponge.

"You should wear your life vest," he reminded me.

"I'm going to be close to shore and you are here, but you're correct, I need to wear it." I am so glad that I did.

Robert retrieved my life vest from the seat of my kayak. He helped me to put on the vest, another rarity that he would offer and I willingly accepted his help.

I peddled gleefully away from the shore, finding myself enjoying that his kayak had a rudder. I playfully peddled in circles. What fun. I could feel the intense workout the peddling was giving my legs. I'm happy.

Robert left the water and returned to the nearby firepit, content that I was occupied and he was relieved from the cold water. He was organizing the shelf, which was a board someone had wedged between two trees to hold gear. His back was to me.

"I have an idea," I thought to myself. "I'll scoot myself off of the kayak and get behind it so he will have to guess where I am. I know I can do this quietly and I'm only about twenty feet from shore, but in deep water."

What happened next was a typical *Lucy* moment that I wouldn't be able to duplicate again even if I tried. As I slid down over the left hand side of the kayak, somehow the corner of my bathing suit on my left leg got caught on the clamp that held the seat backing in place. Had I not had the life jacket on, I would have been strung upside down, face first in the water. The life jacket gave me just enough buoyancy to keep my head above water. I was straddled horizontally alongside the kayak. The hook caught in just the right place to hang me up by my bathing suit bottom, exposing my sixty-year-old butt all the way to its crack, providing a major painful "wedgie." If I was displaying a twenty-year-old butt, maybe, just maybe, I wouldn't have been so humiliated.

Suspending in humility, I had no other choice but to yell to Robert for help. No matter how I tried to maneuver myself, I just couldn't break free. There was no way for me to release myself from the seat clamp that held me hostage. This put a whole new meaning to "being in deep water, up a creek."

Thankfully, the men who were fishing nearby left the area just moments before I slid overboard. They were about my age and I shudder to think what they would have done witnessing my anal blooper. I suspect that, like Robert, they would be laughing too hard to assist me.

"Help, help, babe, help me," I yelled from the helpless state I was in. Helpless is not a frequent word used in my vocabulary.

Robert looked in my direction but didn't move at first. I can only conclude that he wasn't quite sure of what exactly he was looking at.

I yelled again, "Help, move it, I need you," desperate for relief and humiliated beyond belief.

He came down to the water's edge as I was moving the only arm available, to paddle myself closer to shore, thinking there is no way Florida boy will rescue me in the cold water. He assured me later that cold water or not, he would have come to my rescue.

As he surveyed the scene up close he couldn't help himself but say, "Oh, I have got to get a picture of you like this."

"OH. NO. YOU. DON'T. Help me, please!"

He was standing near me with no sense of urgency. I'm not sure at this point if the tears leaking out of my eyes were from humiliation or laughter.

We roared at the idea that I may have exposed more of myself than I was previously willing to bare. All I could think of at the time was if any of the McMansions surrounding the lake, hovering in the mountain tops, housed people who were using their binoculars to view the lake at this time; they got a bull's-eye view.

For the rest of the day and the days that followed, I turned a shade of red every time I tried to have a conversation with Robert. We just belted out laughter.

It's time to move on to the next adventure.

July 2017 Storm

Then they cry out to the Lord in their trouble,
And He brings them out of their distresses.
He calms the storm,
So that its waves are still.
Psalm 107:28, 29

It's a Saturday night, around dinner time. I was camping alone on the southwest side of Penland Island. Nature seemed to have deliberately planned my entertainment. The calmness didn't escape my notice. I remember thinking it's the calm before the storm. Oh, how I wish I was wrong. That was mere minutes before all hell broke loose. I heard a loud boom and what sounded like an explosion in the distance. At first, I thought it was fireworks from the shore line about a half mile away. I was wrong.

The storm came seemingly out of nowhere, no warning, no chance to prepare. The fast-approaching, brilliant flashes of lightning, along with rolling thunder that was married to high winds caught me totally off guard. I rushed to my tent, a false sense of security. I zipped myself into my sleeping bag, as if that would somehow provide me with a hedge of protection. The strong, violent winds howled, the tent shook and shimmied, dancing with rapid movement back and forth. I could hear tree branches falling, hitting the ground all around me. The poles that normally secured my tent bent, one poking me in my hip, keeping me pegged in one spot. I tried to lift it, but couldn't; the strong force of the wind keeping it in place.

I laid still in the fetal position all the while praying, "Lord, I trust You, You are keeping me secure in this spot, protecting me from all the chaos around me." As the tears spilled out of fear, I recall saying, "Is this it? Is this my last stop? Surely, it's not. I have work to do for you Lord, but your will be done." At that moment I felt a profound loss, missing my family and friends. "Surely, Lord, you will allow me to say goodbye?"

With the tent collapsed on top of me, I had only a small window of opportunity to view the outside world. The high winds caused the camp chairs to fly backwards, the plastic food containers went flying through the air, seemingly weightless. A sleep mattress left behind by a friend that visited earlier in the week tumbled away. A plastic red ball that I'd rescued from the lake earlier was making its return to the water's edge. I'm grateful two trees guarded the ball, preventing its exit from the island. A cooler dropped off the shelf that was wedged between two trees.

It was a fast and furious storm. Although only forty-five minutes in duration; it felt like it lasted an eternity. The uncertainty of how long it would last caused momentary fear until I remembered who was in control. "Lord God Almighty, I trust You! You have me right where you want me. Thank you. You helped me to weather the storm."

The storm came to an abrupt halt. Waiting a couple of minutes to be sure it really was over, I got brave and peeked out of my tent. What a mess of chaos the storm left behind. First order of business was the repair the collapsed tent poles, then gather all the camp items blown to the other parts of the island and shoreline. I'm alive. Praise God. Amen!

The Dam at Lake Chatuge

The voice of the Lord is over the waters;
The God of glory thunders;
The Lord is over many waters.
Psalm 29:3

I t started out innocent enough, beginning with a visit to the Lake Chatuge Dam. I was looking for a place to go where I could get some exercise, was close to home, would keep me visible; therefore safe,and have an opportunity to be connected to the world. It didn't take long and I was hooked. I was lured in by the beauty of the surrounding majestic mountains and the healing waters of Lake Chatuge. Looking from the dam, you get a view of Penland Island straight ahead, Gibby Island to the right, complete with a Tarzan swing, which became much more visible in the summer months when screams of joy and laughter can be heard from its repeated use. To the left was what the locals called "The Circle." You can reach it from Hinton Road in the winter or by foot from the dam during the winter months when the lake water is down. At that point, you can walk along an emerged trail amidst the rocks. The Circle has a boat ramp, several spots to picnic complete with picnic benches and outdoor grills.

The dam itself has a paved top that serves as a walkway; it is a half-mile long. It's a safe place to walk. Most people walk across the dam and continue on a walking path through the woods and over to the boat ramp at Gibson Cove. It's approximately a three-mile, round-trip walk. I can only go as far as the length of the dam due to reactions I get from the mega power lines that are overhead along the rest of the trail. I'm thankful to get the half-mile walk in. Many of the locals can be seen there on a daily basis for exercise. They come to the dam to walk, bike, skateboard, or just plain meditate on the surrounding beauty.

I can feel the effects of the power plant, so I don't dawdle. I try to plan my walk across the dam when the power plant is not drawing water.

Everyday holds a new adventure at the dam. New, exciting people to meet, people to project God's love to. I've learned so much more about life and people by being out in the midst of their presence, even if I'm only able to witness their activity from a distance.

Below the dam parking lot is a beach. My heart jumped the first time I saw it. I have, since then, spent countless hours swimming from that beach and grounding on the shoreline. In the past, I was usually by my lonesome during the week. More recently, people are joining in the swim adventure. It feels like it's as close to paradise as it gets.

There is a bench at the end of the dam. I find myself sitting there, projecting prayers of love and healing to those who pass by. Of course, they are completely unaware of my prayer darts. I make it my job. A job I could never have the time or privilege to do if I had to be out in the world, functioning in the capacity that I once was in an office building.

It felt safe to walk on the dam, due to the visibility of it. It is much safer than walking in the woods on a trail by myself. I visited the dam when the least amount of people were there, since I can't be near smart phones or other types of electronics. Most of the locals, the ones who are regular walkers, have gotten to know me. As I became brave enough to share my disability, I found most people, although they didn't completely understand the magnitude of what I'm dealing with, respected my situation. Most of those people turned off or switched their phones to *airplane mode* to block the signal, so we can visit with each other.

This journey began with the word *dam*, not to be confused with the word *damn*. First I had my dam walk, which grew into meeting my dam acquaintances, some acquaintances became my dam friends, and eventually I even had a dam boyfriend. I shared some of my adventures with my dam boyfriend earlier on in the book and there will be more about him later. As an added bonus, I somehow began my "dam ministry." Most recently, I heard that I was referred to as the *dam lady*. Other referrals to me were Island Girl, The Mermaid on Lake Chatuge, Sticks (because I walk with poles) and Pluck.

The goal of my Dam Ministry is to draw people out of their own darkness, into the light. Reclaim their joy. I see a lot of sadness. I want to put a smile on their faces and a new spring in their walk.

Of course, the only people who know I consider it my Dam Ministry, would be my pastors and those closest to me. I don't usually tell many people I consider it my Dam Ministry. I just use my daily walk, or swim, depending on what time of year it is, as a way to project love and hope to those who need it.

Every day that I'm home and not camping on the island, I would drive the short distance between my house and the dam. I walk so frequently in the winter months that I've become a regular and have my regular dam friends. I have *friends*, I have special friends and I have my dam friends.

There are the regulars, which although on occasion, I have asked their names, my compromised short-term memory doesn't allow me to remember what their names are. I often ask their names, but by the time I return from the half-mile walk across and back, I can't recall the names to write down on my ongoing prayer list that I keep in my car. I'm reduced to writing descriptions for my dam friends. There is the *camo couple,* who looked like they could pose for the cover of Cabelos Magazine, especially the female. She meticulously mixes and matches different variations of camouflage fabrics. She comes across as a tough broad who boasts having dated most of the locals, everyone from the past sheriff to the barber, and then some. She is tough. I have a weak stomach and sometimes she shares more than I can process.

She shared that, one time she was walking with her dog, and a guy hid in the bushes along the trail and chased her. I blocked out the end of that story for fear of not being able to process the horror. Or the time she lived at the end of the "tail of the dragon." It's a scenic, windy road dedicated to the daredevils amongst us. She noted that at least five times on a weekend, rescue helicopters and ambulances would remove dead bodies. Those were the reckless, thrill-seekers. They would just literally miss a turn and drive off the mountain.

She followed behind one of the bikers, who passed her a-ways back, only to watch in horror as he slammed into a tree. In graphic, gory detail, she described watching his helmet—with his head still in it—continue down the road without his body intact. I'm still not recovered fully from that gruesome thought or image.

As she continued on, while lighting a cigarette, the wind shifted and I was suddenly aware of the scent of smoke and booze reeking out of her. I guess if I had had those experiences I might need a shot of whiskey to numb my pain as well. But then again I've lived my own horror shows and thankfully never resorted to the bottle for relief. Now she was agitated as she repeated her story and she started to drop F-bombs to emphasize just how gruesome it all was. Under my breath, I was thinking how we as humans are all so fragile, so scared at times. Behind that tough exterior was someone who desperately wants to be heard and understood.

I listened, I acknowledged her stories, and then I did what I always do. I went home to add her to my ongoing, growing prayer list. My heart nearly burst in agony over her pain.

There are so many needs that I couldn't hold onto them all. The burden was just too great. So I wrote all of the needs of everyone who shares anything with me. I wrote them down in my prayer log. Daily, I lift the prayer lists to the One who knows us the best and ask for a healing touch on all those needs.

I pray He crosses the horrific images from her brain and sets her free from all the trauma and the bondage that it has her in.

Some experiences at the dam are more challenging than others. On this particular day I was walking across the dam and I wasn't feeling quite up to par. Looking to my right, down the steep grassy embankment, I noticed four horses. Two of the horses sported cowboys and two cowgirls. That was the first and only time I ever saw horses at the dam and it caught my attention, delighting me in the process.

There seemed to be more people than usual on the dam coming toward me. Thankfully I had my poles with me to walk with, supporting myself. However I wasn't prepared for the strong reaction that overpowered me and even less prepared for the drunken cowboys reenactment of me.

My brain picked up a strong signal, which immediately caused my muscles to weaken substantially. To look at me, trying to hold on to the poles, you would mistake me for a muscular dystrophy patient. My limbs were doing what they wanted to and I found it hard to control not only my muscles, but the onslaught of emotions that followed. I was sobbing out loud.

The drunken cowboy took that as his cue to be entertaining. He cocked his hat sideways making fun of my hat and headband that served as a shield. He slid off of his horse and imitated my unsupported walk and basically laughed at me with enthusiastic pleasure.

I was devastated.

As I tried to continue moving forward, still sobbing out loud, a woman heading swiftly toward me from the other side of the dam said in one rapid breath, "Honey, are you okay? I saw the whole thing take place. What you don't know is after you passed by the cowboy, his horse cold-cocked him with its head and knocked the cowboy off his feet, he was laid out on the ground."

Somehow, she found satisfaction that the horse gave payback to the cowboy's insensitive behavior. But it only saddened me more.

As if his behavior wasn't already out of control. He brought the horse up to the grassy area near the parking lot. By then, I had made my way back to my car and was sitting in it waiting to recover enough to be able to leave. I needed to get home to bed to recover fully.

I couldn't believe what I witnessed next.

The drunken cowboy was an accident waiting to happen. The other riders went on their business of riding and left him there, although I don't think that was intentional. I think they just didn't look behind them to see where he was.

In any case, the drunken cowboy proceeded to walk around his horse, which stood facing the woods. The cowboy walked to the rear of his horse and pulled on its tail. Hard to believe, but the horse never even flinched. The cowboy then got on all fours and crawled from underneath the back of the horse, between the horse's hind legs and proceeded to crawl under and between the two front legs. He stood facing the horse harassing its face.

All I could think was, that is one tolerant horse; he never wavered from his stance. I believe that horse loved its master and performed accordingly. He probably recognized that his owner doesn't always act like a horse's behind, or so the saying goes. It was the alcohol, wreaking havoc.

The horse was in-tune enough to its surroundings to go to bat for me when he saw or felt the humiliation that was bestowed upon me by its owner.

I never saw them again after that day. I also learned a valuable lesson. I can only walk the dam when a minimal amount of people were on it. The risk for exposure to people's cell phones was too great.

On a brighter note, there are my dam friends, Jim and Kathy, a couple that walked every day the same time as me between three and five p.m. They walked their dog, a rescue; although most days, I think the dog walks them. They allowed the dog off his leash to run free. The dog pushes the envelope by running farther than is necessary, but the enjoyment in watching his escape is freeing in itself. One day, they confided in me that they, too, have nicknames for people on the dam. What a surprise to learn that they called me "Sticks." I walk with two Leki poles, so that would be an appropriate name for me. I wasn't quite sure how to feel about that but was happy to be acknowledged.

The next time I saw them, the husband saw me and blurted out, "Here comes Sticks!" The wife followed that with, "I hope we haven't offended you." I said, "Absolutely not, you helped me to feel connected and I love the name."

That couple has relocated since then, but we exchanged contact information and try to keep in touch.

Living alone, the most conversations I hold are with myself. I venture out to the dam to meet new "dam friends" and connect to the outside world. It has become a hobby and a ministry to me. The dam is one of the few places I can still go to.

Another dam friend who is very dear to me is "Brian." He sometimes refers to me as his little sister. That gesture is endearing to me. We pray for each other, since we are both dealing with serious health problems. He is not much older than me and we act as support systems for each other. When I first met him we talked about life. When I shared my story, skeptically at first, he offered me a key to a piece of property he owns so I could use it as a retreat. That was a generous offer, but I couldn't imagine taking someone's key. I'd feel responsible, should anything happen to the prized chickens and dogs that resided there. So I gave the key back. But at least I have another option and a safe place to camp, should I need a new spot.

As time passed, Brian had further trouble with his heart. There was a strong possibility that he would need a defibrillator. Any hope of a future relationship between us was squashed by that realization. I can't be around any type of electronic device, and he would need one to survive. I love him as my Christian brother and pray for him. As his health worsened, he made less visits to the dam. I missed seeing him. It was yet another loss.

Two years passed and although I prayed for Brian, I didn't get to see him. Thankfully, he resurfaced recently and tries to walk daily again. We reconnected, although it was getting closer to the time when he will need to benefit from a defibrillator implant to regulate his heart rhythm. He was upset to have to share that with me, knowing we wouldn't be able to stand next to each other to have a conversation, due to the electronic device he would need. We agreed that we both needed a miracle healing.

I told Brian that we would find a way to communicate even if I have to write him notes, fold the note into a paper airplane and fly the messages to him across the dam.

My healer nurse walks the dam and I'd like to think of her as one of my dam friends, but there is a fine line there. I knew from past experiences when I had a therapist, that they can't cross that line professionally. She would have been a great friend to have, but technically she was my healer when employed at my doctor's office. She now has a private practice and, technically, I'm not her patient yet. So I struggled with this. I wanted her to be my dam friend but I'm afraid of the rejection if I asked her to come by for lunch or dinner. So I respected her space while she was walking the dam. I tried real hard not to infringe on her space. After all; this was her downtime, where she needs space from the demands of her day. She doesn't need me to fill her space. But one day soon I hope she will be my dam friend! I liked and respected her a lot. I loved learning from people who have it all together. She has made a strong impact on my life.

Then there is Robert. In a period of two years we became dam friends, and then he became my dam boyfriend and finally my ex-dam boyfriend. Had I realized I was only the entertainment, we never would have gotten started.

At Christmas time, when I couldn't be where most people were out celebrating. I got creative and decided to do and be where I could be.

Friends from church and family members kept bringing or mailing me Christmas cards. After praying about their usage, I filled out almost one-hundred cards and put together a little Christmas cheer bag, each card holding a different loving message.

Armed with a basket of kindness for Christmas time, I went to the dam to work on my Dam Ministry. The basket included: Christmas cards, candy canes, Hershey's kisses, dog bones, and naughty and nice lists, to add humor.

The message was, "Let's all do one random act of kindness. Together we can make a difference."

Most of the people loved the unexpected gift of a Christmas card from someone they'd encountered. A few scrooges looked at me, putting their hand up to decline my loving offer. Why that hurt me so much, I'm still trying to process. They weren't rejecting me, but rejecting the love of my life—Jesus my King.

I have had so many experiences at the dam since this is my public outing. I've met wonderful locals, foreign visitors, vacationers, all walks of life. Did I mention I love people—all of them? I love hearing people's life stories. How they came to be who they are. The hardest part of meeting people is when I have to ask if they have any electronics on them. Then I have to ask for them to turn them off so we can continue our conversation. I get some peculiar looks. It's embarrassing, but necessary.

Doing my Dam Ministry was much more challenging than I had envisioned. Being out of society for as long as I was, put me in a state of almost Disney-like vision. I don't know whether it's a curse or a blessing, but most times I only see the good in people and have a heart to love them all.

Rejection is painful to me; I suspect its part of all of our humanness. Although the rejection is subtle like the couple on bicycles who rode maybe once a week, they deliberately ride away when they see me approach. It doesn't matter that I'm calling out "Merry

Christmas, I have candy for you." The wife clearly wants no part of me. Go figure.

Thankfully, there was a second couple who rode bikes twice a day. They go out of their way to say *hello*. They even stopped as we exchanged warm greetings. Their loving smiles filled me with warmth.

People are burdened so heavily that they don't see what is right in front of them. Three different men for example, each separate, each burdened, put their hand up to stop me from blessing them with a heartfelt Christmas card. I left a card on one man's truck windshield so he would have it upon return. When I saw him come back to the parking lot, I yelled over, "I left a card for you, I hope you don't mind, Merry Christmas." He grabbed the card anxiously but wasn't particularly happy about it. He raised the card in the air to acknowledge its receipt with his back to me and drove off.

I can remember times that flyers were left on my car and I wasn't happy about it either. Someone was always trying to sell me something. I'm not selling anything except the message, "Let's all do one random act of kindness and make this world a better place." If we can't help each other, what's the point?

One family arrived in the dam parking lot in two car loads. At first, I was timid to approach them. They were of a different descent and I wasn't sure if they would warm to the idea of me trying to make a difference. They ended up being my most profound experience.

The first thing that transpired, while approaching the eight of them, was the unexpected reaction from the rather big-boned woman in her forties. She was standing near two men that were talking to each other. The men were preoccupied so I walked closer to her. She was watching me with a keen eye as I made my way to her. I didn't really notice at first that there was something very different about her, something special. I pursued and in my attempt to win her over. I unintentionally upset her.

My approach: "I have something really fun for you. These are naughty and nice lists. You can fill out both slips." She turned to her family in horror and said very childlike, "She thinks I'm naughty." I retracted with "Here is the nice list, you must have lots to put on that list. Santa knows."

She lit up and said "You know SANTA!" I wasn't prepared for the bone-crushing hug filled with joy that followed. I gave her some candy, a candy cane and a Hershey's kiss, and turned my focus to the mom who was holding the stroller. The stroller was facing away from me. I said, "Merry Christmas. The message for today is to do one random act of kindness." I looked toward the back of the stroller. She said, "Would you like to meet him?" I was unprepared for what I saw, but because I was "prayed up," the Holy Spirit took over.

In the stroller was what I believed to be a young boy; he was so severely deformed it left him almost completely unrecognizable. His mouth hung permanently open. He was under a tent of fabric that revealed lumps from body parts and an opening for his face. He was shielded from the eyes of others. His eyes were wide and distant. By the grace of God, I knelt down close to his face so he could see the Santa hat I was wearing. Out of my mouth spilled these words, "Hello, I love you, I really love you, God is using you to touch people in a mighty way." What I didn't expect was his recognition of me, my words. His face and eyes lit up. When I realized he could comprehend me, I thanked him for the opportunity to meet him. Again and again I said, "I just love you. You are special in God's eyes. I love your spirit, I love your soul."

I spent the rest of the day with a vision of his face in my memory. When I went to bed, I found that I really didn't know if that was a boy or a young man. There was no way to tell the age, nor did I think to ask. Either way, God was using him.

I was so taken aback, I forgot to give the mother the special card I had in my basket for him. So I caught her on the way back to the car. I thanked her for letting me share and handed her the card.

I cried myself to sleep because my heart was so full of love for the spirit and soul that was trapped in such a disfigured body.

I spoke with my pastor about how heavily burdened my heart was. How I felt unqualified to do what I was trying to do to help others. She reminded me that "*God sometimes calls the qualified, but always qualifies the called.*" Those words gave me the courage to continue my attempt at helping others. Those words gave me the fortitude to continue with my Dam Ministry.

I continued to meet the most fascinating people. It's what kept me going, kept me alive. On occasion, I got brave and shared my

EMF status, more often than not, I have to share if the person is carrying any type of electronics or I can't stay near them for very long.

Donnie, my most recent new friend has become very special to me. So you can imagine what a shock to my system it was, when he said he told one of his guy friends about me and my unusual medical condition. His friend's response was, "Why are you hanging around with her? She's whacked." Thankfully, his friend's wife overheard the conversation and offered her opinion. "No dear, she is not whacked. I've heard about and read about electrical sensitivities and it's real. Give the lady a break."

So, Donnie remained my friend and he swam in the lake when the weather is warm. I taught him well. You could see the two of us in our life vests, wearing orange hats to be visible to the boats bobbing in the lake water, laughing over the tales he shared and enjoying the healing waters of Lake Chatuge. He was yet another great guy in transition, grieving the loss of his wife, the love of his life. God sends us friendships to see us through the pain and loss. I thank God for Donnie.

Dam Clean Up – Praise Report

Honor the Lord with your possessions
and with the first fruits of all your increase,
So your barns will be filled with plenty
And your vats will overflow with new wine.
Proverbs 3:9,10

During my normal morning praise and worship time, my spirit was pricked to pray, "Where do you need me today, Lord?" I was given a clear vision of the parking lot at the dam. While I was walking there the other evening, I was made aware of all the recent trash left scattered.

I was heading for the dam with ministry Christmas cards anyway, but now along with the cards I was armed with garbage bags, the pole grabber for easy pick up and a dust pan and broom.

Upon arriving at the dam, I found it was very cold outside. I was alone, the parking lot was empty. This gave me a better view of just how much debris there was to pick up.

I got to work cleaning up the fast food wrappers, cigarette butts, and some things unidentifiable.

None of the regulars came. I never got a chance to hand out any prepared blessings. Little did I know that I was the one to be blessed on this day.

The first blessing was when a red truck pulled in. They parked, exited the truck and passed by me as they went to walk the dam. I said, "Merry Christmas" as they passed by.

I only had one generic card left that I hadn't written in or addressed with someone's name on it. So I wrote what was laid on my heart, put my last two candy canes in the envelope with the card and left in on their windshield.

On the way back from their walk, they stopped to chat. They were curious, I guess, as what I was doing. The two of them: Clark and Lee Mayberry. I thought the name was a hoot since I always lovingly called this area Hooterville.

Anyway, they were both nurses. They were fascinating people. They shared that they'd arrived from Alaska. They had been working with the Eskimos, located three hundred miles north of Anchorage. They had seen polar bears and would bring a photo if I would be at the dam tomorrow.

It wasn't until I was writing this the next day that I realized the card that I'd left for them had a picture of a polar bear on it. It was the only card out of fifty cards that sported a polar bear. It could only be a God thing that I'd left that particular card for them.

Lee is a stunning blond lady who was clearly dressed for outdoors. She was intelligent, well versed, educated, and real. She was very down to earth. After sharing a little bit about the area, the island camping, etc., she said that it sounds like you need to reinvent your life.

I thought about that a lot. Over the years I often had to reinvent me. But being here was about as much reinventing that I could handle for a while.

She shared with me of the people and pastors that they'd recently met while hiking parts of the Appalachian Trail. One of the pastors that they'd met shared that there were camps springing up all over for children to "disconnect." They are so addicted to texting that they needed a break. What a perfect setting that would be for me with my Boy Scouts and Girl Scouts training and history. It would be a perfect fit if I could figure out where this was happening.

I loved the thought of hiking the Appalachian Trail. She told me about a place called Harmony House in Franklin, North Carolina, only forty-five minutes away. They sell freeze-dried food for backpacking and camping.

Clark, Lee's husband, recommended a place called Mt. Lacont in the Smokey Mountains where there is NO cell service.

Thank you, God! There was hope for a future for me. They left after we exchanged hugs.

I got back to the business of cleaning up the parking lot. I was just finished filling my sixth garbage bag with debris, when I decided to squat to sweep up orange peels that were stuck to the pavement. While I was in the process of scraping the fruit from the pavement, I heard another car pull in. I was still lost in my thoughts, thinking about the lovely couple who'd just left. Suddenly I heard a woman's gentle, loving, voice from above me, "Thank you for doing that." I wasn't sure how to respond so I think I said, "It needed to be done. I decided that today I am going to focus on what I can do, not what I can't."

She and her husband seemed curious about me and came closer. I asked if they had any prayer requests. I explained that I do a Dam Ministry. She asked me to tell her about it.

Embarrassed, I said, eyes looking down, "I made it up. I just want God to heal me, use me or take me home. It can only go one of three ways. Today, He is using me!"

I wrote the list of their prayer requests on my tablet. They thanked me and very kindly invited me to their church. Again, embarrassed, I had to explain I couldn't stay in the building long enough to attend a service. "I know the church you go to, it's a mega church. I would never be able to get past the big electronic sign out front." My heart has screamed out a number of times to want to be inside. She explained that, although it was a Baptist Church, we raise our hands to worship.

I excitedly explained that so do I. But I worship in the woods behind my house.

They shared that they just took over the food pantry at church. Their names were Penny and Ralph Bedford. Penny invited me to help out there. She liked my spunk. Oh, how that would be my heart's desire, but it would be too difficult for me to be in town with all the exposure from Wi-Fi and smart phones.

She explained God was laying this on her heart. Sheepishly, I said, "Maybe it's because this time of year the produce stand is closed and I don't have access to produce like I did." As a result of our conversation they are delivering a box of produce to me once a month.

Penny explained the food comes from Manna Food Bank in Asheville. I shared that I use to donate to them when I was able to make my own money. The tables have turned, now I needed help.

I took a good look at Penny and, honestly, I could swear I saw wings—huge angel wings, sprouting out her back sides.

She went on to ask, "Do you can?" I used to but I don't remember how, I would need to learn again. I don't have canning equipment anymore.

We were both so excited for the connection, we were, or I should say, I was talking over her. She stopped me in my tracks. "Hold on, let me finish, your talking is stepping all over my tongue." Ah, the finesse of southern woman.

Okay, that's one I hadn't heard before. We both stopped talking. I processed that.

Penny said, "I have all the canning things and I would love to can soups with you so you have a food stash." Praise the Lord! I had yet another food source.

I told her I have a refrigerator and that I was making soups from the produce stand supplies and freezing them for food. She explained, well if the power failed you will have backup food, yet another survival skill. Do I hear an *amen*?

Penny and Ralph brought the first box of produce on Thursday December 22, 2017. Why was I surprised? Twenty-two is my lucky number.

I put every bit of the produce to good use; every battered, bruised, and delicious last bit of it. "God is giving you the garbage right now," Penny said lovingly. "He wants to see if you will be faithful." Penny was referring to my cleaning up the parking lot and I assumed she meant the produce that I was receiving, the bruised and battered leftovers that the store can't sell.

While at my home, we visited my sanctuary so they could see where I go to church. She expressed that she thought my whole property was a sanctuary.

Penny asked if I played an instrument. I said no. If you were to play an instrument what would it be? "A harp," I replied, not hesitating. "I keep seeing a harp." Her eyes moistened. "Deborah, as I was praying about you yesterday, I saw you playing a harp."

"I have no budget for an instrument or lessons, but it's a dream of mine."

We talked of her consulting work. I was so impressed with her take-charge attitude. She gave presentations for an audience of thirty to, sometimes, five-hundred people. My dream was to be able to give motivational speeches. This was no coincidence we met. It's a God connection.

Penny is an educational, inspirational speaker. She cringed when I said I wanted to be a motivational speaker. She was very clear about the fact that she is not a motivational speaker. She explained that educational and inspirational teachers teach you something you can use. Motivational speakers pump you up and release you. Most people fizzle out after the adrenalin rush subsides.

I had the honor of sitting in on a class she taught on how to think, not *what* to think. She purposely held the class in her home instead of the church hall so I could participate. She and her husband turned off all the modern conveniences so I could be in the house.

They went out of their way to help me, even made arrangements to have a driver pick me up at my house. It was somewhat humiliating to sit in the back seat with my silver mylar poncho on for shielding, so I could tolerate the drive there. I got over that humiliation quickly as the driver very lovingly shared that I looked like a baked potato. I shared that I much rather be a Hershey's kiss. We had a laugh at my expense.

This would be the first real social function I'd successfully attended in seven years. It empowered me to keep moving forward.

Drone Alert

Watch, stand fast in faith, be brave, be strong.
1 Corinthians 16:13

I t was a Sunday afternoon. I was feeling great. I was excited that the recent glutathione IV treatments were having positive effects on my body. I drove to the dam, knowing it would be probably be too crowded to walk across, but I could find solace on the grass by the lake. I laid down on my blanket, let my bare feet lay flat on the ground to reap further healing from grounding. You can't really see me from the parking lot at the spot that I'd chosen.

As I rode in, I spotted two very expensive sports cars parked to the left, before the main parking lot. "How fun," I thought to myself. I've never seen those cars here before.

I parked, walked down the steep grassy incline, and began to get settled. As I was spreading out my blanket, I became aware that I felt tightness in the back of my neck and head. I became somewhat disheveled, but I didn't know why.

I sat down on the blanket and began to remove my boots so I could ground barefooted.

Then it happened. A loud buzzing noise was getting closer and closer to my proximity. I surveyed the lake, thinking it was a boat about to pass by. I didn't see a boat but sat on the blanket with my hand over my ears until the disturbing sound dissipated. There was still no evidence of a boat going by. Confused, I looked around. Hovering above the parking lot was a large drone. I didn't know what to do. I know from past experience that the signal from the drone caused me to be unable to use my legs. I had collapsed on the dam on another occasion when a child was innocently flying a drone above my head. I'd sat frozen, stunned, in a fog that settled into the core of my inner being. Thankfully, with that incident a woman saw me in distress and ran to ask to have the drone brought down. She helped me to my car once I'd recovered.

I looked behind me in the direction of the two sports cars which, previously, were unoccupied and saw four people standing near the cars, one holding a rather large remote.

I needed to get out of there. It will take too long to explain to them to take it down. I won't be able to reach them in time even if my body did not fail me, and chances were they wouldn't hear me from here.

As I was gathering my blanket, I noticed they steered the drone away from where I was. Hopefully, this will give me just enough time to escape. When I got to my car, the drone was nowhere in sight. I decided I'd pull down to the beach and ground there. I pulled down onto the beach parking area, turning in the circle, facing the parking lot above. As I was regrouping myself, sitting in the car, I looked up and couldn't believe my eyes. The drone had followed me and was hovering fifteen feet ahead of me. Maybe they were just curious as to where my car went. I believe a camera was attached to the drone. Anyway, I didn't leave my car and was too afraid to chance driving. Less than a minute later it was gone. *Whew.*

I drove up to the parking lot, all the while thinking, "I had better get out of here while I still can." I could see the drone heading off in the distance across the field at the back side of the dam. The two sports cars were gone. That was confusing. After all, they had the remote.

As I drove down the road to leave while I still could, the confusion was cleared up. Ahead of me, I could clearly see the drone hovering above the convertible sports car as they drove down the road. Are you kidding me? *Really?* How horrifying that would be for an older person coming down the road to see this alien-looking drone following the car and not understanding what it was.

The sports cars took a right, turning into an area with a large open field. They looked like they were settling in there. I was furious that I was wasting all this time and energy on things out of my control. I turned my car around and went back to the dam to reclaim my space on the grass. I can't give up my happy place. No sooner did I lay on my blanket when I passed out cold. Chronic fatigue had set in. According to the placement of the sun, I would say I had been passed out about one hour.

There was no sign of the drone returning. However, the parking lot was full so I left for home.

Early Monday morning at around 3:00 a.m., I awakened, feeling like I had a thousand needles in my brain. The sound in my ears was really loud, like one hundred bees had taken up residence there. My back, outer arms, hands and the bottoms of my feet felt like they were on fire. I sat up to take a drink of water and my hand could barely hold the glass that I kept on my bedside table. My muscles were weak and I felt nauseous. I knew it was a delayed reaction to the stress of the drone exposure; a very disturbing predicament to be in.

Some of my reactions are accumulative. I may not feel the effects while I am being exposed but different exposures seem to add up to a disturbing outcome.

Saturday Night Rap

But he who hates his brother is in darkness and walks in darkness,
and does not know where he is going,
because the darkness has blinded his eyes.
1 John 2:11

It was a Saturday night. I took my usual walk at the dam. It was perfect timing at 4:30 p.m., that is when most people go home for dinner, providing minimal exposure. It was cold outside, brisk. I arrived to an empty parking lot. No one was around. I wondered where everyone was at. Usually there is at least a handful of people. No matter. My goal would be to walk across the half-mile stretch and back three times. It's an aggressive goal for me but I'm trying to push through the pain.

On my way back from my second go-round, I saw what looked like something dark jumping upon the rocks that support the dam. At first, I thought it was an animal because of its quick movements.

As I came closer I noticed three people; one guy and two girls walking on the dam, almost simultaneously with the dark movement on the lower rocks.

The noise was getting louder but I couldn't identify it yet. What was it, angry noise, growls? I can't quite figure out what I'm seeing or hearing.

Now as they came into closer proximity, I saw a guy jumping from rock to rock like a monkey, he is very flexible, balancing on his hands. Somewhere stored on his being is a recorder of some kind. It's playing loud, angry music with extremely offensive lyrics. Words filled with racial hate. There were lots of F-bombs. The

"Mother-F'n" "N" words were all I could process before I had to tune it out.

I'm looking at the three people on the dam. The two women were shielding their bodies from the cold. The guy walking seems okay. Then the second guy—the monkey—climbs up the rocks to join them. I wasn't real sure about him. He had a wild look in his eyes and the angry music emanated throughout his being. Sweat dressed his brow, his dark hair damp and curly from the sweat that he'd worked up with his aggressive jungle moves. He had an olive complexion.

I knew I was in trouble. The music caused me to get confused and my brain felt like it was going into spasms. It felt like someone had a vise grip on the back of my neck and brain, I was going into reactive mode.

As I continued walking past them I said, "Hello," making contact with the one guy walking on the dam. The guy nodded in response, the woman shyly smiled.

I wanted so badly to talk to them. This was my ministry. But I was unsure in my spirit if I should open conversation. I had a limited window of opportunity to get away before I wouldn't be able to function from the audio bombardment climbing towards us from the rocks.

I certainly wasn't going to ask an already, clearly, angry person to turn it off. I don't want to even guess the outcome on that. So, I retreated.

If I knew how to dance to rap. . .I thought about the shock value of dorky-looking me breaking it down on the dam. That definitely would have gotten their attention. Just the thought of that indicated to me it's time to go home. I felt defeated. It wouldn't be possible to do a third round without passing them twice. I couldn't take the hits to my nervous system.

I still wondered what would be the draw to listening to such hateful music? I prayed for them all from a distance. The prayers were especially to break the strong negative hateful words and replace them with loving thoughts. Nothing is impossible for the God we serve.

Costumes

I will praise You, for I am fearfully and wonderfully made,
Marvelous are Your works, and that my soul knows very well.
Psalm 139:14

As a child I would create characters. They were nothing really unusual. I wanted to make people happy, put a smile on their faces.

On Easter, when I was about ten years old, I pretended to be E-bunny. I wore my pajamas, made paper ears, a paper tail, and paper feet out of construction paper. The feet resembled more of a duck than a bunny. I made a wagon out of the base of a cardboard box, adding a string to pull it around the inside of the house to deliver the goodies within. There were flowers for my mother that my Dad bought and candies for my brothers and sisters.

I imagine dressing up is not that significant being a child. However the love of costumes never left my spirit and stayed with me into my adulthood.

Over the years I would create costumes to become a different character. It's a great way to leave *you* behind and become someone or something else, as a means of escape. Creating costumes has always been a strong passion of mine. It masks the seriousness of everyday life. In my new reality, a costume allows me to become that character and leave behind my EMF-afflicted status.

In the past, I'd created a new character yearly when Halloween rolled around. I took myself way too seriously the rest of the year. I no longer celebrate Halloween, for spiritual reasons, but I do celebrate costumes. It is just more acceptable to dress in costume during that holiday period.

For the first four years of my affliction, costumes were not an option. Creating and designing just wasn't going to happen. I couldn't function in that capacity. My brain just couldn't hold its thoughts long enough to create anything. I couldn't stay on task.

Around the fifth year of my condition a friend from Asheville sent me People Magazine as a gift. While perusing the pages, designs made an impression on me once again. The creative part of my brain was starting to slowly surface again. Now that the shock of my diagnosis has settled into my spirit, I am working hard to try to get back on track.

I began to emerge from the cocoon that held me in darkening bondage for these past several years. I came to the realization that, although I couldn't have the same quality of life that I once had, it is possible to create a new life, to invent a different life. Find a new hope. I needed to reach outside of my circumstances to reach others. To feel connected to the people in the world that we live in.

Costuming was a way to be creative. It became a diversion from my new reality.

While I was camping on Penland Island, I had the life scared out of me by a local exhibitionist who frequented the lake in his "Pirate Ship" with his accompanying "Wench." It wasn't a real pirate ship, but it's the next best thing. He took a pontoon boat, built a cabin around the steering part with a window big enough to view him. He painted it black and hung pirate flags. He sported a lifelike cannon at the back of the ship that blew and made loud noises. No real ammo escaped the chamber. He looked for the places that had the most campers and then lets the cannon blow.

Since I created the illusion that I'm not out on the island by myself, by adding extra furniture or tents, he targeted my campsite quite frequently. He went where the most people were. Sometimes he blew as many as eight rounds of ammo. It created a noisy, very heart-pounding, gut-wrenching sound. The noise from the blast of the cannon was quite painful to my hypersensitive ears.

He dressed in full pirate garb and held his face in the scary, spooky stance of a mean pirate, glaring right at and through you. You just never knew when he would grace you with his powerful presence.

Thankfully his wenches, dressed in skimpy wench attire, were always beautiful model-like females that held a smile and some-times a wink, sign language, to let you know it was all in good fun. At times, looking at his angry, intimidating demeanor, I wasn't so sure fun is what he was going for.

The occasional friends who visited me in the daytime, by boat, didn't seem to appreciate all the unnecessary noise. The racket didn't happen all that often, so I learned to just cover my ears. The noise from the cannon defeated the point of going out to the island for quiet and relief, since I'm sound sensitive. However, the diversion from my solitary life made it worth the discomfort. I secretly admired the pirate's creativity.

Upon discussing my dilemma with the pirate's continuous visits, my friend Ted inquired rather boldly, "Deborah, if he can be a pirate, why can't you be a mermaid?" I thought about it but didn't comment at the time. And so, the seed of a mermaid character was planted. It was shortly after that conversation that the mermaid came to life in my imagination. I was coming back to life.

I asked my girlfriend Margaret if she would take a photo of me so I could send it to my mom. She said, "I could but I'm not very good at taking photos. However, my son Randy will be visiting in a couple of weeks. He is a semi-pro photographer and I know he would love to help you." This started the beginning of a series of photo shoots, egged on by my friend, her son, my mom, and my church family. Oh, I know that I know that they were all just being polite and wanting to keep me motivated. It was a way to keep me focused on anything other than my EMF status. It worked. I had fun, *real fun*, for the first time in a very long time. There is healing in fun and laughter.

Sewing anything was a challenge and I paid a price with the jolts I felt from using my sewing machine. I ran an extension cord to another room to plug in my sewing machine. It didn't matter that the breaker was off in the room that I sewed in. I still felt the juice of the electrical from the sewing machine each time I pushed the pedal to sew. I'd sew during the day only, so I could see with the use of the sunlight from the windows. Since my house is pitch black at night, with the exception of a candle or flashlight. Despite my precautions, the sewing machine is electrical and wore me down quickly. I found I could sew in ten minute intervals. I constantly had to stop to step away and take breaks. What I used to be able to accomplish in an afternoon would now take me weeks to finish because I couldn't last using the machine. I persevered. I wasn't giving up my dream of creating a mermaid costume. I made sure to go outside to ground to get relief and to bed early to recover. The point is I didn't give up on my dream to create.

The ideal would be to own a treadle old-fashioned non-electric sewing machine. I simply didn't have a budget for one. It's not like I can go out shopping for the best buy. I was thankful for what I had and I continued to think outside the box to be able to use it.

Mermaid

A merry heart does good, like medicine,
But a broken spirit dries the bones.
Proverbs 17:22

I started taking a sketch Pad out to the island where I camped for relief. My first thought was Ted was right, if someone can be a pirate and a wench on Lake Chatuge, why couldn't I be a mermaid? Why not? No budget for fabric, so what? Recycling things made for great homemade costumes.

Dilemma—I can't shop. I would need fabric, notions, and my imagination to pull the mermaid costume together. So I prayed about how I was going to manage this. It was laid on my heart. . .

If Scarlet O'Hara could use her drapes to make a gown, I could use my curtains.

So, curtains it was!

I had curtains left over from my condo that seemed appropriate in color. Purple and green panels came to life in my imagination in the form of a mermaid.

In order to create the tail, I cut a piece of cardboard into the shape of the end of the tail so it would be stiff enough to stand on end and not lay flat. I then put two balloons between the two pieces of cardboard to hold it open, giving the illusion of the mermaids tail flapping. Finally I covered the tail with the curtain fabric. The party box that I mentioned was in storage for years; it was time to resurrect it. The box was left over from the long ago days when I once mimicked Martha Stewart when hosting a party.

I took a standard old-fashioned headband and covered it with purple fabric that I scrunched together to use as my crown. I added shells that I had collected to create a nautical atmosphere.

To add more excitement to the photo, I came up with a handwritten sign to egg on the pirate. It read, "Pirates Welcome." I had the photo session down on the dam beach where I frequently swim. Thankfully the Pirate wasn't on the lake that day. The sign was meant for photos only and not to entice that scary-looking dude of a pirate.

I was coming out of the closet in full swing. The passion of costumes has been reawakened. I now had something to look forward to.

There was a double reason for this reemerging passion for costumes. One reason was the inner need to create for expression of self. But the most important reason was that it kept my mom going. It gave her something to look forward to. She has been on dialysis for seven years and shares how tired she is. The photos I mailed to her bring her to life as she lived precariously through me with each photo session. I'm not sure who gets more joy out of my sessions her or me. In any case, it serves two healing purposes. We keep each other motivated.

I basked in my glory on the beach dressed as a mermaid. After the photographer left, I stayed sitting among the rocks to praise and worship. I was so at peace, filled with God's love and serenity. I had the complete joy of the Lord. I began to believe I would be healed.

Every so often, an occasional couple walked by on the dam behind and above me. I simply yelled out, "I'm getting in touch with my inner child." It brought a pleasurable smile to their faces and filled me with joy.

This mermaid photo was taken on the beach, below the dam,
on Lake Chatuge. The costume is made out of recycled curtains.
Photo credit: R. A. Bond

237

Angel

Do not forget to entertain strangers,
for by so doing some here
unwittingly entertained Angels.
Hebrews 13:2

The creation of costumes continued as my life unfolded.
Pastor Linda brought me a blue shower curtain one day and said, "I want to see what you will do with this." She was intrigued that I'd used curtains for the mermaid. I could see an angel coming to life with the blue shower curtain fabric. Again, yet another group effort. Shirley brought me a halo and wings from her dentist's office. On one of her visits there, all of the staff were dressed as angels. When she inquired where to get the halo and wings, one of the staff said she could have hers to give to me. It was yet another blessing. Margaret brought me extra fabric to use as I like. I used this for the backside panels of the gown, since one shower curtain wasn't enough fabric to fit around all of me.

I was thrilled to use the angel photo as a Christmas card. Thankfully, the local print shop comes outside to assist me with all of my photo needs. In the photo my face showed reverence for the Lord.

This angel photo was taken in my back yard on my swing.
This costume is made out of a recycled shower curtain.
Photo credit: R. A. Bond

Pilgrim

Let us come before His presence with Thanksgiving
Let us shout joyfully to Him with psalms.
Psalm 95:2

Thanksgiving was arriving soon and I needed a way to celebrate. I had made this costume a few years earlier and retrieved it from storage from the back of my closet. I decided to use the photo to make cards for my family, especially my mom who waited to see what I would come up with next. She empowers me.

Looking at this photo helps me to envision a simpler era. In a lot of ways people were so much healthier years ago when there weren't so many distractions. Sometimes I think I was born in the wrong era. I am drawn to a simpler way of life, due to my sensitivities.

Pilgrim pattern made years prior for Thanksgivings past.
Photo credit: R. A. Bond

Little Red Riding Hood

Then they cried out to the Lord in their trouble,
And He saved them out of their distresses.
Psalm 107:13

After being half-scared out of my wits by the pack of wolves on Penland Island, it only made sense that Little Red Riding Hood would surface. Apparently, *I am afraid* of the big bad wolves!

To create Red Riding Hood, I used a dress that my dear friend Margaret supplied me with. It was a tea-length dress, navy with red and white flowers that she'd purchased at a local thrift store. My mom, cashing in on the excitement sent me red fabric and a pattern for the hooded cape. As the photo day got closer, she also sent me a tube of red lipstick. My dear friend Shirley brought me red thread. Another group effort.

I have Pastor Bob to thank for my debut of "Red." He knew I'd made the Little Red Riding Hood costume for my next photo shoot.

"So, Deborah, will you be wearing your red cape on the dam for Valentine's Day?" Pastor Bob nudged my spirit.

"I hadn't planned on it," I responded, thinking, "I feel like I'm about to die. My heart hurts after a recent breakup. How could I possibly go out in public? Wouldn't my broken heart bleed through for the entire world to see."

But the seed was planted and what I took to be a challenge, a dare, was on.

Days later, I was praying about Valentine's Day. I had two visions. One of me walking—rather skipping—across the dam with the joy of the Lord and a basket of treats, and, yes, dressed in costume. The second vision was of my recent boyfriend, Robert, coming across the dam dressed as the Big Bad Wolf, getting down on one knee and proposing making an "honest woman out of me" or so the saying goes.

The first vision of my skipping across the dam was realized; in fact I did eight slow laps across and back. I didn't know it until later but I wore the heels right off of my boots. The pavement wasn't forgiving. The second vision was just a disappointing fantasy. He did not show, he did not propose, and the confusing part about that is I'm the one who broke it off, always feeling left behind. The thought of him proposing confused even me.

I was created to shine God's love on a lot of people. Being in a relationship where the expectations are to love one person only would suffocate me.

So, on Valentine's Day I prayed myself up and spread the joy of the Lord all over the dam at Lake Chatuge.

During my eight laps walking the dam, I encountered approximately forty people over the span of four hours. That is not a lot of people for that time span but it was the perfect number for me to encounter. Any more than that and I would have been overwhelmed by the stimulation. As it was, I was exhausted and needed one week's rest to recover from Valentine's Day.

In between people showing up to walk the dam, when I knew I was alone, I sang songs like *Ha-ley-lu-yah to the Lord*. Chanting, *Jesus, Jesus, Jesus*. Switching back and forth to more secular songs of, *Who's afraid of the Big Bad Wolf* to *Hey there Little Red Riding Hood, you sure are looking good*. I felt elated to be used by God to bring smiles to people's faces.

You never knew what kind of response you will get from the public when you catch them off guard. Let's face it, no one expects a sixty-year-old Red to be skipping across the dam. They certainly don't expect her to go in to the whole spiel of "Hi, I was on my way to Grandma's house when suddenly I got chased by a pack of wolves and ended up here. Happy Valentine's Day, would you like a treat?" as I held out my well stocked basket of candy and valentines with printed inspirational notes.

I thank Pastor Bob for encouraging me. I love a good dare.

I loved watching people's responses; the positive responses, of course. The first couple that I encountered laughed until they cried. They loved it. They actually thanked me for doing this, it made their day. They especially liked the old-fashioned candy treats.

The next young man actually caught me off guard. I was standing at the gate entrance to the dam. Leaning against the gate, I saw a man running across the dam for exercise. As he approached my vicinity he stopped, took a hard look at me, and said, "I was so hoping when I got to the end of the dam there would be someone waiting for me dressed in costume." He gave the biggest empowering smile and went on to say, "I appreciate you and what you are trying to do. Thank you." I handed him a box of confection hearts on his way by and basked in the warmth of his huge smile.

Another young man, in his late twenties, a regular walker at the dam, was walking his dog. I carry dog biscuits for an opportunity to approach the owner. This guy never smiled. He hid behind his headset, leaving very little opportunity to get his attention. I've tried for two years on different holidays and chance meetings to just smile or wave. I've tried to have a conversation. I would have been content if he would've just acknowledged me.

He wasn't buying any of it. He was happy in his solitude. This day would prove differently. I skipped along with my basket. He didn't see me approaching because his back was to me. I tapped him on the shoulder. I reached into my basket and pulled out a dog biscuit. I held the biscuit up so he could see it as he turned around to face me. I heard myself say, "Happy Valentine's Day, I have a biscuit for your dog." *Success!* He pulled the headset off of one ear. I repeated my spiel. He gave me the biggest smile, revealing that he was actually quite handsome when he wasn't so intense in his own thoughts. As I continued to say, "I was on my way to grandma's house but got lost. . ." Every time that I have seen him since then, he smiled. Mission accomplished. We connected.

From two o'clock to three o'clock is a low point for visitors at the dam during February, so I took that opportunity to go home for a potty break. There were no restrooms at the dam. I knew if I tried to cop a squat in the woods, the red cape would give me away. I'd have some *'splaining* to do. The Lucy in me was surfacing.

Upon my return to the dam, I stood at the yellow gate. Just another typical day at the dam hanging out dressed as Little Red Riding Hood. I could see a very tall man approaching from a distance. I'd say he was all of six-foot, five-inches tall, it's only him walking across the dam and me awaiting his arrival. No one else was around. As he came closer he was looking at me, not quite sure what to make of me. My spirit was frozen. I didn't go into my usual Red Riding Hood gig, I simply said, "Happy Valentine's Day." and held out my basket for him to take a piece of candy. He reached into the basket to take a treat, all the while obsessively focused on my red lips. He said, "That was so kind of you I feel like I should kiss you." I backed away to get some more distance between us. I heard myself say, "That's not what I was going for. I was looking for a 'God bless you.'" Why was I scared? I know I'd prayed myself up to do God's work. He started to back away, mesmerized with my mouth, still maintaining focus. "I better leave before I get carried away with those red lips," he said as he started to retreat. I think maybe he was the real Big Bad Wolf.

Phew. I made a mental note to thank my mother for encouraging the red lipstick to complete my outfit. *Not.* The lipstick mom mailed me was called Love that Red, the reddest-red tube made by Revlon. It occurred to me later, that maybe I should have mentioned to him that I was on my way to Grandma's because I think he thought I was selling more than a basket of kindness.

Recovered from the last encounter, I walked to the end of the dam. I was standing there talking with someone. Not paying attention, I got caught off guard. A dog sitter was walking toward us holding on to the dog leash for dear life, but she couldn't contain the dog. He jumped up and pounced on me, temporarily knocking the wind out of me. She stopped but couldn't help but laugh when she realized what just happened. "I'm sorry; he thinks he is the big bad wolf. I'm dog sitting. Can I take a picture to show the owner what a good time her dog is having while she is away?" Why not? After all this is a Kodak moment. I nodded yes in response, still taken back at the unexpected pounce from the dog.

Next I saw my special friend and nurse, Edwina, walking toward me. She was about a quarter-mile away. I could see her wheels spinning in her brain trying to figure out if that was me. If it is me, I imagined her thinking that I have finally gone over the edge trying to deal with my EMF status. Sheepishly, she approached me. I played it for all it was worth. "Hi, I'm on my way to Grandma's house, I got chased by a pack of wolves and ended up here at the dam, so now I can be with my dam friends." Unsure of how she was going to react, I stood holding my breath, waiting for a response. It didn't take long before the shock wore off and she laughed out loud. "I am so happy to see that you are doing your life the way you want to and not how someone else thinks it should be done." She examined the construction of my cape. She loved it. I felt free. She confirmed that I was free to be who God had made me to be.

I think the most joyful memory of the whole LRRH (Little Red Riding Hood) ministry was the man and wife that were approaching from the woods side of the dam. I was initially walking towards them about three-quarters of a mile away. As I got closer, maybe within a quarter mile, I notice that the wife was overlooking the water the whole time but the husband was looking in my direction out of sheer curiosity. I was tired because I had already done eight laps by this time. Thinking I already had addressed them, I turned around and headed back to the main gate. My back was to them. They were power walking, so I could hear them fast approaching. This is how that conversation went between them:

The husband said to the wife, "Honey, that's Little Red Riding Hood."

"IT IS NOT Little Red Riding Hood," the wife replied briskly and with emphasis.

"No honey, really, I think that is Little Red Riding Hood." He was frustrated that she doesn't believe him.

"Honey, please stop, that IS NOT Little Red Riding Hood." Now she is frustrated with him as well.

They got within ten feet of me and I just couldn't help myself. Very seriously I turned around, looked right at the wife, and said, "I was on my way to Grandma's house—" I never got to finish. She turned to her husband in shock and said, "IT IS Little Red Riding Hood."

She went on to say, "Oh, no one is going to believe me, can I take a picture?" She just couldn't get over that I was there, in character, true to life. They loved it. In fact they loved it so much the wife said they weren't going to walk this way today but they were so glad they did. As they went to leave, they said, "Will you be here for St. Patrick's Day?" "We will be back if you will." That wasn't the plan at this point, I was exhausted.

In an attempt to pay kindness forward, the blessing actually came back at me. What a wonderful surprise to see that one lady who had an encounter with me at the dam actually wrote a wonderful article under The View section of the local newspaper thanking me for being there.

Thursday, Feb. 16, 2017: Clay County Progress
Little Red Riding Hood's basket of kindness

On Valentine's Day, my husband and I walked the dam. It was a nice stroll (post op orders) when we see a gal with a red cape and basket walking towards us. Is that who we think? She approaches and I ask, "Red is that you?" Low and behold, she introduces herself as Little Red Riding Hood on her way to Grandma's house and wants to share her sweets with us. Sharing her candy hearts and an inspirational greeting, she was paying it forward. Her message said, "Hi you! The world needs you. Thanks for showing up today!" Well Red, thank you and thanks for showing up today, you made our day.

Nancy Steck

I am continuously amazed at the people God places in our paths. Thank you, Lord for Nancy Steck, bless her for her kindred spirit.

For the five hours that I visited the dam on Valentine's Day, I wasn't focused on my EMF suffering, I wasn't focused on my losses. I was Little Red Riding Hood. God had a sense of humor when he made me.

After the fact, I thought to myself, *I blew it. I could have used Little Red Riding Hood to send out a bigger message.*

The message should have been:

"I'm lost, are you lost too? Jesus is the way, the truth and the light. Give your heart to him today, just by inviting him in."

What a powerful heartfelt message that would have been. Why is it always easier in hindsight to think of what you should have said? Maybe Red will have to resurrect herself at some point to deliver that message.

After sharing with my brother Chris that I had dressed up as Little Red Riding Hood and had walked the dam. His quick witted response was, "The next time you go to visit your doctor for the IV treatments, ask her what she is putting in the IV that would make you act out in this way." Leave it to my brother to boldly point out my abnormal behavior. We laughed about it at the expense of me.

I'd have glimpses of sadness as I reminisced about having a boyfriend. I felt sad for not having a lover on the biggest lovers' holiday of the year. It's tough being a strong Christian. Doing things the "right" way isn't always easy. I try with everything within me—but sometimes I fall. When I fall, I fall hard.

Most recently, my pastor found drapes in a thrift store. I was still dreaming up what that might turn in to. At first glance, I saw a Victorian gown. Look out Scarlet O'Hara!

Little Red Riding Hood Photo Shoot
Feast of Joy, Famine of Misery

My brethren, count it all joy when you fall into various trials,
knowing that the testing of your faith produces patience.
James 1:2,3

I had hoped it would snow, so the red cape would really stand out in the photo. My photographer friend was planning a trip from Florida to North Carolina during the next snowfall for landscape photos. No snow in sight, but he arrived anyway.

Today would prove to be a fun, but exhausting day. I had a photo shoot scheduled for 8:00 a.m. My body wasn't used to being vertical so early in the morning. I knew my energy level was low but you can't be around Randy for long when his high energy, which, when un-bottled, rubs off on you.

Randy, who calls himself a semi-pro photographer, whom I consider a pro, is back in town to visit his mom. While he is in town, he always finds the time to bless me with his talents of photography creativity. He has a way of capturing the characters that I dreamed up. Between his imagination and mine the result is a visual keepsake.

The shoot for Little Red Riding Hood was to be taken at the dam, only two minutes from my home. We all met at my house. His mother, my friend Margaret, doesn't trust the two of us together, so she always chaperones. She tells me Randy is so full of life, with a strong worldly appetite for woman, and she knows I'm compromised. Despite her warnings, he has always been a gentleman with me. He is playful. But he never crossed any lines. Put him with a Christian goodie-two-shoe and Satan would have a heyday with that scenario.

Randy went ahead of Margaret and I to survey the area. He was very excited to announce that he found "Grandma's house." So, we made our first stop at the V in the road on the way to the dam. Randy pushed down some brush in front of the abandoned building to clear the doorway and helped me to get in position to stand there. He left to go back to the car to get his camera, leaving me standing there feeling vulnerable that some critter might emerge or slither by me from the contents of the vacant house behind me. The missing door unnerved me a bit.

When I looked up to see Randy approaching, I had to blink twice to be sure of what I was seeing. Approaching in front of me was "The Big Bad Wolf," literally. Randy had on a large latex mask, which covered his whole head. It was a large wolf's head with Grandma's night cap and spectacles on its nose. I laughed until I cried from the thought and effort that he put into surprising me, although it was a bit of a shock.

At that point, Randy recruited his mom to take photos while he staged being the Big Bad Wolf. He positioned himself so that he was peeking out from behind Grandma's house without Red suspecting a thing.

Next stop, a minute further down the road was a path in the woods. We tried two different places to get the lighting right; one path at the far end of the dam and this one on the side of the road.

We were having so much fun that I lost sight of all the things I was being exposed to. It wasn't until we were halfway across the dam (a quarter mile into the walk) that my knees felt weak and I felt like I would drop to the pavement.

"Randy, do you have your smart phone on?" I asked to rule it out as a possible cause of weakness.

"Well, yah," he said matter-of-factly.

"You need to turn it off or at least put in on airplane mode to cut the signal. I will walk ahead to get away from you."

"No problem," he said, still not getting the impact the signal's exposure has on me. His mother had told him I was getting better. He must have assumed it was okay to use electronics now. I guess I can't expect those who are not afflicted to completely understand.

When we got to the wooded area at the far side of the dam, Randy set up his tripod, had me stand in the woods, stood behind me with the mask on to have a photo taken. I thought the camera was on a timer. Before I knew it, Randy hit a remote button. That was a wireless signal. I was between the remote and the camera. Then the camera flashed three times. Normally a flash trips my system up and I go into seize mode. This time I held my ground, no immediate reaction other than intensity in my all-over body weakness.

As an added bonus, we stopped alongside the road at an opening to the woods. It presented a rather wide path. Randy set up his tripod. He had his mom manning the camera to video tape while we staged the reenactment of Little Red Riding Hood skipping through the woods and the Big Bad Wolf jumping out from behind the bushes as Red screamed, "Aah, aah, aah!"

All of the exposures, to me, turned out to be accumulative. I didn't feel the full effects at first. By mid afternoon the next day, I wasn't well. I was in slow motion. Then the intense inner-brain pain presented itself. The pain was excruciating. My body and mind were completely exhausted. This would be a five-day process to recover to function again. Bed rest, grounding, oxygen therapy, keeping quiet, and calming complete silence seemed to be the only antidotes.

On Sunday, now the second day of debilitating reactions, I managed to make it to my sanctuary in my backyard but couldn't muster up the energy to sing. All I could do was sit in the outdoor chapel and stare at the wooden cross. Feeling isolated and defeated, I just sat in the Lord's presence.

A squirrel climbed up the tree to my right and stood on a short, jagged branch looking down upon me. Its head was cocking curiously in all different directions. I looked at him and thought, "You are a squirrel." Then I thanked God for sending the squirrel to me at that moment. It was a reminder that God is everywhere all around us. If we just open our eyes to the many ways He tries to get our attention.

I made it back to my house and spent the rest of the day on the couch.

This photo was taken on Meyers Chapel Road at the fork in the road
that leads to the Lake Chatuge dam.
Photo Credit: Margaret Bond

Pastors' Visit

And not only that, but we also glory in tribulations,
knowing that tribulation produces perseverance,
and perseverance, character; and character, hope.
Romans 5:3,4

By mid-afternoon my pastors, Bob and Linda, had stopped by to say hello. Suspecting that they might try to visit this day, I tried with all my might to get a grip on my emotions. That just wasn't going to happen.

I saw them through the living room window from the confines of my couch. I managed to get up long enough to unlock the front door so they could let themselves in. Somehow irrationally thinking that they wouldn't notice I was completely wiped out and an emotional basket case.

Pastor Linda entered the doorway first. She is incredibly loving and so in-tuned to me. The Lord knew what He was doing when He called her to ministry. She announced her arrival. As she walked in, she took one look at me and very lovingly said, "Did Little Red Riding Hood overdo it?"

"Yesss," I sobbed.

"It's okay, you can't help it," meaning I can't help the reactive mode.

I felt humiliated being caught in such a helpless, vulnerable state of mind. Anyone who knows me knows I am a doer. Being a doer makes it all the more frustrating to not be able to do all that I once did. Like the once simple task of shopping for myself.

Pastor Bob walked in behind her, apprehensive of what he might be walking into. I could see the concerned look on his face in the mirror across the room as he stood behind me. I could also see the reflection of defeat in my own face. I couldn't get a grip on my emotions. I sobbed openly with a raw pain expelling from the words out of my mouth.

"It shouldn't be!" I blurted out with raw pain reflecting in my voice.

"Ingles is right there," I pointed in the direction of the grocery store across the fields, behind my house.

"I can't even go in long enough to get toilet paper. I need toilet paper. I haven't been able to get anyone to shop for me for three weeks. The girlfriend I had lined up to grocery shop for me had hurt her back and has been out of commission." I wasn't sure what hurt worse; the fact that I needed groceries or the guilt I felt in not being able to help my friend when she was in pain from her back injury. My friend's house is all electronics, going to her house is not an option for me. Each time someone came to visit, I just couldn't ask them to shop. I had been in verbal bondage, feeling defeated.

I explained to the Pastors that I didn't want to ask them to shop, even though they told me they would any time I needed anything. They do so much for so many I didn't want to abuse their good intentions.

I went on in my hysterics. "Hearing about Robert is just too painful."

The grief, pain, suffering, and panic that set in was all-consuming. It was yet another loss.

Pastor Linda didn't hesitate. "We are here to help you. I had a feeling you needed us today." That could only be the Holy Spirit pricking her heart.

Pastor Bob said, "Let's get some nutrition in her and she should start to feel better."

They left to go get what, was now, a lengthy grocery list. The list had accumulated over the weeks. I was out of everything from milk to toilet paper. I was out of all the basic essentials.

They returned carting my groceries in. I was surprised when they remained to visit. I had taken up so much of their Sunday with the shopping already.

Before they left, we joined hands and Pastor Linda led prayer for healing. Praying that my brain would be healed and work again as it was intended to.

By the time they left, although I was completely exhausted, I had restored hope. They threw me a lifeline by infilling me with the profound love of Christ. Along with that, I now had a case of toilet paper.

> "For your Father knows the things you have need of before you ask Him".
>
> Mathew 6:8

Part V:

Relationships and Recovery

Dam Boyfriend

Who shall separate us from the love of Christ?
Shall tribulation, or distress, or persecution,
or famine, or nakedness, or peril or sword?
Romans 8:35

Here's how our story began. It was October 5, 2015 and I was sitting on my car in the dam parking lot with my binoculars focused in the direction of Penland Island. I was searching the island for evidence of wildlife inhabitants. I was scouting for any relatives to the bear that I had an encounter with during a recent camping experience there.

A Classic Volkswagen van pulled in two parking spaces over from me. A very tall, quiet, reserved man, stepped out of the van and went around the back to retrieve his dog. I have seen him here before at a distance but he was always so preoccupied that we never connected. He gave the appearance that he was a "hippie want-to-be from the sixties," so I wasn't planning on getting too chummy with him. Little did I know that over time he would tantalize my desires.

"There is a vacancy on Penland Island because I won't be going back any time soon." I blurted out before I could stop myself.

"Tell me about that." He said in a calm, soothing, polished voice as he stood a few feet from me to my left.

I went into the whole bear encounter that I had on Penland Island just two weeks prior to our chance meeting here.

"Want to walk across the dam?" he asked inquisitively.

"Actually, I was just getting ready to walk across anyway so why not?"

259

On the way across the dam, we spoke polite, first-time meeting talk. Then catching me by surprise he asked, "Do you have anyone in your heart?" "There's a new approach", I was thinking to myself. I didn't say anything. How do you comment on the many times you have been let down. How many ways can your heart actually break?

He shared that his dog was in his heart. I waited a while and said, "Jesus is in mine and he's not leaving any time soon." I was daring him to defy the Lord's existence. He didn't. That was a plus.

He stopped, looked directly at me, and slowly, in a cultured manner, said, "I like that."

I'm thinking, "This guy's smooth, real smooth. He has been around the block a couple of times. What's his deal anyway?"

"Do you want to go out sometime?" he continued.

"Noooo!" was my knee-jerk reaction.

"What do you mean, no?" He seemed to be surprised to be told no.

"I can't, so let's not even get started. I can't do the things others can do. I can't go out to the movies or dinner or shop like most people can," thinking that should be enough to discourage anybody.

"Well, what can you do?" he went on to say in a matter-of-fact way.

How desperate is this guy? Didn't he hear what I just said?

Then I heard myself say, "I can hike, camp, play cards."

"Do you want to go on a hike?"

What is with this guy? Why would he even want to get started?

"Look, I don't come here to date. I come here because it's my big outing. I'm always here, I'll see you again sometime."

We made it back to the parking lot.

"Can I call you?'

"Noooo. I can't use the phone like others, I don't give out my number."

"Want to go for a ride in my van? We can listen to music." He was quite persistent.

I blurted in defense, "I can't listen to music, it hurts." All the while I'm thinking you mentioned you had a daughter. Would you want your daughter to get in a van with someone she'd just met? This was getting scary, spooky. I left, all the while looking in my rear mirror to make sure I wasn't being followed.

Robert and I came across each other a couple more times at the dam. Sometimes he would pull out some chairs from his van and we'd sit in the grass to talk. He could only talk a few minutes, he had a short attention span, and then I felt dismissed, because basically I was. He had an uncanny way of both flattering me and dismissing me at the same time. I felt like I was being interviewed. It was almost like he was wondering if he really wanted to pursue me or not. A mirror image of how I was feeling about him.

I wanted to believe that maybe, just maybe, I could be in a normal relationship, despite my affliction. Over time, he was so convincing in his approach that I actually believed he saw past my restrictions, past my dorky head wrap and protective cap, past my walking sticks and into my soul. I thought he could see the real me; the loving, intelligent being that God made me to be.

Forgive me for wallowing in self-pity Lord, that isn't usually my style. I've fallen. I pray before I fall too deeply that you will cast your safety net to reel me back, before I hit rock bottom.

We would accidentally run into each other and the verbal dance we played went on a couple more times. Then a period of months lapsed with the time change and we didn't see each other again for a while. When our paths finally crossed again at the dam it was the week of Christmas. He offered to do a grocery run for me. And, well, being that he caught me during a very hungry time, since the new Ingles manager made the decision that Ingles wasn't going to provide my grocery monthly run, I caved. I allowed him to shop for me. That would mean he would need to deliver the groceries to me.

I noticed how strikingly handsome he was in his red sweat pants and grey sweatshirt as he stood at the end of my walkway. Boldly, I asked him if he was just being a Good Samaritan by getting my groceries or did he have an ulterior motive. He said he was being a Good Samaritan but hoped to see me again. And then he left for the holidays to be with his daughter.

I didn't hear from him for New Year's Eve, so I made the assumption that he was out on the town. All the while kicking myself for showing any interest at all, there was no way around being left out, being left behind.

Rather than dwell on the obvious. I have learned to entertain myself on holidays. So I put together a production. A production complete with dressing up and singing songs. Okay so it wasn't all that great without having music for a back drop but it was entertaining. All the while I was thinking if he had called he could have been the MC and I would be the show.

On January 2nd he called, because now he had my number. He asked me how my New Year's was. I replied, "Fantastic."

"Oh," He said, rather surprised which frankly lit a flame under me; like I'm not supposed to have fun with my limitations?

"I put on a production for myself complete with rewriting songs and costumes," I boasted unable to stop myself.

"I wish I had known. I would have loved to have joined you."

"I don't call guys. This is something I do for me to keep me uplifted."

Hard to believe, we agreed to go on a hike. The plan was that we would meet at the dam. It was a surprise to realize once I got to the dam that that was his idea of a hike to walk across the dam.

"I thought you said we were going on a hike? This is a wussy walk!"

"I thought that was all you could do." He sounded defeated.

"Nooo, I wanted to go on a real hike." I couldn't help but show my disappointment.

We agreed to meet again for a real hike. Next time, he would be more prepared. So I settled and we walked across the dam.

When we got back to the car, I told him I thought we were going on an aggressive hike so I put stew in my crock pot. I asked him if he would like to join me for dinner.

"Are you asking me to come to your house for dinner?" he asked as if I'd shocked him.

"Well, only if you are hungry."

"Yes, I'd love to."

Ok, he was a little too enthusiastic. Does he get he is only coming for dinner and then he's out of there?

This started the pattern of me cooking and us eating together. Could this be my Prince Charming?

For one year, I heard how wonderful I am. He wanted to spend the rest of his life with me and on and on and on. Only to conclude the next year by giving me his best offer.

"Would you consider being married to me, but living in separate houses?"

I thought someone tore a hole in my spirit. I was numb, imploding; disappointment would be too mild a reaction. So I didn't react. I imploded this information into my psyche. Am I not worth more than that? Forgive my bluntness, but that's just a license to conquer. That is not what the God I serve wants for me. I disconnected at that point and never could get back to where we'd worked so hard to be. He was NOT stepping up to the plate. I knew, that I knew, that I knew he wasn't going to! That's not love. My insides screamed for relief. "Not even if you were the last man on this planet," I thought. It is time for me to give up the dream of Cinderella and wait for Tarzan. After all, Tarzan fits much better into my life style of camping and living in the woods. At this point Cheeta was starting to look good to me.

Oh, how I wished I could have verbalized my pent-up emotion. It was the beginning of our demise. I heard, but didn't take seriously, anything he had to say from that moment forward.

It would be another six months, to include a breakup during that time before we discussed that proposal and resolved our so-called miscommunication. He retracted what he meant by saying he meant living in both places together. Suggesting we would live back and forth between properties until he could sell his and we could find a more suitable arrangement. Good save, but hogwash. I wasn't buying it but hung in to see how this would play itself out.

Originally, I took it to heart, thinking he meant due to my disability he wasn't going to give up modern conveniences to be with me. That he would visit, eat dinner, make love and then go back to his McMansion. Communication! Something I used to be good at. I shut down for a couple of months, only to resurface after serious prayer time. I prayed about what to do with our demise.

Wednesday morning, while doing my morning devotion, a letter slipped from the pages of my Bible. I had put the letter from Robert, now my ex-dam boyfriend, in my Bible for safe keeping. I decided to read it again. Maybe reading it would ease the pain somehow. I felt like I was reading the letter for the first time. The contents became so much clearer, loving.

"What do I do, Lord?" I prayed.

It was laid on my heart to *"just say you are sorry."*

I pondered that thought but wasn't sure that could possibly heal the situation.

It took me until Wednesday, the day the ladies come for knitting circle to be able to sit and look and act somewhat human again since my setback from our breakup. I still had bouts of confusion and my brain was exhausted, but I held my own.

I was very aware that my sensitivities were heightened. The floodgates in my eyes were holding back my tears. I knew at any second I wouldn't be able to control the flow if anyone noticed my slow responses and brought it to my attention. No one did.

It took all day of walking by the phone several times just to place the call. I had every excuse made to wait; it's not the right timing. Fear is a powerful emotion. He's at work, can't call. He's at lunch with friends, can't call now. The ladies from church are here now, too late to call. He's working out after work, can't call now. I waited until dark, thankful, but disappointed when he didn't answer. Panicked, I hung up the phone receiver. Take a deep breath. I called back a second time and was brave enough to leave a message.

"I'm so sorry. I never thought our story would end this way. If it's any consolation, I was vulnerable, too."

I went to bed, never expecting to hear from him again. I needed to say I was sorry for my part in the break up. That was all.

The next night, Thursday night, Robert called. He thanked me for calling and asked if he could come over to just hold me—just a hug.

I was unable to respond. As I was nodding my head up and down to give permission, permission he could not see, I heard myself answer very timidly, "Yes."

He came over, held me dearly and said, "Let it out!"

I wailed out loud. I wailed for what seemed like forever.

"Let it out like I did for Evelyn." Evelyn was his dog that had passed recently. We played reversed roles in that instant.

The raw pain and emotion were crippling at first and then freeing.

Our communication had been reopened. We could now rationally sort out what the heck happened. After all, this is the man I allowed to seduce me verbally with my full cooperation and what I believed was true love. We weren't exempt from make-out sessions, however, Robert respected my wishes to not cross any lines until we became husband and wife. I have learned from past experience that crossing that line would change everything and we were both comfortable with the way things were for now. I knew it would be worth the wait. I wanted God's blessings on our union when the time came.

We were happily back together again, however brief in duration. We were trying to find a way to combine our worlds or so I was led to believe. I was thinking, "Nothing is impossible with the God we serve." However, God gives us free will. Free will would prove to be my downfall in allowing Robert back into my life. He turned out to be a seasoned player. Since my mind couldn't get a grip around that concept it would still be a while before that notion would be realized. I wasn't the brightest bulb in the box in this instance. I allowed my heart to rule my brains. I wanted to believe he actually was capable of loving me in the disabled condition I found myself to be in.

We coasted for a few months. Nothing changed from before. I started praying for discernment in regards to my relationship with Robert. I asked for discernment one way or the other. I asked to bring clarity to the direction I should take. I shared in prayer with God my concerns. Lord, he talks a good talk but I've seen no evidence of him following through and putting his words into actions.

One thing about the God we serve, if you are going to ask for help which I have done repeatedly, we need to listen for clarity. It felt like God hit me upside the head with a two by four. I was pricked in my spirit to just listen and observe. So for the next two camp-outs I did just that; I listened and watched.

Memorial Day weekend we camped in his backyard. Holiday outings would be a nightmare in public for me with the overuse of electronics everywhere. We were able to explore a new remote lake, one without cell towers housed around it and only thirty minutes from his house. The first day we explored by launching our kayaks, the second we took a chance on using his boat. We had fun and, by the grace of God, I could tolerate his boat if I sat at the farthest point from the engine. I felt strong currents but didn't seize. It felt great to do something normal that other people do for a change.

I prepared food for the weekend, ahead of time, so we wouldn't have to think about what to eat. We would have all the time we needed to discuss our future; the topic never surfaced. I listened for it but didn't provoke it.

When the food I brought was exhausted we had a delicious meal of surf and turf, compliments of Robert.

"I'm going to put the shells in the woods," he stated.

"Please don't do that, put them in a baggie in the garbage can. The shells will attract animals. Or do what you have in the past and store in the freezer until you are ready to take the garbage out," I pleaded.

Since he agreed to put the shells in the garbage, it never occurred to me he was just giving me lip service.

Shortly after we cleaned up from lunch Robert hung his double hammock so we could nap. We both passed out after two days of kayaking and boating. As we were waking, Robert said "I smelled a strong odor when you were sleeping."

"Oh." I didn't really think much of it coming out of my sleep state. But minutes later, while we were still lying in the hammock, I looked across the back lawn to the forest that bordered his backyard. In between the trees, next to the balding grass was a large, dark shadow-like movement. After the third time, the reflection presented itself. It was a black bear.

"Babe, get off the hammock slowly, don't run, just walk to the house," I commanded.

"Why?" He was questioning my motive.

"There is a bear right between those two trees," I said, while pointing the trees out. "See the balding grass, look right above that area, its right there."

"You are not going to believe this but that is exactly where I put the shells," he said in disbelief.

"You what? We talked about that. Now the bear will associate your yard, us, with a food source."

So much for a safe backyard camping experience!

At this point I just wanted to go home. I felt defeated.

The next week I let Robert know that I was going to be camping out on Penland Island to get much-needed relief and work on my book.

"Now I feel left behind," he stated,

He works full time, so he sees me when he can. He called from work the morning I was getting ready to leave for my campout to let me know he would bring out dinner on Saturday night. Okay, I thought, he is trying. I would be out there three nights by then and will be in short supply of food items since refrigeration is hard to come by while camping.

Robert arrived at 3:00 p.m. on Saturday. Along with some sandwiches, he showed up with all of his camping gear.

"I hope you don't mind that I am inviting myself," he said carefully.

"I wouldn't say that you are inviting yourself since I've been wanting you to come out here for an overnight for over a year now."

He was trying, he really was, but he was way out of his element. He asked me to help set up his tent. He sawed wood, adding unnecessary amounts of wood to make a bonfire, not taking into consideration that I was going to be there several nights and would need the wood. But hey, he was trying to impress me with a bonfire. Enough said.

It was June and I was struggling with the usual emotions that have haunted me since my Dad's death so many years ago. It's as if my June GPS is set for sadness so I allowed myself to grieve. Although each year was less painful, it is still very much alive in my emotional state.

We took to the water to get cooled off and get some relief. While in the water, he discussed his career, his wanting to email the church to let them know he would not be attending the next day, and the stress of his job. He just couldn't turn his engine off. I couldn't help myself. I was compelled to let him know that this is my healing space, my happy place. All stress gets left at home.

He seemed to enjoy floating around in the water. He was finally able to disconnect. *Hallelujah!*

Toward the evening, we were sitting around the campfire relaxing. Another zinger was presented to me. "Deborah, how far away from you do I have to be to use my smartphone? I'm thinking I'll look up what time the moon will be rising," he said, impressed with himself.

"Really! I mean really!" I couldn't stop myself the words just jolted out of my mouth. "Here is a revelation for you, how about you look up and watch for the moon to arrive, and then look at your watch. That is the time the moon comes up!"

Clueless, he responded, "Was that a bad thing?"

"You think!" Unbelievable, he just doesn't get it. I'm out here to get away from the exposure of electronics, not call it into my vibration.

Regardless, he walked away to check his emails, both work and personal. He felt compelled to call his daughter to let her know where he was. She is thirty-six and married, but he couldn't relax enough to just be in the moment. She asked him to text her since she was at a concert and could barely hear him. Then he emailed the church to let them know he wouldn't be there in the morning.

He has to be connected. It seemed like too much of a sacrifice to just enjoy nature in the paradise that surrounded us. His actions were really stressing me out. It felt like an invasion of my safe zone, *because it was*.

Sunday morning rolled around and I woke up to the sound of movement on the other side of the campsite. I peeked out of my tent to see Robert in fast-forward mode dismantling his tent.

"What are you doing?" I asked, still half asleep.

"There is another storm coming and I don't want my tent to get wet," he exclaimed.

"Huhh," leaked out of my mouth.

Unfortunately for Robert, his first night camping on Penland wasn't a pleasant one for him. It rained, thundered, and lightning in the middle of the night. Not a good first experience. He seemed overly stressed to me. I'm used to living in the elements and take it as it comes.

The rain started to come down just as he'd finished packing up his tent. He proceeded to take all of his "now wet" gear to my tent. I was in disbelief as he says to let him into my tent, carting with him all of his baggage. He didn't want his things to get further saturated, not taking into consideration the inside of my tent was now wet from him and his wet stuff.

Once inside he said, "I've never seen the inside of your tent, this is luxury."

"Define luxury," I'm thinking. It's a basic four-man tent which really is only big enough for one once you bring in your sleeping bag, gear, and change of clothes.

"It's my safe zone; I don't entertain people in it," I responded.

He should have left his tent up as shelter or, if for no other reason but to keep his gear dry. I could tell he was really stressed and looking for any excuse to leave.

The rain let up within the half hour.

Looking at me intensely, he blurted out, "You are a brave woman, Deborah."

"I do what I need to do," I responded, skeptically waiting for his next move.

"I need to leave while I have a window of opportunity, there is another storm coming," he shared nervously.

As he loaded up his gear I took the opportunity to use my camp shovel to dig out the wet base of the fire pit so that I could start a fire to cook breakfast. Knowing it would take a while for the water to heat, I gathered my biodegradable soap and shampoo to bathe and headed for the lake.

We had discussed the experience of bathing in the lake the night before and he seemed open to the idea at the time. As I was bathing in the lake I called out to him to join me.

"Come in Babe, time for our bath," I offered.

"I don't need one," he replied defensively.

Oh boy, this guy is miserable. He is clearly out of his element.

I continued to bathe. It took a couple of attempts of coaching him but he finally gave into the idea.

"Okay, maybe I will." He sheepishly entered the lake.

I wanted his first bath in the lake to be pleasurable so I asked him to submerge himself to be wet and I applied shampoo to his scalp and rubbed rather aggressively in the hopes of ridding some of his stress. Instead of being in the moment, all he could say was, "I can't wait to tell my friend Randal," his lifetime friend.

After our baths, the water on the campfire was heated enough for me to prepare our oatmeal cereal. I added dried blueberries to make it a special treat.

Robert passed on breakfast despite the fact that it was already prepared. He just wanted to leave. He went on rather anxiously about his boat.

"What if the motor doesn't start? I had problems with it the day before. I would have to paddle to shore."

"It's only a twenty-minute paddle. I do it all the time," I offered, not impressed that he was leaving prematurely. I actually felt bad for him; he was way too stressed to enjoy the camping experience. As he left, he claimed he enjoyed the experience, but that was not my take, looking in on the scene. He was so stressed out that he made me feel stressed out, which defeated the reason I go to the island to begin with, to de-stress!

The canoe with a motor, thankfully, started right up. As quickly as Robert showed up, he was gone. Arriving at 3:00 p.m. on Saturday and gone by 10:00 a.m. on Sunday. I was grateful that he'd made the attempt but can't help but see the answers to all of my prayers in this equation.

The confirmation I prayed for was loud and clear, "He couldn't weather the storm!"

I gave him credit for trying, but we both have to be honest with ourselves. We exist in different worlds. I'm in the woods and he is in the concrete jungle of modern society. He gets three stars for trying.

I had brought three good books, so for the next couple of days bound to my tent due to torrential rain and an occasional thunderstorm, I happily read. I finally got the downtime and healing I was looking for.

Thankfully, the weather broke, in intervals just long enough for a potty break and a food fix. I had a secondary tarp draped over my tent, but even with that extra protection, water seeped in as I watched small streams of water surrounding me inside the tent. I still had plenty of dry clothes in my dry sack. The long johns I packed came in handy with the dampness in the air.

I always try to remember that the more difficult your circumstances, the more you gain through it. The spirit of the Lord empowers you.

A rather large, black raven stole my Ziploc plastic bag which held my matches. Thankfully, I didn't panic when it went missing. I prayed about the whereabouts and, just twenty feet into the woods,

I found the missing bag. I had to chuckle. I knew from past experiences that the raven is mischievous and had taken my newspaper, also in a Ziploc bag, and deposited it many times in different spots. It has become a game of hide and seek for us. The raven hides my things and I try to find and retrieve them.

Monday morning in-between storms I swam around Penland Island. The water was clear, crisp, and mirrored a sheet of glass. There were no boats out. I had the lake to myself. I sang songs of praise and worship while I was swimming. It felt like a sense of accomplishment each time I completed the course. On a good day, I can complete the swim in an hour and fifteen minutes. I walk taller and heal a little bit more with each successful workout. After all, I'm in my happy place.

Upon my return, I decided to chill out and float on my blowup raft. What a treat it was to have two ducks circle up close and personal to me while I was floating. These appear to be the same ducks that have frequented my campsite in the past for a piece of bread. At that time they waddled up to me, snatched a piece of bread from the nearby ground where I tossed the pieces, took the piece of bread to the water, wet it, eat it, and returned for another piece.

This trip taught me a lot. I need the guy who was able to be on the island with me and have my back. The one who knew I needed to go there for healing purposes and doesn't stress out, but is able to join me. I concluded that his name is Jesus. He has protected me all along. No mortal man can come close to the shield that my Lord provides me. Praise God!

Why do we keep doing the same things expecting different results?

It was the middle of August and I ended my relationship with Robert abruptly in mid-June. I recognized our different worlds and didn't think it would be fair to keep pursuing this course. I also felt in my spirit that something wasn't right. I felt played with.

I know our relationship wasn't perfect but whose is? I just couldn't shake the feeling. I was just getting past the point of working through my grief from the breakup when he resurfaced again.

I tried moving forward. I spent a week on Penland Island with Mark, another friend of mine. My friend was kind and generous enough to help me get my gear to and from the island and supplied the necessary grocery runs complete with ice refills. Along with that, he purchased his own tent, mattress, gas one-burner stove, a canopy, a lantern, a sleeping bag; enough stuff to justify luxury camping.

He had been overly concerned about my camping alone and offered to have my back. How could I refuse that offer?

We spent our days cooking wholesome meals, swimming, and fishing without a single catch. We took note that none of the fisherman caught anything either. Spying on them with binoculars felt like peeping Toms.

Upon my return home, I went about the business of putting my house back in order. There was always so much to do to catch up after a campout. There were clothes to wash, camp dishes to rewash and disinfect, a backlog of mail to be processed, houseplants to tend to. Getting back into a daily routine of wellness in general is a process.

There will always be people who are open to your truth and those that will shun you. Ironically, Mark was everything Robert wasn't and Robert is everything that Mark isn't. Mark was generous to a fault with food supplies, repairing things around my house, availability, and time to give me. Robert was romantic and a gentleman, trained in sales and is proficient at telling me what I wanted to hear.

After returning from the campout, Mark left abruptly. We sorted out our gear, he gathered all of what belonged to him. He said he would be busy for the next three weeks. The three weeks turned into two months of busyness. He was agitated and disappointed. I prayed about the situation and was led to write a letter to him. I needed to nip this situation in the bud. He never responded, although I saw him from a distance in the area where I swim, so I knew he was okay. I continued to pray for him.

My spirit could sense that Mark just couldn't get the concept of my disability. He had no clue of what I was dealing with. He would comment, "I don't know anyone else suffering from EMF. My son doesn't know anyone. My friends don't know anyone." As if that alone was enough to discredit me.

As we paddled back to shore on our separate kayaks, side by side, so we could be sure none of the gear would be lost, I tried to make small talk.

"My heart is burdened to get the word out to those who don't know to shield themselves. There are pregnant women who are holding the smart phones to their engorged bellies. It was a bit of a shock for him to attack my words by saying, "That's just your opinion." If I were thinking clearly, I would have responded, "Yes, and my opinion counts." But I held my tongue counting the minutes to be home.

I picked up my P.O. Box mail a week ago on Saturday, just prior to leaving. In the box at that time was a yellow slip, indicating I had a package. This is the third time I was given a yellow slip. The two previous times I was told that the slip was put in the wrong box, so not expecting anything I put the slip aside until my return from camping one week later. Besides it was a Saturday and the Post Office window was closed for business so this would have to wait.

It is now Friday afternoon, first day back from camping. I entered the Post Office, retrieved my mail and was surprised to learn that; indeed, I did have a package addressed to me. But wait, it was from Robert. He must be returning the blue-ice block I left in his freezer. Why is he doing this now? I asked myself, after all two months have passed. I put the package aside, unsure of its contents but not ready to visit it yet. How much can my heart take?

I tried to remember though we go through trouble and heartache, we can face anything without fear as long as our faces are turned toward God. He is our "refuge."

Finally, I got brave enough to open the package. I was totally unprepared for its contents.

Enclosed was a beautifully, well thought-out love letter, professing his longing for me, along with that, a single glass slipper. Okay, so you needed to use your imagination here, it was a hard, clear-plastic *painting* the illusion of glass. The shoe also sported a stiletto heal. The front of the shoe covered in sparkling glitter. It mimicked Cinderella's slipper. Did he have to send the slipper? I mean REALLY!

I gasped with shock and surprise as I held the slipper in my hand. The impact of the gift emotionally shot an arrow straight through my already-fractured heart, shattering the neatly-guarded walls that held in its contents. The all-consuming fantasy flared up like a hot flame of fire, then was quickly doused with a pinch of reality. I sobbed for what seemed like hours.

When the well of tears went dry, I composed myself. I took the box, the letter, and the glass slipper to my sanctuary. I reread the contents of the letter and couldn't resist trying on the glass slipper. It fit! Not only did it fit, but it was the most amazing shoe I've ever put on. It held a magic all of its own. Oh, how my heart wanted to embrace Robert. I wanted his hand to slip deep into the back of my pants to the base of my spine and hold on to the place where my electrical meets. Laying a flat hand on the base of one's spine is a technique used to balance your electrical system. I missed having someone willing to hold that spot. I wanted to pour out my love, completely emerging myself in the love that we once shared.

Right there in the sanctuary, before God to see and share, I cried out, "Lord, I need you, is this just a temptation or is it the real deal? Please lead guide and direct me."

I couldn't move. Like flood works, the tears poured out again like a river overflowing and out of control.

Don't move, do nothing, pray, and sit still, all these thoughts crowded my mind. So, for a couple of days I couldn't respond. I had to allow myself to absorb the shock. . . and then after continuous praying for guidance, I responded by written word, finding myself getting harsher with each edited version. Deep down I wanted so badly for him to be my prince, I just wasn't sure he was capable of being who I needed him to be. My disability being so unique that he just couldn't see beyond his connected world to join me in my unconnected world.

I can't be his plaything. I wrote a brutally honest letter, outlining my needs on all levels. I stuck the letter in my Bible for God to deal with. I want His will for the outcome. After rereading the letter and eight edited versions later, I mailed it, expecting never to hear from Prince Charming again; although my heart screamed the desire to be otherwise.

I expected that the prince wanted a loving, fantasy response, expecting me to show up in Cinderella's gown in pursuit of the other slipper, but my intellect kicked in and could not allow myself to be sucked back in to the fantasy world that we'd created for short term pleasure.

Reality hit, we can't keep doing this to each other. I gravitated to the woods and he lives in the concrete jungle—the world.

As tears flowed steadily down my face, with that realization I heard myself singing. "Impossible for a plain yellow pumpkin to become a horse and carriage. . . Impossible things are happening every day!"

In that moment, I asked myself. Could I choose love and desire over the compulsion to be seen as right? Could I muster the courage to speak my truth? How can I empower more of what I want rather than what I do not want?

Romance was the component missing in my life. Robert and I had romance; if nothing else, we had that down. His touch awakened me to repressed sensual knowledge of myself. For so many years I played both the male and female role by going it alone. With him, I felt what it was like to be a woman again. He knew how to be a gentleman. He knew to hold out the chair for a lady when seated at the dinner table. We enjoyed dressing up and dining formally in the seclusion of our different homes. We prayed blessing over our meals.

Why then do we keep making up only to keep breaking up?

I stored the letter in my Bible for safe keeping. *Lord, are you working behind the scenes on the two of us? All I see is IMPOSSIBLE!*

Journal to My Lover
Whoever You Are

*Husbands love your wives, just as Christ
also loved the Church and gave Himself for her
Ephesians 5:25*

Another day passes and you are not here.
*Lord send me the strong male, Christian partner,
you have designed especially for me. Send me the
man who desires to know everything about me and
loves me anyway.*

*One who shares my dreams and desires. One
who has my back and will guard and protect me.*

*One who will love me even as my body ages;
despite my body aging. One who loves my soul
and spirit.*

*Since I can no longer provide for myself – let him
feel compelled to do so lovingly and not begrudgingly.*

*Send me my best friend, confident, lover, pro-
vider, one who will not depart easily. One who sees
my needs and fills them.*

******

*After reading this, yet again, I realize I'm
speaking of you, Lord. You are always here and
available to me.*
Praise God!

I love you Lord God Almighty.

Holistic Doctors Visit – Georgia

To another faith by the same Spirit,
to another gifts of healings by the same Spirit.
1 Corinthians 12:9

On Thursday, I went in for my weekly appointment of acupuncture and Glutathione IV treatments. I was drained, struggled to get dressed, and was ready for some physical relief.

This was a week I had yet another major setback. I would need to share my feelings with my doctor. How else would she be able to help me?

"There is one thing about hitting bottom, doctor, there is only one way to go and that's up."

I shared that I was discouraged from failed attempts at getting food. I was frustrated because I could see the back of Ingles grocery store but can't function even in the parking lot due to Wi-Fi, so going into the store was still not an option.

I was denied shopping by the new manager a year ago. I was feeling the loss of a recent breakup. Strong feelings of being left behind. The whole world seemed to be singing but I couldn't even murmur a tune. I'd lost my joy.

Wallowing in self-pity isn't typically my style. This time however, I had a pity party, didn't invite anyone, therefore no one came.

I was still distraught. I couldn't even fake my status to get through the visit. Sobbing out loud, I heard myself exclaim, "I have no coping skills." The lack of coping skills happens when I have exposure. It is also a side effect of poor nutrition. Let's face it, if you can't shop or get anyone to shop for you, you don't eat, period.

Oh, sure there was always something I could eat, such as a reserve of peanut butter in an emergency. But chronic stress leaves me with no appetite or desire to make the effort to eat.

I was dehydrated, frustrated, humiliated, and utterly defeated.

I hit ROCK BOTTOM!

I arrived at my Thursday doctor's appointment. It has been a week of raw emotion. "I just needed to keep it together long enough to benefit from the treatments," I'm thinking.

Upon my entrance through the sitting room, which brings me through to my exam room, I saw four large photos displayed around the room. They weren't here a week ago, this is something new.

I could instantly feel a transformation in my spirit as I took in the magic of these photos. I stopped in my tracks with the realization that these spiritual, creative displays were underwater photos. The models were gorgeous, free, gowns and hair flowing through the water that held them secure.

The photographer captured my truest happy place. All four photos were underwater photos of models. Each one of the photos was more beautiful than the last. Portraits of hair flowing, big expressive eyes, a hint of air bubbles from the mouth. Their dresses were free-floating in the water that contained them. Joy, joy, explicit joy! I just wanted to absorb the photographer's vision. I was submerged in the magic displayed in front of me.

I arrived in the exam room and readied myself for treatments. The doctor came in to the room; usually she just gets to the task at hand.

Today as she entered I said, "Those photos out there, they captured my happy place."

"Really, tell me about that," she said inquisitively. She was looking at me as if she was having a breakthrough moment in my health.

"Every day, during summer I swim for healing. The place I feel no pain, physically and emotionally is under the water. I'm free."

She stopped in her tracks. She pulled up a stool and sat eye level with me. I was horizontal on the table. I could tell her wheels were churning. She was onto something.

"What was your childhood like?" she started.

"Scary," I blurted out, without too much thought.

"It is possible it felt safer to be in the womb than what you experienced after being born"?" she asked inquisitively.

"Humh." Food for thought.

We went into this whole conversation on growing up, different feelings surrounding different events. Knowing that doesn't change my experiences but it somehow made sense to my spirit. It would be several more months when I had the good fortune to speak with a gentleman at the dam, who had a scientific background and worked with radar in the past. Somehow the subject of feeling better while swimming under water surfaced. He was emphatic that the reason I felt better swimming underwater was because microwaves, which are airborne, can't penetrate water. My toxic body hurts when subject to microwaves.

Next, the doctor and I talked about my relationship. "If he loves you, he'll be back," the doctor said smugly.

This was confusing to me. After all, she was the one that said it takes all of my energy to try to get well. Starting a relationship and working on wellness are two major life stressors.

I'm thinking a relationship: the support, the need to be hugged, should prove healing in itself. For those reasons, along with the fact that I can't shop for myself, seemed proof enough to me that I not only wanted to be able to be in a relationship, but I needed to be in one. I needed someone who cared whether I have food supplies or not. I'm thinking wellness and a healthy relationship go together. Having someone pour love into you and being able to love someone back is a healer. It's how we are built.

After our discussion and more flood works of tears, we determined together that I was purging. It doesn't happen every week with acupuncture but for whatever reason it happened all seven days of this week. It was a cleansing, a release.

After the new treatment, I felt physical and emotional relief. The treatment and the fact that the doctor validated my existence in her discussions brought comfort to me. She listened, she heard me, she commented. She believed in me. She believed that I can beat this thing.

With childlike wonder, I looked at her and asked, "Do you really believe I can beat this? Or are you telling me so you think that is giving me hope?"

She said matter-of-factly that, "I believe you can beat this, but you have to believe it, too."

She feels it may be safer for me to stay in the state that I'm in. Confusing, I know. I need to process that theory.

After discussing all this with the doctor, I felt like I could put on my big girl panties again and somehow strive to move forward.

She told me not to underestimate the treatments I was going through. The doctor commended me for all the hard work I was doing to seek wellness.

At the end of the appointment, I got off of the exam table, got dressed, turned back towards the exam table to fold the sheets. At that moment, I felt a sharp pain rip through my chest and my heart. My knees buckled, I grabbed the exam table for support, and yelled for the nurse. At that instant of shocking pain sensation and panic I couldn't even remember the nurse's name. I thought I had a heart attack. I moved to look toward the door and the slight shift of my body made the pain subside. That's when I put my hand to my chest only to find one of the acupuncture needles was still in my chest on an angle. It was an honest mistake to forget to remove one when you have fifty needles put in you. One needle was accidently left inserted in me.

When the acupuncture needle pierced my skin deeper, it felt as if my heart were sliced open. The contents of my heart had nothing left to retain them. The repressed, denied contents spilled out, causing a landslide of emotional pain to be released. It was a purging from the inner chambers of my heart.

I'm not sure which hurt worse the pain from the needle being pushed further in or the shocked look of horror on my nurse's face when she realized it wasn't removed when the other needles were taken out.

Left Behind

Let your conduct be without covetousness,
be content with such things as you have.
For He Himself has said,
"I will never leave you nor forsake you."
Hebrews 13:5

There is no way around not being left behind. The world is upping its game with electronics faster than I can heal my body.

For the past seven years it's as if I no longer exist. Invitations stopped coming. The phone was not an option for the first couple of years to reach me and, even now, I pay a price every time I use the phone.

Family and friends have to go on with the business of living in the world as it exists now. Wi-Fi is still so incredibly debilitating to me that I have to avoid it at all cost.

The cost to avoid Wi-Fi is great. It has cost me friendships, wedding and shower invitations, worship on Sunday in a public church with other believers, and dinner invitations are non-existent.

The most painful memories of being left behind are those that involve family members. While tenting at my brother's farm in West Virginia, the family; two brothers, sister and sister–in–law decided to take mom on a "family outing." They were going to the zoo.

I love the zoo. In my heart I'm thinking maybe this is something I can do too. But my younger brother came to tell me of their plans. Along with that to share that the animals all have electronic fences, cages around them. "There is no way you can go." As I heard those words come out of my brother's mouth I thought my heart had been ripped out of my chest.

When it was nearing the time for them to leave, I made myself scarce.

This would be a good time to use the bathroom to shower and dress. I was in the bathroom so no one could see the disturbed look on my face. They all knew I can't be in there for long but I made every excuse to stay there. It was just easier.

"Sis, come out I want to hug you good bye."

"I'm one foot in the shower; I'll see you when you get back." I tried to hide the emotion in my voice but I don't think I did a very good job of it. The tears were streaming down my face and a good shower is what I needed to rinse away my grief, or so I thought.

They drove off. I don't know if I can begin to describe the emptiness I felt. If this is my future, what I can expect going forward, how was I going to cope with always being left behind?

I will never leave you or forsake you.

As this thought was laid on my spirit I replied, "Yes, Lord, I trust you. My tears dried up until the next challenge.

Two years prior, a special friend, my boyfriend at the time, asked me to join him at a family gathering for Thanksgiving. I was still living in Asheville, North Carolina. Trying to do something "normal" and not yet understanding the severity of my affliction, I agreed to go.

The ride to his family's house was taxing, leaving me with chronic fatigue. I ended up not being able to function in the townhouse where his sister and her family resided.

I walked in the front door and literally walked right out the back door. This was not before passing by a huge big screen TV, the kitchen with the mixer going, overhead lights and fan, electric stove in the cooking process, and lots of chatter from everyone helping. The last straw was an electronic remote control toy truck that whizzed by. It was a war zone for me.

I felt useless. I would always step up to the plate to help. I knew I was severely afflicted and had to leave out of the nearest exit, which at this point was the back door.

Needless to say, I ended up staying outside, away from the town-house, down on a sandy beach next to the community pond. There I could ground to get relief.

I knew that day if there was any hope of being in a normal situation, a normal relationship, it wasn't going to happen here.

My guy friend seemed empathetic but sometimes the looks I got convinced me he just didn't get it. How could he? I'm not sure I understood the magnitude of my setback at that point.

The church that I had been an active member of, for the whole time I had been in Asheville, was now presenting challenges just to enter the building.

Thankfully, the Sunday school teacher was willing to turn off the florescent lights in the class room so I could still participate. That was a challenge on days that were cloudy since it was hard to see our lesson booklets. But we persevered.

I was asked to be an usher and took pride in being one of the first female ushers in the church. They were trying to be supportive by giving me a bigger role in the church. I still didn't have a clue that I just couldn't function due to exposures in the building.

After passing the collection plate, all ushers were to stand closest to the pulpit while a blessing was said. I would learn later that the electronic band equipment, microphones, and wiring right behind me were causing my body to react in strange ways. I had lead legs and couldn't move forward. Still unaware of what the problem was, I had to nod to the head usher in the back of the church to come forward to help me walk out. Humiliated, confused, tears flowing, I had to leave the church building yet again to get relief where there seemed to be none.

I just wanted to belong. Be part of something. At this point I could no longer go back to my job. It was becoming harder to stay in the building at the YMCA. I was having trouble functioning in my condo. What was I to do next?

I prayed that God has a plan and sought direction through prayer.

Relationships

Let each of you look out not only for his own interests,
but also for the interest of others.
Philippians 2:4

I have been blessed with a strong support system. This is a really important aspect to the healing process. If you don't have a support system, reach out to others until you do.

I have openly embraced the love of Christ, the love from family, the love of my church family, and the support and love of endless friendships.

Using a phone for any length of time was still a hardship. Much of my communication was still by snail mail. Occasional calls came in to check up on my well-being. Those calls are bittersweet. Most went like this, "I know you can't talk long so I want you to know I'm thinking of you. Ok I'm sure you have to go now so goodbye." It's awesome that someone was reaching out to me and equally as frustrating that they abruptly hung up.

On other occasions when I pushed the envelope by staying on longer than I should I became deathly ill. The result was muscle weakness, flashes of light behind my closed eyelids, and lack of oxygen to my brain causing serious discomfort. But sometimes loneliness to speak to someone replaced my logic and I used the phone for an extended period only to pay a debilitating price.

Relationships can be challenging enough under normal conditions but throw in a disability and the challenges become insurmountable.

Thankfully, my son calls me a couple times during the month now, always instilling positive input. Although it is still difficult to use the phone for any length of time we stay on long enough for him to keep me in the loop of how his life is progressing and he checks on my progress. He sees me getting well. He feeds me uplifting positive affirmations, becoming one of my biggest cheerleaders along the wellness path.

Although I had left a message for my daughter, she doesn't seem to have found the time to always return my calls—at least not what I would consider in a timely manner. I felt abandoned. Serves me right, I thought. This is how she must have felt when I had a demanding career like the one she has now. Okay, now I'm being ridiculous. I lived for my children. I recognized that we have come to a point in our lives when I want more from my daughter than my daughter needs or wants from me. Why is that so painful? Sometimes I think my daughter keeps an emotional distance because I have been sick for so long. Maybe she expects me to die and distances herself to break the emotional fall that occurs after the loss of a loved one. Regardless, I love her dearly and gave her the space she seems to need. My brain was tired, so tired. I added this self-inflicted wound to my list of woes.

When we finally connected, my daughter couldn't be more loving. She commented on how glad she was that I was passionate about helping others by writing my story. She has blossomed in her own right.

Love relationships were almost impossible to sustain. I'm not in the world like everyone else. I'm the minority. I felt like an abandoned soul left behind by the computer age, forced into a lonely exile by the inescapable radiation of the wireless revolution. I was in denial to think I could maintain a relationship with all of the distractions tugging at my partner.

First there was Davey, a good ole boy, a great guy. He was absolutely adorable, I should be so lucky. He was the guy I tried having Thanksgiving dinner with, years prior. The therapist that introduced us made it very clear, after I let him take a piece of my heart, that Davey was young, early fifties, and will want to go out on the town. Really? You tell me after the fact? Apparently not even the therapist got the seriousness of my predicament or she wouldn't have set me up for this fall. Oh I tried, but public dinner dates were no longer an option. I knew Davey didn't get the seriousness of my affliction when he asked me to go to a car show in Charlotte. The conversation went something like this:

"There is a huge car show in Charlotte in a couple of weeks, will you go with me?" he pleaded.

"How many people to you expect to be there?" I inquired.

"Oh, maybe a thousand," he said, like it was no big deal.

"Out of that thousand, how many do you expect to have a cell phone?"

"I don't know, maybe nine hundred."

"If I can't be around my one cell phone, how do you expect me to survive nine hundred of them?"

He was offended and felt rejected. But I wasn't rejecting him, I simply knew I couldn't handle the cell phone exposure. What a nightmare.

That was the straw that broke the camel's back. Where do you go from there? I couldn't be what he needed. I couldn't go public places but I was too afraid to say those words out loud.

The price from exposure would just be too high. I ended up having to get out of society completely leaving my new love behind. I had high hopes he might come to get me since I could no longer drive myself during that period of darkness. But instead he disclosed his desire to work in the city and get a smart phone. *Ouch.* Still in his early fifties, I wished him good luck and prayed for the right and perfect partner for him. Then I did what I always do and got down on my hands and knees and prayed for deliverance. It wasn't time. He must not be the one for me, long term. Another ouch. I thanked God for meeting Davey and for the special dinners we'd shared before I could no longer.

After settling in Hayesville, I met the man who would become my Sunday school teacher; that is, if I were able to stay in the building long enough. The professor and I became good friends. We shared stories of our lives. He was in serious grief over the recent death of his wife, the love of his life. We shared dinner together and he would travel often leaving Waggie, his little black and white dog, behind. I happily took care of Waggie.

Waggie was also in serious grief from the loss of his human mommy. I spent six weeks working with him. I would get down on the floor to spend quality time with the dog who was really a kid in a dog suit. I let him know his mom didn't leave him intentionally, it was just her time. The dog ignored me for the first couple of days. After that I got down on the floor to meet his eye level. I looked him right in the face and said, "You are here for six weeks, we can have fun or you can be miserable." Miraculously, he seemed to get my drift. The first day he watched me doing yoga, spread out on the floor. The second day he watched me from my bed. The third day he was sitting on my belly while I did my morning stretches on my back. We had a blast. I too, now had a dog companion to walk in the dog parade at the dam, which was a constant stream of different dogs that walk with their owners for exercise.

In helping Waggie with his grief, it somehow came back to me as a healing as well. After all, I had been grieving the changes in my life. This was no coincidence that we were able to spend quality time together. Praise God for the unconditional love of a pet.

Neal was a tall, long and lean, good-looking professor. Somehow in the process of helping him with his grief, I fell for him. That story ended poorly when we just couldn't agree on some major issues. He felt led to a different part of the country after the sale of his house.

I've talked about another guy friend, Ted, and his island visits elsewhere in the book; however I wanted to mention he is a great guy who also was widowed from the love of his life. It broke my heart to see the intensity of the repressed grief that he held. His new life included the desire to go on cruises, so even if I could help him with his grief, our shared grief was that I couldn't accompany him on a cruise. He drove a Harley—I can no longer ride on the back. Deal breakers. I know God has someone very special in mind for him. I pray for that.

Is there no end to this madness?

Total Solar Eclipse

But in those days after the tribulation
The sun will be darkened,
and the moon will not give its light;
Mark 13:24

After months of anticipation and preparation by the locals, the day of the August 21, 2017 eclipse finally arrived. Hayesville was in the path of totality. Everyone was anticipating this extraordinary experience.

My stress was building due to newspaper articles emphasizing the exorbitant amount of people who were expected to merge upon us. Scientists, spectators, Europeans were to grace our mountains.

My bigger concern: should one million extra people occupy the seven counties around me, what would the effect that all of their electronics have on the area, on me?

It was presumed that we would have power outages, no food left on store shelves, traffic jams, accidents, and gas rationing. The tension was building as each day passed, bringing us one step closer to the eclipse. I was tempted to leave the area but driving myself wasn't an option and no one else was leaving. I simply couldn't get a ride out.

Days before the eclipse, flashing electronic signs along Route 64 indicated slow moving traffic ahead, although there wasn't any traffic. Handmade signs to "Park your car here for $20.00" surfaced everywhere. Tent sites for $100.00 were popping up. Hotels were booked solid, so I was told.

Speaking with my nurse practitioner friend at the dam (the one I requested to balance my energy by applying pressure to my pressure points), she shared with me that the sun is all energy, when the eclipse happens there will be a major shift in energy. She suggested grounding and centering myself in front of my fire pit.

I had already planned to light the fire pit and praise and worship throughout the eclipse. Grounding goes without saying, I do it automatically.

It was 2:00 p.m., I built my fire pit, layering newspaper, tinder, kindling, and seasoned logs. It torched easily in the heat of the day and all its dryness.

I began to praise and worship in anticipation of the big black out. I wanted to sit alone to benefit from the full spiritual effects with no distractions.

Its time was near. Slowly around 2:20 p.m., the sunlight started to dim. I started singing praise and worship songs louder and louder. The darkness was creeping in slowly but surely. I expected a total blackout but was disappointed that although it was dark I could still look around my yard and see its surrounding. This had nothing to do with the light from the fire pit.

At the height of the darkness, everything stopped. I was calling out, "Lord God Almighty" while tears flowed heavily down my face. I'm not clear on why I was so overwhelmed, maybe it was just a release.

I went through the trouble of buying two pairs of special eclipse glasses to have on hand to be able to view this awe-inspiring site. However the day before the eclipse, my brother called from West Virginia. He had been to his Ophthalmologist. The Ophthalmologist warned of the dangers of looking at the eclipse. He shared with me that if there is even a pinhole or a scratch on the viewing glasses, and you looked up, the damage to your eyes would be irreversible. It would result in a sunburn effect on your eyes.

Since my eyes are still a major concern since my setback seven years ago; I elected not to look up. I went through a two year period where I had to wear dark glasses even in the house, I was so light sensitive.

Not looking up to view the eclipse didn't take away from the magical effects of sitting outside as the natural lighting changed from light to dark and back to light again. It was as if the world just stopped. The silence, although not for long, was deafening.

A local man made comment in our home town paper that summed the experience up best when he said,

"As I move on in years, wonderment gets scarce, but today's eclipse was stunning. Primal and beautiful, strumming a chord deep within the soul. I didn't attempt any photos of totality as I wanted to be present in body, mind, and spirit. Everything got still and quiet. A sky like no other. Streams of the corona, like white fire, upon the deepest blue I've ever seen. It was a moment. As I reflect on today, I think for a few moments we all were bound looking skyward in awe."

Well said, Keith Gibby, I felt like I saw the eclipse through your eyes. Thank you.

At the height of the darkness I could hear whoops and hollers all around town. I couldn't stop myself, I too let out a loud, "Woo hoo—thank you, Lord!

Then the sunlight came back full force and I could hear people going about their business once again. A lawn mower started up. Dogs barked, cars were back in route to their destinations, a truck bellowed in the distance. I could hear a helicopter flying by.

Do I feel any different? Yes, major relief that the time has passed and the anxiety melted away. I'm not sure if the anxiety melting was due to my sitting near a fire pit in 95 degree weather or just plain glad to get back to the normal routine of the day.

Anyway, the hordes of people that were expected to arrive never came. The town was prepared for crowd control and I'm sure the well-stocked vendors were disappointed.

I waited an hour and decided that I would attempt the three-minute drive to the dam. Thankfully the beach was empty. I swam my usual workout along the shoreline of the lake and around the buoy at The Circle and back again. Then I removed my vest and retrieved my pink noodle from shore. I used the noodle as a floating marker to show I'm swimming. I love underwater swimming. When I heard or felt the vibration of an approaching water craft, I surfaced and held the bright pink noodle up to identify that I'm in the water. Most of the time, the sight of the bright noodle was sufficient to avoid a boat or Jet Ski from coming too close. On occasion, someone may push the envelope and come within an uncomfortable proximity to me.

Those moments I don't welcome. I prayed a whole lot harder when I thought there was even a chance that a boater didn't see me.

Most days on the beach or in the water I meet someone new. On the day of the eclipse, I had a double blessing of meeting two different families. I had the good fortune to meet Heather, a young beauty in her early forties, who was recovering from a motorcycle accident from two years earlier. She and her handsome friend Lenny were visiting from Virginia. Lenny was originally from Guatemala. Heather promised to return here to visit me. I put them both on my prayer list.

Shortly after they left, I returned to the water for an aggressive swim both on and under water. Once I'd exhausted myself, I simply floated with the pink noodle under my arms and wore my bright orange hat to be visible. I mimic a buoy.

What happened next could not be a coincidence. Besides, I don't believe in coincidences. I was looking towards the grass to the right of the beach as I witnessed three people walk to the water's edge. I would learn later that it's a step-father, mother and son. The mother walked past my car, which I had parked near the beach and where I displayed my chair. I called to her from the water to let her know she could use my chair if she wanted to get more comfortable. She looked at one me with a rather blank stare. I was unaware she spoke little English. She dabbled her toes at the water's edge, then returned to her husband and son. Her son was laid out on the grass. I thought to myself, "He's grounding," but then dismissed my thoughts and got back to the business of swimming.

Shortly after, the mother, in a full T-shirt dress, walked onto the beach and into the water. It was such a hot day she needed relief from the heat. We struck up a conversation as best we could with her limited English. They originated from Czechoslovakia, but currently lived outside of Atlanta, Georgia. The three of them came here specifically for the eclipse. They got lost and ended up at the dam.

Feeling the comfort of the lake water, the mother, Rosetta, yelled out for her son, calling him by his birth name, to join her. I couldn't believe my eyes—Fabio lives! A tall, well built, handsome man, who I assumed was in his early forties, dropped his shorts and, sporting a tight-fitting pair of Calvin Klein underwear, strolled across the lawn, onto the beach and into the water directly in front of me. . .and then with an accent that would make any heart melt said, "I hope you don't mind, but I forgot my swim trunks—I hope I do not offend you."

"Oh no, not in the least, I have NO problem with that." Do I hear a REALLY here. Do I get an Amen!

Okay, so I'm past the moment when I realized I'm not dead yet. I too, like eye candy. Get a grip, I told myself. He was young enough to be your son's friend. He was living proof that God doesn't make junk, he was gorgeous. During our conversation I learned that I am his mother's age of 61 and he is all of 39 years young. Okay, so it was a short-lived fantasy.

As the three of us finished making our introductions and I welcomed them to the area. I'm thinking to myself, I am not going to mention EMF today. Today I'm just Deborah. Minor chitchat surfaced and then Fabio decided to share a little about himself. He displayed a distraught, uptight, and frustrated demeanor. He shared with me that he was writing a book because he got fired from his job for spouting off. This, he explained, was not his normal behavior, he never spouted out before and definitely not to the boss. His wife was divorcing him, he has two small children. He went on to say that he doesn't understand what is happening to him. When he drives his electric car his arms tingle, numbness sets in to both his arms and face and he can't make a decision. He is agitated, he can't think and he is scrambled. BINGO! So much for me NOT mentioning my EMF status today!

Okay so I wasn't going to intercept but it is my obligation to pass along what took me years to learn. "Fabio, I'm not a doctor, but I, too, am writing a book, but I do know what is wrong with me. I hope you don't mind me sharing but I believe I know what is wrong with you. It sounds like a clear-cut case of EMF."

He was so overwhelmed with meeting me because I was someone who could help him. He was searching for answers. Wanting to learn more about the EMF disease, we continued our conversation on land.

At some point he will be visiting so I can share all that I have learned. I asked him to be sure to bring his mother!

The mother, a petite, attractive woman who has a strong passionate love for her family had a great deal of wisdom. She shared in her broken English language, "I try to tell him cell phone not good, he no listen."

I explained to Fabio that when he is laid out on the ground, he is grounding, his spirit knew what he needed, and he was drawn to the earth for healing.

"How's your faith?" I boldly asked.

"I am spiritual," he replied.

"Fabio, when you wake up tomorrow I want you to give thanks for this experience, give thanks in advance for healing. Turn the tide. This moment in time is not forever."

I wanted to make him aware of his condition so that he can heal his body, his marriage and make sense out of what happened at his job.

We exchanged contact information. I mailed him a letter with the latest EMF catalog, invited him to come to see me and bring his wife as well. Maybe if she saw that he was not losing his mind, he was suffering from exposure, they could make some changes for him to adjust to his condition. I put them all on my prayer list. Then I said a brief prayer to forgive me for my wayward thoughts. This is the first time I'd wished I was twenty years younger. God help me.

As I got to know him, I learned that Fabio was so much more than a handsome face and a well-built structure. He had substance, depth. He was educated, cultured, and open to new ideas. He was a devoted father and an all-around good guy. He displayed actions of care and concern and was generous with his time and resources. He had integrity.

I felt blessed that we have called our new friendship into each other's vibration. We had an appreciation for each other's expression of the written word and connected on a spiritual level. Although he is twenty-two years my junior, there didn't seem to be an age gap when we spent time together. We held a mutual respect for each other's life experiences as we continued to learn from each other and grow in our friendship.

It always amazes me how God plants people in our paths when we need them the most. I was helping to expand Fabio's knowledge and connecting him to key people who could help him. He would visit with his precious children, giving me the priceless gift of their joy and wonder. We both gained from our encounters.

Gifts

Every good gift and every perfect gift
Is from above, and comes down from
The father of lights, with whom
There is no variation or shadow of turning.
James 1:17

Despite my limited world, I wanted and needed to find a way to be productive. I invented projects to make as gifts. Since going to work or going shopping were no longer options for me, I took to recycling things from my house.

I tried to think outside the box by recycling magazines. How many ways could I put them to use? I started small by inventing different greeting cards; each unique to the recipients attributes. Then I graduated to a little larger project of custom made collages. Using the diploma-sized black frames to encase them.

At first, I didn't have the confidence of their worth. But the positive feedback I received from the recipients of those gifts encouraged me to continue.

The largest collage project I did was to create a collage for my blessed buddy's 50th birthday. Since travelling to her wasn't an option I had to come up with something that she would remember forever. That was a three-month project. Slow and steady won the race in this scenario.

Not having a budget to buy gifts for my church family, for my pastors and friends that visit me weekly, most times twice a week, I prayed about a way to bless them back for all the ways they enhanced my life. I had a clear vision of a calendar. All I could think of was, surely Lord, you don't mean I need to take this on. Ah, but it was meant to be. This would mean taking four years of the church bulletins they'd blessed me with each week and recycling them into twelve collages—one for each month of the year.

Each heartfelt gift became grander in appearance; each gift more ambitious than the last.

The visions and gifts we are given are direct from God. We all have hidden talents that can bloom if we allow ourselves to let those visions take hold. I am living proof that God is in the mix. He can use us in the broken state we are in if we let Him.

The very best gift we can give is the gift of ourselves. Despite what we are dealing with in our own life, a smile in someone else's direction can change someone's day into a more positive experience.

Spending a few minutes by lending an ear to listen to someone or providing a hug can go a long way in making someone's day. You never know how one random act of kindness could profoundly impact someone's life.

I benefitted greatly from other people's generosity since my setback. As a result my goal this lifetime is to pay forward all the love, gifts and concern that I have been privileged to receive.

Be a *Pluck* in all ways; use your spirit to bless the world. Who says one person can't make a difference!

Dam Boyfriend Deliberation

My face is flushed from weeping,
And on my eyelids is the shadow of death.
Job 16:16

As it turned out, some of us have to learn the hard way and some of us learn the easy way. Maybe since all of my lessons have been learned the hard way, it will be engrained in me to never do this again. Because had I realized I was being played like a fiddle, the song never would have been started. Always seeing the good in people was a handicap for me—in this instance.

Hard to believe after all we'd put each other through, we tried, yet again, to be a couple. I state this because our lifestyles are so different. I spent most of my time in the woods and he was in the world; the concrete jungle. At some point during this attempt, Robert became detached. I could tell he wasn't himself. It never occurred to me he was looking for a way out of this relationship, but he was.

A tell-all clue was so obvious but still I chose not to see it. We were tired, so we laid down on my bed to snuggle. We were almost at the two-year mark in our relationship. Inquisitively I asked, "If we were walking across the dam and ran into someone you knew how would you introduce me?" He thought about that for a while and said, "Well, you're my friend, I'd say you were my girlfriend but you think that is too high school. I guess I'd say you were my soul mate. Let me turn that question around on you. How would you introduce me?" I didn't hesitate. "That's easy," I said confidently, "I'd say, this is my fiancé. After all, we are planning a future together." "That's where we differ. That would mean we'd set a date to marry and

296

we haven't," he responded slyly. *Where I come from a fiancé is the intent to marry.* I was so stunned I only thought this line. I couldn't speak the words. And then another bomb was dropped.

He slipped in the conversation and said I was a "potential" wife. Gingerly I said, "Excuse me, run that by me again." He retracted by saying, "Scratch the potential."

Despite that conversation, Robert pumped me up, excited about our October 5th anniversary date coming up. This was the anniversary of the date we'd met, so we agreed to meet on the beach at the dam to celebrate. Always the romantic, he brought the van to dine in, two take-out scrumptious dinners, a dozen red roses, a loving card and candlelight. I supplied dessert cakes, chocolate, a card with an attempt at humor sporting a wolf, using a play on words from Red Riding Hood.

Although the atmosphere was romantic I could sense something tense about him, he just wasn't himself. His voice was impersonal. He talked about everything except us or our future.

After dinner, we walked the dam and enjoyed the moonlit views. My spirit felt disconnected from his as if he'd already made a break from me. We returned to the van and Robert brought out two lounge chairs with sleeping bags for each. We sat side by side in companionable silence to continue enjoying the views of the moon lit lake. The scenery was stunning.

We'd started to look at housing just a couple of weeks ago. I'm daydreaming thinking we will be married soon and I will finally be able to physically love him the way I've dreamed about doing for the past two years. I was just about to tell him that we could spend the winter loving on each other and in the spring resume the search for a place to live; since the search seemed to be stressing him out needlessly. I never got the words out.

And this is how our story ended.

After an hour of awkward and strained silence, I very lovingly and gently asked, "Where are we at babe?" I was hoping to open conversation about our future. As it turned out, that was a loaded question. I guess you could say I was blindsided, I didn't anticipate what came next. Most of what transpired is a blur, however I do remember the following words, voiced loudly and curtly at me in a harsh and frantic tone, "I love you, Deborah. I don't want to be with anyone else, Deborah. I visit you when I can. Why isn't that enough for you? Just because I can't commit to you, you're going to throw me to the curb?"

After I received the burden of what he actually was trying to communicate, I imploded with the following thoughts. *"Wait, what? Did I just hear that correctly? You can't commit? When were you going to tell me? You had me looking at houses only two weeks ago. What's your game? I thought you were going to propose tonight so we could set a date, elevating our status to include the 'F' word— fiancé."* I thought this but was too numb to say out loud. I thought about screaming to drown out his words but what good would that do? There was nothing I could do to pacify my annoyance.

Maybe he was rejecting me because he saw how sick I got when he drove me to look at houses. I don't do well in a vehicle for any length of time. Since we went so few places he never really witnessed my meltdowns. I had shared my reality many times with him in the past, but having him see it for himself brought it to life. It was a strong possibility that he may not be able to cope with my illness but was in too deep to say so. It doesn't matter that I have always been brutally honest; he chose not to see what was always right in front of him. We were mirror images in that regard.

It is hard being disabled recognizing that I once was able to financially supply my own needs and now not being able to remain in a building long enough to produce my own income.

I had expectations that the love and strength of my partner could keep me functioning. I had to ask myself, when did I allow the other person to have such control over me? I wanted and needed more of him than he was willing to give. I got tired of hearing what he was giving up so he could be with me. "I was supposed to sell hotdogs tonight at the game, but I'd rather be with you." He felt the need to tell me blow-by-blow with every opportunity lost because he was spending time with me. Did he not get that he stabbed a blade deeper into my heart each time he reminded me of what I could no longer do? Did he not think I could hear the resentment in his voice and actions?

I was devoted to this man. Sadly, he didn't see the value of my love, forgiveness and devotion. Those things were not worth their weight in gold in this scenario.

Contemplating me with a strange look of dispassion in his eyes, he ended our relationship. It became a surreal situation. He held an intense look of regret with a hint of unraveling sanity. Thankfully, he reserved judgment of me other than the fact that he said he *tried* to understand my disability.

THAT'S IT. . .you tried to understand? Inside my head, these thoughts were imploding, screaming out loud in the confines of my brain, but the sound of it couldn't funnel to my lips. The reality and raw pain in the words he was conveying were borderline unbearable. The burden weighed on my heart. The thought that this guy who supposedly was "in love" with me couldn't hold up, how would anyone want to be in a committed relationship with me? It is not their sentence, its mine.

It's not rocket science. I can't be around anything electrical or wireless. That hasn't changed since the day Robert and I had met two years earlier. I was honest with him. What happened to the loving guy I met? The one who said we would go through this together? The one who said he would help me get through this winter? He clearly doesn't exist.

He manipulated the conversation to make it appear that I was the one ending it. He clearly had his running shoes on and they were laced and tied at the top. For a few minutes we stood looking at each other in a silent, speechless battle. I stood there in startled shock; everything I was hearing was in opposition of what I believed to be true. I had no choice but to let him go. Spiritually, I envisioned a ball and chain falling away from my ankle. It was yet another response to my request for discernment. It was time to let him go once and for all. I could no longer be fed false promises or false hope.

Recently, I'd read the book entitled "Joni." It is the story of Joni Eareckson Tada, which gave me unbelievable inner strength. She is a quadriplegic who spent more than thirty years in a wheel chair. She shares, in one section of her book, about a love relationship that ended. Her partner walked away, stating he couldn't do this anymore and walked out the door. In her frozen state, all she could do was let the tears flow. She couldn't lift her hands to throw something; she couldn't run after him, she could only sit there and feel the intense emotional pain.

As Robert walked away from me I envisioned Joni sitting in her wheelchair to the left of me. If she could go on after her guy walked out on her, so could I. Outwardly I remained calm however inside I was riddled with confusion but felt it best to restrain my voice. I had to fight against my desire to cling to him. After he left, I released the breath I didn't know I was holding.

His timing to run couldn't have been worse. I had a treatment that day and was exhausted. I put a good front up but had very little to give. I was halfway through my weekly IV treatments and needed all of my strength to accomplish that task for the next several weeks. Two weeks later, Klepto was killed when he was hit by a car. He was the neighborhood dog who guarded my house for a cookie a day. I always knew that his fetish for chasing cars would take him from me one day. True to form, he died doing what he loved best; he just couldn't help himself. Although I hadn't yet learned that he was dead, my spirit knew. I could hear the un-conveyed news in my heart. He was laid to rest on October 17th. The overwhelming impact that these two major losses inflicted was pushing me to the brink of emotional collapse. Just when I thought my heart wasn't capable of breaking any further, the news of Klepto found the last hidden spot left in my heart and shattered its remains. I felt the depth of both losses.

The next six weeks were a blur. I functioned in a fog of despair along with emotional and physical numbness. I couldn't even say the words out loud for weeks for fear that it was true. How did I process this new reality—a dead relationship that once kept me vibrant and hopeful, and a dead dog that once filled my spirit with joy? I prayed God would invade my despondency and release it from my current circumstances. There was nothing further I could do for myself to restore my heart after these profound losses except to hand it over to a higher source and rest it all at the foot of the cross.

Joni's story renewed my faith that there is a bigger, better plan.

Despite the raw pain I felt, I still prayed that Robert's heart and mind would heal so he doesn't repeat the cycle with the next relationship.

I questioned my error of believing him to be my future, my end-of-life partner. The person that I thought I wanted to grow young with. It was difficult to admit to myself that I'd made a mistake, yet again.

For months I searched in my mind for the cause of his look on the brink of insanity. Was it pain? In my humanness, I thought he was led astray by someone else. His breaking off our relationship and blaming me just didn't hold logic.

Then, as if a light bulb came on in my brain, I wondered if he too wasn't suffering from the effects of EMF bombardment. After all, he was silently assaulted at his house and at work with the invisible yet powerful forces of Wi-Fi and EMFs.

Could it be true? Or was it karma? What goes around comes around? He had that same crazed look in his eyes that I did years ago when I had no idea what was happening to me. When all I could do was flee my marriage, not exactly knowing why I needed to run, but running regardless of the consequences.

Although Robert and I weren't married, I observed for the last year of our relationship that he would say one thing yet do another. Was this his true personality or symptoms from a much bigger cause?

Maybe I was grabbing at straws here. After all, it would be much too painful to admit that he just couldn't be who I needed him to be. I'm trying to make sense out of something that makes no sense at all.

People everywhere are affected by the silent killer. Most are completely unaware of the invisible dangers. Even though Robert was armed with the knowledge and awareness of the EMF condition, through the sharing of my experiences, I can only assume he chose to think it couldn't happen to him. He kept upping his game with more and more of the latest technology. When will enough stimulation be enough? Denial is a powerful predicament to be in.

When I think back to the times I shared my EMF experiences with him, I recall him gazing at me with affectionate tolerance. He was appeasing me but never actually got the concept of my reality or what I was trying to convey. This was evidenced in his reactions or non-reactions of the same.

The sad part was that Robert was torn out of my life while I still loved him. It was like burying someone who is alive and won't stay dead. At times he would force his way into my mind. At one time I was so vibrant; so passionately and overwhelmingly alive. Now I felt void and empty. It has taken months to release him, yet at times he still surfaced in my mind re-squashing my spirit all over again. I'm beginning to think that loving someone so passionately, and being in love, must be a mental illness. It's haunting and all-consuming, provoking feelings that don't dissipate overnight. Unfortunately for me, I picked the wrong one to fall for. Robert was bigger than life to me and wasn't an easy guy to forget. God help me; take this burden from me.

Can I be free of resentment and forgive this person who has wronged me? Only with God as my source would that be possible, somehow I have to view this from a higher source—but right now I still felt the need to vent.

When I looked back over how smooth he had been, I concluded that he either wrote the book on how to make a woman fall in love with him or he read one, because he had all the right moves down. He said all the right things that a woman wants to hear. I didn't know how to handle all of his compliments. I felt physically exhilarated as though it wasn't me but I became the exotic spiritual beauty that he seemed to think I was. He had unexpected qualities that drew me in. Robert was easy on the eyes, intelligent, reserved, soft spoken, patient, romantic, and kind. All of the attributes I dreamed of in a life partner. The only thing he didn't have, which would be the most important component was staying power.

Then I asked myself what was lacking in me that I fully cooperated in allowing him to seduce me verbally. He snow-balled me with what I thought were verbal gifts at the time but, in the end, meant nothing. They were simply words meant to entice me. Words like, *"You are so wonderful, Deborah, I won't disappoint you, Deborah, I want to spend the rest of my life with you, Deborah, you are so beautiful, Deborah, I'd rather go nowhere with you than everywhere with anybody else, blah, blah, blah, blah, blah."*

I know this sounds like a woman scorned, because, well, I am a scorned woman. For two years I feel like I've been taken as a fool. I willingly, lovingly, prayed for, cooked for, and planned a future with this man, despite personal struggles with my health. Looking back, I can only surmise that he saw me as a challenge. It was a game to him while I struggled to survive.

I had to remind myself that God doesn't make junk. I know I am perfectly and wonderfully made by God as we all are. We are perfect in God's eyes just as we are, it doesn't matter if we are disabled or not. I stand strong in that knowledge. I thank God for each new day.

As I began to step away from my raw pain and pray, I had to remind myself that God made Robert as well. The difference being Robert is still an unenlightened soul. He is still very much influenced by the world. As the layers of our relationship began to unfold, I spied glimpses of him displaying unhealthy, destructive, tendencies of selfishness and jealousy that could not be denied. Despite those traits, I still loved this man. When jealousy and selfishness reared their ugly heads it made our relationship more challenging and, at times, broke my spirit. I kept hoping God's love, through me, would heal those damaged parts of him. And that his love being poured into me would heal my damaged parts as well.

A true Christian man would lay his life down for his partner. He would promise (and mean it) to love, protect, and cherish her. For reasons undisclosed to me, Robert just wasn't capable of filling those preordained needs in me. He shared that he wasn't a wealthy man, but that excuse was lame at best. He took the coward's way out. He was a coward in the sense that he didn't trust God to make a way for us.

There were so many clues that he wasn't being legit. I guess I chose to be blinded to the truth. The truth would have been too painful. He had no intention of following through on his promises. He was a poser; only pretending to be what I needed. How can I possibly process my unexpressed grief?

All he did was tease and bait my desires, then took away any possibility of fulfilling the long-awaited expectations of all I'd anticipated. How was I to know he was not a sincere guy? Is it too much to expect to be the second most important person in someone else's life; God first, me next?

I had no choice but to put my big girl panties on and walk forward one step at a time.

Doing God's work and living His will made me vulnerable for predators. Discernment has set me free. I know that I can meet and exceed any of life's difficulties because I am filled with faith. God has his loving arms around me. My faith has started to allow me to discern what actions are not *of Him*. This chapter of my life had come to a close. I look beyond my current circumstances and can't wait to see what God has in store for my future.

Ironically, Robert and my story began and ended at the dam. *Damn.*

Now that I have carried on so and told my truth, I recognize there are always two sides to any situation, any story. But after analyzing and praying about it, I see that there may be three sides to this one.

If my love wasn't enough, then I don't think anyone could fill the void in his spirit; at least no earthly person. I do believe if he would open himself up to receive Jesus Christ in His entirety, inviting Him into his vibration, having a relationship with Him, that and only that, will fill his void. No earthly possessions. No amount of money. No other relationship can fill what is lacking. Nothing but the living waters of God can quench his thirst, can satisfy his search but he has to recognize that and want it.

After spilling my heart out onto these pages I stopped, took a deep breath and a giant step back. I prayed about it, yet again. This is what I got. . .I'm far from perfect. I strive to be Christ-like but have fallen so far from that in this relationship. In my humanness after the final break-up of my relationship with Robert, I found myself resorting to all kinds of sin. I judged him. I cursed him. I felt bitterness at his tactics. I was resentful of his worldliness. I felt love, but the weakness of my flesh leaned heavier towards lust. I felt prideful, betrayed, misunderstood, unforgiving, abandoned, rage, and lastly, left behind.

Try as I may I can't seem to stop my mouth from purging explicits. Releasing the raw pain, intense disappointment and loss of what could have been an unbelievable long term relationship if it was Christ based, as I originally was led to believe it was.

Lord, I want to forgive Robert of the offense of abandonment, as you forgave all of my offenses. I need you, Lord, to close the deep wounds engraved in my spirit. Please rip away the raw pain that exists. Restore my joy. Separate me from all this human drama. Help me to not complain about my disappointment to others.

I'm trying to work through the fact that I willingly opened my heart and soul to Robert. I allowed him to skip into my heart, giving him full access in a two-year window of exploration—allowing him to occupy its contents with false hope, only to have him walk away and take it all with him. I didn't take heed to the signs of his fleeting. Some part of me must have needed to believe all the lies he conjured up.

What I'm trying to say is that God must be working behind the scene, He is the third side. Only God can use our circumstances, even our suffering, especially our suffering, to mold us into the gems He strives for us to be. He can take this from us if we surrender it all to Him.

I get that I'm not perfect, just forgiven when I repent of all that I have fallen short on. Being greatly blessed is so much more than I deserve. Forgive me, again, Lord God Almighty, I know that I am a work in progress. And Lord, help me to forgive Robert. I feel you are using this circumstance to refine me and possibly to refine him. After all, I keep asking in prayer to be more Christ-like. How can I accomplish that task if my focus is set on a narcissistic man?

See? There I go again. I'm judging him. Cleanse me of the need to do so. Remove the residual of bitterness that remains in my heart.

Never give up on your dreams. If you are with someone who doesn't support those dreams (regardless of how big or little) you are with the wrong person. Don't settle. Thinking back, we had different dreams, different goals. I guess you could say neither settled; him by choice, me by force.

When I prayed about it again, I recognized God is in control. He is grooming both Robert and I to move in different directions. He wants to use us both for His glory, but we must be willing vessels.

The physical day-to-day bondage of our relationship was severed but I chose to believe we both learned powerful lessons from the experience. It couldn't have been for nothing. My heart ached with the things that were said and the things unsaid. I missed loving him and being loved by him. I missed the life we never had. Sometimes I think I was in love with the idea of being in a love relationship and maybe so was he. Fantasy over. Hopefully when the flames of passion and disappointment subside, we will have grown into better, more refined people in the process.

After all, isn't that what life is all about? Learning and growing?

In our combined brokenness, even after all we'd inflicted on each other, I still had hopes that he would come to his senses and work towards putting the shattered fragments of our hearts back together as one unit. After months of unfulfilled expectations I had to come to the realization that it wasn't meant to be. We were done. But it was still so hard for me to swallow that idea. He left me no choice but to turn to the next page in my life's story. Time to release the limitations this relationship has put on us both.

The question I still cannot seem to answer was, why are we so afraid of each other? In our vulnerable state, we did more harm in the long run than good.

It feels like I have bled onto these pages a vulnerable opening of myself. More intimate than even I was aware of.

I surrender it all and put this relationship, which has become toxic, at the foot of the cross, yet again. *Amen.*

It took several months, but acceptance was starting to take hold. I got the joy of the Lord back. Sometimes we have to take a couple of steps back to finally move forward.

I can't wait to see what God has in store for my future.

Thank you, Lord, for not abandoning me when I fell short and needed you the most. No one can take your place.

Valentine's Day 2018

Lady Almina

My heart is overflowing with a good theme
I recite my composition concerning the King
My tongue is the pen of a ready writer.
Psalm 45:1

I t stood to reason that the next character to emerge for my dam ministry would be Lady Almina. She is a lady in waiting. . .waiting to see what God has in store for her next.

Six week's worth of anticipation, involving the creation and presentation of the character Lady Almina and the day has finally arrived for her to come out.

As I was preparing for the royal debut, hair in curlers, no make-up, I heard a knock on, what I pretended to be, my dressing room door. It was a special delivery. I opened the door to view the most gorgeous bouquet of roses, displayed beautifully with the largest red bow imaginable. They were stunning. I couldn't give any energy to the source in which they came since my focus needed to be on helping others this day. My interpretation was, the show must go on!

Despite the dreariness of the rainy day, prayers were answered for a window of opportunity with no rain from 2:30 p.m. until dark.

This day Lady Almina will walk the dam at Lake Chatuge, in the hope of bringing joy, love, and peace to those she encounters.

It was somewhat of a shock to her system to have so many rejections—people who skirted around her, avoided her or ran past

307

her royal majesty. Those were the people who needed the loving message the most, but they weren't open to it. I sometimes forget how fearful people have become due to the toxicity they receive from watching the news via TV, radio, and the internet. I live free of those negative sources, so my approach to people is at times Disney-like, one of pure unconditional love.

Visitors straggled in and Lady Almina prepared herself for each new encounter; never knowing quite what the response would be. Her heart was pure and, for those who would stop long enough for her to perform her spiel, they were able to see and feel the peace and love of God that she so willingly offered.

Some of her regular dam friends went out of their way to acknowledge her efforts, openly embracing her exuberant, animated character. One couple and their son stopped their bikes, jumped off, and took turns hugging Lady Almina repeatedly as the joy of what they were seeing registered. Two long-distance bikers circled her in playful disbelief of what they had stumbled upon. Provoking her with, "What do we have here?"

Lady Almina had prayed that there be at least one soul who could be touched deeply by her actions. A gentleman, preoccupied in thought, skin greyish in color, body language displaying a cry for help in its hunched manner, crossed the dam, peering at her as she blurted her spiel, all the while looking at her in disbelief gaining distance away from her in a circle like motion. She thought he thought her a lunatic. But to her surprise, on his way back across the dam, he stopped within three feet of her, looked directly into her eyes and said, "You have no idea what you have done for me today, thank you."

Several people, families mostly, thanked her for her desire to make a difference. One couple added candy to the stash of handouts, the wife made sure she told Lady Almina how much Lady Almina was needed. That was an unexpected blessing and uplift to contin-ueforward. The wife didn't know it, but her kind words were greatly needed that day.

Photo credit Lord Richard and Lady Lynn

The most heartwarming surprises were in the wide-eyed, precious faces of the young children who peeked at the heiress in wonder; some openly ran up to Lady Almina to embrace her in an open display of affection. One young lady, guestimated at eight years old, whispered, "God Bless You," after hugging the storybook character in a tight embrace. Lady Almina's response, *"He just did."* A close male friend wandered across the dam and looked everywhere except at Lady Almina, he seemed in disbelief of what she conveyed. He seemed embarrassed for her. He clearly will never look at her the same way again. He had never experienced this side of her.

People with pets asked for a photo with their dog. Cameras were flashing from afar. It was the closest thing to being a celebrity that would be realized in this lifetime. What fun! I had to come to grip with not participating with others in public buildings so I created my own world as a way to reach out to others with God's love.

Lady Almina got two invites to local churches. Oh, if only she weren't afflicted by Wi-Fi—what a show she could put on! If only it were possible to stay in a building long enough.

Her spiel:

The most amazing thing happened

I was in a storybook on page 7 to be exact (7 being a God number)

When suddenly, someone turned the page abruptly and I fell out of the book

And I landed here on the dam.

I'm lost.

Then I remembered that Jesus is the way!

Happy Valentine's Day!

As the day continued on, one curious gentleman, another dam friend, asked if there even was a Valentine's Day in 1890, the year Lady Almina claimed to have come from. That was a very good question. So after some research it was conveyed that in the year 269AD, St. Valentine came to be.

The origin of this holiday for the expression of love really wasn't romantic at all—at least not in the traditional sense.

An emperor Claudius prohibited the marriage of young people; he based it on the hypothesis that unmarried soldiers fought better than married soldiers because married soldiers might be afraid of what might happen to them or their wives or families if they died.

A guy name Valentine, a Roman Priest, encouraged the young to marry within the Christian Church, so he secretly married them. Valentine was eventually caught, imprisoned and tortured for performing marriage ceremonies against command of Emperor Claudius the second.

One of the men who came to judge Valentine was called Asterius, whose daughter was blind. Supposedly Valentine prayed with and healed the young girl. Asterius was so astonished he became a Christian as a result.

Valentine was sentenced to a three-part execution of a beating, stoning, and finally, a gruesome decapitation all for his stand for Christian marriage.

As the story goes the last words he wrote were in a note to Asterius's daughter. He inspired today's romantic missives by signing it "from your Valentine." Not exactly what we think about with today's flowers, candy, red hearts, and romance.

Back to Lady Almina. The day was coming to a close, maybe another hour of daylight. Lady Almina was deeply touched when one of her Christian brothers recognized she was on her own, vulnerable to her surroundings, and only dribbles of people were coming and going. He made it a point, in front of a gentleman who had stopped to visit, letting her know he would be sitting in his truck until 5:30 p.m. until which time he needed to pick up his wife; also a mutual friend.

He was letting Lady Almina know he had her back. That is the love of Christ. That is the whole point of God's love. As brothers and sisters we need to love and care for others around us.

That loving gesture from a brother made Valentine's Day all the more special.

Amen.

Pluck: What does it mean?

Be strong and of good courage
Do not fear nor be afraid of them;
For the Lord your god, He is the One who goes with you.
He will not leave you nor forsake you.
Deuteronomy 31:6

At first, I found offense in the word *pluck*, being ignorant of its meaning. Then I discovered that the American Heritage Dictionary refers to the word "pluck" as a verb, meaning resourceful courage and daring in the face of difficulties; spirit. It also means to remove or detach by grasping and pulling abruptly.

As I thought about the different meanings, I began to see clearly why I have been graced with the nickname, "PLUCK."

After writing this book and reviewing the sequences of events that led me to today I concluded that I was plucked out corporate America, plucked out of the lifestyle I took so much pride in maintaining, plucked out of my condo, plucked away from all the people who I'd held so dearly in my heart, plucked out of church buildings, plucked out of public, plucked away from mainstream society, and most recently, plucked out of a relationship I thought was long term. It's true. It took resourceful courage to continue on.

As humans, we go through life experiencing many changes. To keep pace we find ourselves being plucked from one situation to another, or at least that is how my history has played out.

To stand up for what one believes to be true takes courage—profound, resourceful courage—especially when put in the predicament of being a canary; a silent sufferer. It is not easy to remain vertical when everything you've treasured got plucked away. It becomes difficult at times to not let other people's opinions define me.

Having been diagnosed long before the knowledge of EMF surfaced to the general public's eye, I took a lot of guff. It didn't help that I thought I lost my mind to have such strong reactions to my surroundings. I didn't understand. The terms "chemically sensitive" and "electromagnetic fields" were foreign to me.

I may be naïve to think that my book can make a difference, but I am pursuing the goal of trying to help you and others before things you treasure most are plucked away.

No one plans a major setback; it just sneaks up on you. But I believe that old saying, that knowledge is power.

Educate yourself about the effects of EMF. Don't be kept in the dark. Use resourceful courage to protect yourself and your loved ones. Pray to your higher power. The one thing I am certain of is that nothing can pluck us out of His hand.

Be a Pluck. Don't give up!

Don't give up when life throws you a curve ball. Whether you lost your job, your home, your health, a loved one, a partner, or gotten passed over for the much-deserved promotion you were waiting on. Maintain resourceful courage; show the world you have what it takes, you have pluck, let your new nickname reflect PLUCK as well!

In Closing

And my God shall supply all of your need according to
His riches in glory by Christ Jesus.
Philippians 4:19

My way of life seems absurd to most. But it only makes sense to me to play out the hand that life dealt me.

I have learned to be grateful for what I can still do. I have the joy of the Lord, although that has been tested repeatedly. To date, now eight years into my setback, I can see and hear and walk and talk as long as I remain within my safe zone, providing me a non-reactive state of being.

Some see my world as a prison sentence. I see it as a way to survive.

Although my outings are few, I am able to go to the local rural post office every week or two to retrieve my P.O. Box mail. I recognize, through trial and error, that I have about eight minutes, due to the adverse reactions I sustain from the fluorescent lighting and other exposures so I do not dawdle.

I still manage to drive to the refuse department mere minutes away, once a week, to rid my household garbage. It is getting harder to time it when the least amount of people are there and the diesel equipment is turned off. I don't do well around either. The attendants know that and fully cooperate in turning off machinery when they see me approach. They go above and beyond to accommodate me.

Thankfully Ingles grocery store has reassigned a shopper to me. About every three weeks I make a list of basic needs that they deliver.

My big outing is going to the Lake Chatuge Dam to walk or swim, depending on the season. Most of the regulars at the dam know to turn off their cell phones if they want to strike up a conversation with me. If they don't remember, it is my job to remind them. The price is simply too high if turning off a cell phone goes unnoticed. I walk the dam when the least amount of people are there, or ground away from others.

In my toxic state, I simply cannot tolerate further exposure. Just because we can't see the invisible rays doesn't mean they don't exist.

Most likely if I am not at the dam, in the summer I am camping somewhere for relief—either on one of the islands or at the Park and Rec. In the winter I merely try to cope indoors by turning the breakers off.

Having the refrigerator in the garage and the breakers off in the house gives me some relief, but camping is the ultimate comfort.

I have been told I am taking my EMF status to the extreme. This was not said to be malicious; it was merely an observation. The person commenting is currently unaffiliated and doesn't suffer like I do, at least not yet. Hopefully, he will never have to find out.

As the technology ups its game, I shudder to think what that will mean. If the silent killer is this painful now—what will be the outcome as new, more improved, more powerful signals emerge? I would be lying if I didn't tell you how frightened this knowledge makes me feel at times.

The consolation to my fears is that, whether I am able to survive in my physical body or not, I still win. I know that I will be transformed to a better place spiritually when I can no longer sustain myself here. I know without a shadow of a doubt that heaven awaits me.

I have had to do whatever it takes to get relief and to heal. So if kayaking out to Penland Island for four days to get relief and two days at home to repack supplies is my course of action, then so be it. That is exactly what I did the first two years in Hayesville.

That theory worked for a while before the invasion of multiple new towers around the lake. I need a new plan if I am going to be successful in healing my brain and body.

If I focused on the facts that follow, I would clearly lose my mind. I am sixty-two years young, yet find it nearly impossible to maintain a relationship due to my restrictions. I cannot be employed because I cannot maintain my composure, my muscle status, long enough to be in a building. I cannot walk the streets due to exposure from the power lines, so I seek out places free of power lines.

It is impossible to be in the presence of other people who aren't willing or able to leave electronics behind. . .whether it be due to lack of knowledge or simply an unwillingness to disconnect or believe in the adverse effects. Cell phones, hearing aids, pacemakers, laptops, tablets, oxygen machines—anything with a frequency is my enemy.

I can no longer travel, fly, go to a library, to an indoor church, a restaurant, movie theatre, or sleep in a hotel. All realities I once knew and, quite frankly, I took for granted without even realizing it.

I would lose my mind if my focus were on my limitations. I choose to rise above it all. My focus is on what I can do, not what I can no longer do.

I had hopes that my EMF condition was a short-term problem. However, now eight years into it, I knew I was in a different reality; this wasn't just a bad dream, it was a nightmare. Sometimes I wish I could push CTRL-ALT-DELETE and make it all go away. But then again I realize that through my setback I found my voice.

At this point with my EMF issues, it is not possible to have the same "hooked up, connected" life style as everybody else. However, it is possible to have a different, better quality of life, a life free of all of the electronic distractions; a life that encourages direct contact with nature with God as our guidance. A life filled with joy. God is the only wireless connection that won't cause discomfort.

I try to live in the present moment. Otherwise, fear could rear its ugly head into my psyche. Just the thought of the rate in which the electronic age is progressing is enough to put me into an emotionally comatose state. I don't allow that even though, at times, it feels like I am running out of places to hide, places left that are free of Wi-Fi. I pray for the day that signs say Wi-fi Free instead of Free Wi-fi.

Once all of the worldly distractions of entertainment are removed you are left facing yourself. I feel as though I have gained through losing. Most people are running so hard and fast it is as if they think they can out run themselves. I use to be one of those people. You can't outrun God. Eventually He gets your attention. I feel like He plucked me out of Corporate America and set me down on Penland

Island until I got it right. You have my attention, Lord. Use me. Thank you for contentment just as I am.

If you are disabled in any way, always remember to do what you can do and don't worry about what you can't. We are precious, perfectly and wonderfully made, in God's eyes.

Words are powerful. I choose to release negative words and thoughts, replacing them with positive ones that heal and renew me. I choose to release old resentments so I can embrace new loving relationships through the power of forgiveness. I speak loving, life-giving words into my spirit. I speak healing words to my body, I bless my body, I praise it for its wonderful, amazing works; it's healing properties. Giving gratitude is healing. Adding humor is healing. I am grateful as I remember to NEVER give up! That's why people have called me "Pluck." Although I may not be cured of the EMF sensitivities, I am healed from the emotional wounds that held me captive for so many years. It has been a slow, gradual improvement of health. I am whole. I have the joy of the Lord by living in the guarded world that I have had to create.

I am empowered to share God's love with anyone I cross paths with. I've never met a stranger. I wrote this book because I have a profound love of people. I care about what happens to you, your families, and friends. It is my hope that by sharing my story it will serve as a wakeup call on two levels. One: to help prevent toxic exposure to you and yours by limiting the time you subject yourself to electronics, and two: to bring a heightened awareness of Christ. I don't want anyone else to have to suffer the loss of health and well-being the way that I did due to this man-made illness. I pray you will learn valuable information that will help you both in your walk in the world and on your spiritual journey.

I pray you recognize that this could happen to anyone, even you. Denying its existence will not shield you from its toxicity. It is my hope that you will read this book and pass it along as a learning tool about environmental illnesses. A page in the back of the book offers a place to write your name, city, state and country. After you have read this book I pray you will recognize its value and pass it along to others. Passing this book along will serve as your contribution to bringing public awareness to this EMF man-made disorder and to the love of Christ that sustains us.

I give praise and thanks to my Lord and Savior, Jesus Christ, for sustaining me on my journey. There truly is a God. If it were not for my belief in God, I could not have survived. God is my wireless connection; invite Him to be yours!

I start each day acknowledging Him. I take whatever time it takes to read through my daily readings and lift my ongoing prayer lists to Him. My favorite readings are from Sarah Young's "Jesus Calling" and/or "Jesus Always." I look up the coordinating scriptures and let the scriptures permeate my soul.

We have no control over the environment. The man-made towers, computers, and cell phones cause a bombardment to our senses in this electronic age. But we do have control over our spiritual safety.

Put down those cell phones, disconnect, and connect to the One who truly matters. LOOK UP before it's too late! Acknowledge Jesus Christ and the higher power that exists.

Humble yourself to repent. I know a lot of people shun the word *repent*. I was one of them. But it is a simple process. Just admit that you are truly sorry for those things you did or said that didn't glorify God.

Wouldn't you rather pray to a loving God and later find out He is real, than to not pray and miss out on His glory? It's your choice.

Be open and flexible to move in the path that God leads you. It will lead you to your highest good.

If you don't know Jesus and you want to invite him into your life, it is as simple as saying the following prayer:

> *Dear Lord,*
> *I believe that You are the son of God. I believe that You died and rose again from the dead. I repent to You that I am less than perfect and that I have done things in my humanness that didn't always honor You. I invite You into my heart and into my life. Amen.*

You can talk to Jesus like He is your best friend and confident, because He is if you will allow him to be. It is the energy of God that fuels and empowers me to live boldly, exciting me to take action to live with purpose. I trust Him for the strength to follow my goals.

It is easy to trust Him when things are going well. I challenge you to trust Him in the darkness; that is the meaning of true faith. God bless you and I pray you will let Jesus take the wheel!

> *The Lord bless you and keep you;*
> *The Lord make His face shine upon you,*
> *And be gracious to you;*
> *The Lord lift up His countenance upon you,*
> *And give you peace.*
> *Numbers 6:24-26*

> *Jesus turned and seeing her said,*
> *"Take heart daughter, your faith has made you well."*
> *Mathew 9:22*

My daily readings include the following prayer that I use to glorify Him:

> *I acknowledge and affirm that my body is a temple that houses You, Lord, God Almighty.*
> *I forgive myself for all the ways I may not have found worth in or honored my body in the past.*
> *As I open my mind and heart to You, Christ, my conscious awareness of other people and things are enhanced.*
> *I am unashamed of my humble reliance and total dependence on You, and I place my total trust and confidence in Your hands.*
> *My heart is filled with appreciation, a deeper love, and serenity as a result of Your constant presence.*
> *I repent that I am less than perfect, that I need to release old expectations of myself and strive to "just be" in Your presence.*
> *You are my precious treasure, my Master. You light my way. You are really all I ever needed.*
> *I thank You, God, for loving me when I felt unlovable. In the profound deep pit of my brokenness*

You nurtured and restored me. No one can take Your place.

Jesus, Lord God Almighty, You are my heart's deepest desire. You are everything to me. Healing is continuously taking place in me, through You, all the time. Every cell in my body is being restored as a result of Your unfailing, undying presence.

Thank You, Lord, for Your hand in renewing my mind, and body, and restoring my soul. I adore you.

With abundant Love in Your name,
Deborah

A note About the Author

And whatever things you ask in prayer,
believing, you will receive.
Mathew 21:22

Deborah Hyatt is a sixty-two-year old, divorced, born-again, Christian female. She is disabled from the profound effects that EMFs have havocked on her body, mind and spirit. She prefers you say *compromised* rather than *disabled* when referring to her condition. "Differently-abled" would be even a better choice of words to describe her condition as meticulously described by the nurse practitioner that cares for her.

Prior to her setback, Deborah spent much of her life working in different corporations in administrative, coordinator roles. However, she openly admits that her best, most rewarding, yet challenging roles have been being a proud mother to her two now-adult children. She taught them freedom of expression as they were growing up and she kids that they took it up a couple of notches in their flamboyant outward appearances, reflected through their very artistic tattoos and creative hair styles. They both live life to the fullest. Praise God!

Deborah currently resides in the rural mountains of North Carolina in a small town she lovingly refers to as Hooterville. She moved to Hayesville due to the town's boasting of being twenty years behind the times. To her surprise, six months after relocating to the town, Wi-Fi was introduced. Unable financially to relocate, yet again, she makes the best of it by avoiding town and group gatherings. To escape the effects of Wi-Fi, she spends most of her time camping on the nearby islands on Lake Chatuge. It is there that she found the much needed physical relief from the effects of society. If you ask her she will tell you that she found her "Happy Place" with God's lead.

Although healing is being realized by taking precautions to avoid Wi-Fi and electromagnetic fields, her life remains in a private sector still unable to participate in public gatherings. She is grateful for all she can do and rarely focuses on what she can't.

Her writing was used as both a tool to enlighten the public of the severity long term EMF can afflict, as well as a journal to shed the experience into writing. Hoping somehow that writing would remove the burden she felt to share with so many.

Of all her prayers the one that resurfaces the most is that no one else should ever have to suffer the pain, humiliation and isolation that this debilitating illness causes.

It has been said by one of her friends that:
> She doesn't have faith, she lives faith.
> She doesn't believe in God, she believes God.
> She listens to God, doesn't just sing about wanting to listen.
> She follows the SPIRIT of God
> which led her to her happy place on and near Lake Chatuge.

She is filled with spiritual contentment as reflected by the joy of the Lord that shines through her. She trusts God and believes she is doing exactly what God has called her to do by sharing her story and glorifying His name in the process.

She hopes her story will help others to be proactive in guarding their health and give hope to those who are already afflicted. She wants *Pluck* to become a household word. Be courageous. Have pluck. Be a Pluck! Never give up! The author wishes to thank you for taking the time to read her story and would love to hear from you. Snail mail is the only method of communication for her at this time. Sorry, she is still unable to use email. God Bless you.

Please send any correspondence to:
Deborah Hyatt
C/o Pluck
P.O. Box 1062
Hayesville, NC 28904

An Attitude of Gratitude

Rejoice always, pray without ceasing,
In everything give thanks;
For this is the will of God in Christ Jesus for you.
1 Thessalonians 5:16-18

I choose an attitude of gratitude. Like most people, I have endured through the pain, losses, disappointments, betrayals, and hardships of everyday life. The difference being, I have arrived at a place of profound joy. As a result of living through heartache, my attitude has softened considerably. Looking around, I see that many people are stuck in their grief. I am overflowing with an attitude of gratitude that has been engraved in my heart. I read somewhere that attitude is more important than facts. It is more important than the past, than education, than money, than circumstances, than failures, than successes, than what other people think or say or do. It is more important than appearance, gifts, or skill. It will make or break a love relationship. . .a company. . .a church. . .a friendship. . .a home.

We have a choice every day regarding the attitude we will embrace for that day. We cannot change our past. We cannot change the way other people will act. We cannot change the inevitable. The only thing we can do is adjust our attitudes, be aware of our thoughts. I am convinced that life is 10% what happens to us and 90% how we react to it. We can change our world and change the outcome of things just by taking charge of our attitude.

An attitude of gratitude is healing. As a result of gratitude, some of the numbness in my soul has begun to wear off. It is nurturing to be grateful for all aspects of our lives. As I pushed through the darkness I was in, I reflect back and choose to acknowledge all of the positive things and wonderful people I have to be grateful for. The list seems manic because it goes on and on.

Along with that, I am thankful for the hidden blessing and the miraculous countless ways joy has been instilled in my life. Had I not had my setback I wouldn't be available at the dam for the many people who have crossed my path. They have enhanced my life and taught me about the many different kinds of challenges that we all face in this lifetime.

When we search our hearts and look around with eyes filled with the spirit of God we see, truly see, what has been right in front of us and has been there all the time. With God's guidance, I am able to rise above my circumstances and "just be" in His presence.

I am grateful for fresh starts and new beginnings. For finding my happy place, enabling me to enjoy the healing waters of Lake Chatuge, Penland Island, and my home and Sanctuary. I have never enjoyed or appreciated the outdoors like I do now. It's a whole new life. It's a whole new awareness.

I am grateful for the ability to be creative and the sensitivity I have acquired for others that my disability enhanced.

I am grateful for the domestic animals and wildlife, of all of God's creatures.

I am grateful for the profound love of being raised by a mother and a father, for being Daddy's little girl. I am grateful for the ability to be a daughter, a mother, a sister, a friend, worshipper, and mostly grateful for being the daughter of a King, the Lord Jesus. I am grateful for having the faith to receive salvation. I am profoundly grateful for my Bible; it opened my eyes to the Truth.

I am grateful for the right to vote—even though that has to be by snail mail. I am extremely grateful for winning my social security disability case, enabling me an income to be able to feed myself. I am ever so grateful for the ability to eat, sing and dance (even if that means without music) and swim. I am grateful for my kayak, for all campsites everywhere, hiking trails, and walking sticks.

I am profoundly grateful to my loving, devoted family for their endless support, especially when none of us had any idea the magnitude of what had happened to me or what was yet to come. They never gave up on me. They continued to love me unconditionally throughout the course of my illness. I love you all and am most beholden for your love and support.

The reason I carry on so when it comes to being grateful is because, if you find yourself in a slump, look around. We have so many things to be grateful for.

To my earthly father, my daddy, I honor you daily by keeping you alive in my thoughts. Life hasn't been the same since your passing in 1975. On some level I will always be daddy's little girl. Our love is not bound to this earth.

To my mother who loves her children with a passion, despite the dysfunction that exists among us. There is no love like a mother's love. My mother endlessly poured love in my direction by any means possible. During the days when my using a phone was not possible I could still feel her love via prayers and snail mail. It didn't matter that she was on dialysis three times a week. She always asked how I was doing, putting my condition ahead of her own. Mom has been my biggest fan throughout the wellness and writing process. She always encouraged me by saying she wants the first signed copy. Your belief, and sometimes disbelief, in me got me through the composing process of writing. She once told me she was holding on just to see how my life played out. She was convinced my life would heal, and repeatedly tried to convince me of the same stating "everything will fall into place." The first finished copy is yours, Mom. Thank you for your undying love and your faith in me.

My sister Candace poured continuous emotional, financial, and spiritual support into me. With her nursing background, she believed in me when the mainstream medical system didn't. She made frequent visits when I lived in New York State, assessing me with the keen eye of her profession. She provided companionship when I needed it the most. It was comforting to know she had my back. Sis, you were my strength when I had nothing left to offer. You refueled my spirit, reminding me often of who I was and what I am capable of. Having both been born June babies we understand each other more than most. We get the Gemini conflict. I treasure you. I cannot imagine my life without you in it.

My brother Chris lovingly known as Badder, and his wife Jeannine, lovingly known as Neene, selflessly gave me a place to retreat on their secluded fifty acres surrounded by undeveloped forest land. They, again, offered me retreat on their farm in West Virginia where I found solace in my tent. A special thanks to Chris for his upbeat persona and infectious smile that he displayed every day that I was with him—despite whatever he was dealing with in his own life. The healing from his laughter and smiles were contagious. Badder, I will always be grateful to you for challenging me to write my story. You planted that seed. I took the risk. It was your confidence in me that made it flourish. Your no-nonsense can-do attitude set a flame under me. You relit my fire. I simply love you. Despite your black and white views on life, you rose above that, not having facts laid out before you and believed in me regardless. You didn't know what was wrong with me, but you stood by me, believed in me, empowered me to move towards wellness. Neene, I so enjoy witnessing you play the role of the farmer's wife, after all Green Acres IS the place to be. You were both in tune to me and always seemed to know when to throw me a lifeline, emotionally and financially. Thank you for loving me and blessing me in so many ways.

To my older, worldly, brother David, for his brutally honest assessment of me. When I told him I was sensitive to cell phones and Wi-Fi, he blurted out something that sounded like, "You're screwed!" As painful as it was to hear the vulgarity of those words— they were, in fact, an honest assessment of my situation and a correct observation of my predicament, as if I didn't already know that. As a Christian woman, I like to think I'm compromised, even the word disabled sounds like a curse word to my ears.

To Trish, looking into your eyes reflects a mirror image that cannot be denied. You are in my heart and prayers, and will remain there. Some bonds just can't be tampered with. I simply love you. Your unconditional love for me emanates from your spirit. You are an amazing lady who I am proud to call my sister.

To my ex-husband Eric for graciously seeing to our children's needs when I couldn't, for rescuing me years ago from a horrific situation when I didn't know I needed rescuing. Thank you. I loved you the best I knew how, I'm sorry it wasn't enough.

To my grown children, Derrick and Erica, for knowing something was critically wrong, but loving and emotionally supporting me through the learning process of finding out exactly what it was.

For giving me positive feedback when the world wasn't feeding me positive. Thank you for being there for me when I wasn't capable of being available to you. I know it had to be scary witnessing me as I continued to disconnect. I'm sorry for all the times I couldn't be available to you, especially during the two years I was unable to use a phone to be connected to you. . .to hear your voices. Although the geographical distance keeps us apart, you are both tattooed on my heart. I love you both to the moon and back a trillion times over.

Derrick, YOU ARE Mr. Amazing. I'm impressed with your take-charge, can-do outlook on life. Life threw a hardball, you got hit upside the head with it, but came through stronger and better than before. I believe you found yourself in the process. I love that you are not afraid to express yourself through your art, your corporate position, your partnership at the gym. Your workouts at thirty-six years old is something that most people wouldn't even attempt at twenty. You totally rock!

Erica, not only have you grown in leaps and bounds as a young woman, but you have overcome many obstacles. I am so proud of your take-charge attitude. Being an Office Manager is no light task; you make it sound easy. I am so grateful for the time we spent together while I was out of society in New York State. That time span was healing and made up for all the mother/daughter challenges we had during your teen years. I am so thankful and proud of all that you are and all that you do. Besides your busy schedule, you managed to remain drop-dead gorgeous. How do you do it all?

To Julie and Peter, for your endless love and concern. Thank you for following my journey through life. You will never know how much it meant to me that you drove from Connecticut to North Carolina to visit and to see for yourself where I ended up and that I was safe. Thank you, I love you.

To Cynthia and Roland, I apologize for not making it to your home on Thanksgiving. I was slipping fast back then and didn't recognize why it was so hard to accomplish anything or follow through on the promise made.

Cynthia, you were a major positive influence in my life. I will always remember you as the best boss ever, my role model in the workplace, and my mentor as a friend. Not a day goes by where I don't miss you. I pray you are well.

To my Aunt Edna, for upholding me with your warm, loving, continuous letters of compassion. Your confidence in me never wavered. I am so blessed to be the recipient of the love that God has instilled in you. Despite all that you deal with in your immediate family, you always find time to connect. I love you. I'll treasure our tea time forever.

To my blessed buddy, Miss Laura, my sister in Christ who resides in Alaska. You never gave up on me. It is times like this that we find out who are true friends are, and a sister you are. Thank you for encouraging me with scripture and old-fashioned letter writing when no other means of communication was possible. For reconnecting by landline when our talks were brief. For your heartfelt, endless projected prayers of healing. For listening in ways that no one else could. For knowing who I am and loving me anyway. You rock, girlfriend! You are truly a friend for life, because let's face it—you know too much! Only you can appreciate when I say, "Who's Pablo and bad bye."

To Jack and Louise, my brother and sister in Christ and my mentors. We met at our mutual church in Asheville, NC. Your continued love and support through prayers, letters, Bible Studies, and photos kept me in check. Your love never ceased. I am in awe of the two of you. You are amazing. Despite all that you deal with in your own lives, you always found time to acknowledge me. I adore you both. Louise, you may be legally blind, but you see better than anyone I know. Your vision takes me back at times. You set a strong example of doing what you can do and don't worry about what you can't. Mere words could never describe how I feel about you. I have no doubt God has always been in the mix of our relationship. I love and adore you both. Thank you for believing in me.

To Pastor Bob and Carol for your love, visits, and support through the process. It has taken me three more years of healing, since the day you presented the pinwheel as a gift to me from the two of you and Jack and Louise. The gift I proudly displayed in my yard. I can finally look in its direction and tolerate the movement of the wheels—prior to now, that type of movement would have sent me into a tailspin. I get profound pleasure from its colorful spokes reeling in the breeze. Thank you.

To my condo family: Teresa, Ruth, John, Cliff and Marie, Dale and Janice, Dr Dick and Sue, Phil and Dorothy, thank you for all of the wonderful and less than wonderful memories; I miss you all terribly. We were definitely family during the years we lived side by side. As with any family there is always love and conflict. I'm thankful we had an abundance of love. You all remain in my prayers.

To T, for opening my eyes, for blessing me on the Texas trip and being supportive until I could no longer be who you needed me to be in a friend. You remain on my prayer list.

In memory of Ruth, who persevered with me every single step of the way until her life was cut short abruptly. You are sincerely missed.

To my long-ago work family, Tonya, Sheila, Linda, Jackie, Carl, Jesse, Barbara, Ann, Theresa, Frantz, and Paul, I know there are so many more people not mentioned, but forgive me when I say you know who you are. Sadly, the name part of my memory bank appears to be wiped clean, but not entirely deleted; your faces remain but your names escape me. I'll always felt regret that my health deteriorated so quickly I never got the opportunity to say goodbye. I look forward to our paths crossing again one day. In the meantime, know that you are loved and missed dearly.

To my Asheville Church family, Pastor James and Judy, for loving me the best you could. If I didn't know what was happening to me, I can see how it would be confusing to you. You all remain on my prayer lists and in my heart. I miss you all.

To Sylvia, I'm so sorry my life became too difficult for you to bare. Never a day passes that I don't think of you. You will always remain on my prayer list. I love you enough to respect your wishes and let you go. You are missed. I pray for a miracle healing so I can come visit you as a whole person instead of the little bit I could offer you in the past.

To Davey, the only reason I giggled when you said *you had three words for me* was because you had those words from me at hello—unconditionally. I wish I understood my illness better at the time so we could have made a clean break, instead of the lingering wait for me to get well. I had hopes that you knew the seriousness of my condition and would come for me anyway. Despina loves you and wants only good things for you. Live your life to the fullest. You have a big heart. You remain on my prayer list.

To Marion, my therapist while I was in Asheville, for your love and support during a major transition period in my life. You had no way of knowing my condition would worsen to the degree that it did. Thank you for believing in me and guiding me along the way. You are missed.

To Joska, for your visits, for researching online since I was unable to, for your heartfelt advice in trying to protect me from the elements, for all of the fabulous ballroom dances we shared when I could still dance. Promise me you will never stop dancing. You give joy to a lot of women with your playfulness and dancing abilities. We have a friendship that has weathered the throws of life. Thank you for believing in me.

To Owen and his wife Virginia at the Park and Recreation, for their care and concern when I tented there for the month of October in 2013, and subsequent stays after that. You made me feel like I was right at home. Owen, you were the first person I really got to know upon arrival to Hayesville. I figured if the folks around there were half the man you are then I'm in the right place. . .I'm home. May God continue to bless you and your family for all that you do for so many.

To all of my dam friends and acquaintances, I am grateful to you all and treasure the stories and fellowship we share. I am grateful for friends in passing, long-term friends, and people of all walks of life, people in general. I was able to go through my ongoing prayer log and came up with the following names: Henry, wife Cornelia, son Matt, dog Taco, Butch, Bob, Bobbie, Kim, Clark, Robert, Gary and his two precious miniature kids in dog suits, Tara, Gabriel, Elaine, Karen, Andrew, Pam, Dan, Mary Ester, "Grasshopper" Dennis, Stephanie, Cherie, Jan, Cindy, Linda and Ben, Judy and Tim, Joan—the author of poetry, Jo and David, Ginny and Herman, Mari and George, Charlene, Charlotte, Keith, April, Tommy, Luke, Missy, Dusty, Paul and Danielle, Donna, Ana, Craig—a brother, Julie, Laurie, Anna, Shawn, Gena, Nell, Dwayne, Carolyn and David, Clark and Barb, Marie and dog Precious, Big Rob, Alison, Dave and dog, Richard and Lynn, Bernadette, Frasier, Veronica, Jim and Cathy (I miss you both dearly), Larry, Judy, Pat, Aiden, James and Luisa, Paul and Cheryl, Winy, George and Joanne, Lynn, Susan, Christopher, Mandy, Maria—a loving young mother and daughter Kimberly, a very special young lady; Lois, David and Clark (brothers), Sonya who works in Electronic Marketing, Tyler, Med student, Ed, Dude, Father Neal and wife Susan, Velma and baby Rupa, Donny, Donna, Alvin, Mabel, Jenny and Richard, Kay, Tom with his German Shepherd, June, Louis, Ann, Gordon, Steve on jet ski, Lynn, Stacey, Haden and Piper, Carmen, Bubba and Michelle, Avery, Spencer, Brantley, Heidi, Ray, Scott, Mary and Corey, Leo, Loretta and Neal, Sharon and Frank, Jim and Bella, Gary, Darren, Robin, Regina and Harley, Myleigh, Jeff, Ellen, and Susi, and to all those whose names have escaped my conscious memory, but you know who you are, thank you for blessing me with your presence; you have enhanced my life.

To Ted for being a really great friend and brother. Thank you for playing chauffer when I couldn't drive myself to the doctors. You did a really good job of pretending to love me when I asked you to. I know God has someone very special in mind for your future. God bless you.

To John and Maria, for the strong connection our lives made to one another in just a couple of months. The summer of 2015, when you visited me at my campsite on Lake Chatuge will always hold a special place in my heart as the best summer of my life. It was the beginning of some real healing. John, your loving advice and wisdom about pressure points and positive thinking remains useful and in my demeanor, after all we are all "Outstanding!" Maria, I missed you like nobody's business when you moved away, yet again. We just *get* each other. I am so thankful for the time we had together. I love you both dearly.

To Robert, my dam ex-boyfriend, your endless run to Ingles had been a blessing when I needed something in a pinch. Although you never really understood the magnitude of what I dealt with, I give you a standing ovation for trying. Your carefree attitude had helped me at times to lighten up when I became locked in gear with my battle to survive. Although we want to believe that love is enough, with our worlds so far apart, it would take a miracle to co-habit. In any case, the time we spent together was a learning experience, with moments I will treasure in my memory bank forever. I miss what was never allowed to flourish. One more thing, "There is a vacancy on Penland Island, so you better watch it, Buster!"

To Clark, me, myself, you, yours, ours, my very special fishing buddy, thank you for selflessly teaching me how to fish. Not only did you supply the fishing pole, and all of the supplies necessary, but you taught me the skills to be successful should I need to find food while staying on the island. It matters not that I never actually caught a fish, we developed a very special friendship in the process. I appreciated all that you did for me. Take care of you.

To Louis: thank you for all the ways you have blessed me. Your passion in researching my condition has not gone unnoticed. I appreciate all the ways you have helped me to find new ways to get relief from my EMF. I will be forever grateful for your compassionate heart and for taking the time to share part of your day with me. You continually surprise me with your ability to think outside the box to come up with ways to help improve my situation. I am thankful for your friendship. The necklace rocks!

To Grasshopper for your friendship, supply of eggs, the romance novel, and puzzle. I am grateful to you and appreciate your friendship.

To George and Joanne, Our meeting was not by chance, it was a God connection. You both emanate love to one another and to everyone who is fortunate enough to cross your paths. I simply love the two of you. God knew I needed a retired dentist and an retired x-ray technician to help solve my root canal dilemma, not to mention two wonderful new friends. Timing is everything in life. I can't wait until we can see each other again.

To Brian, I treasured our visits at the dam. Who would have thought health issues would keep us apart. I pray for your wellness and that you remain free from electronics where your heart is concerned. You were missed for the two years we both dealt with our own health concerns, but I'm very glad to see you back walking at the dam. You touched my heart when you let me know you thought of me as your little sister. I meant it when I said "If you need to have an electronic device surgically implanted to get relief, I'll write you notes. Then send them via paper airplanes across the dam." When we can no longer stand side by side, we will find a way to communicate. You were right when you said we both needed a miracle.

To Lord Richard and Lady Lynn who never ceased to make my day special. Richard's "old and mean" demeanor loves to yell out "shark" when I'm about to dive under-water. . .which cracks me up. Your two very-well trained poodles enhanced Lady Almina's drapery. Thank you both for your continued support, friendship, playfulness, and for caring so deeply,

To Bob, we should be rivals for the part you played in invention of the cell phone, however, your friendship overrides our differences. Remember, fill yourself with God and he will give you the desires of your heart. It's a timing thing.

To Steve, we are living proof of what can be done when you put two heads together. Thank you for being willing to think outside the box to come up with a solution to minimize the EMF exposure in my house so I could walk down my hallway. You are a talented electrician and I'm proud to call you my friend. Thank you for sharing your story of Alice, the love of your life. Your story inspired me.

To the guys at the Hayesville Refuse Department: Kevin, Randy, Adam and Tim, you never flinch when I ask for a weather report. Thank you for always being available to help. When you turn off the machinery so I can approach, I consider that going way beyond the call of duty. Thank you all. You help me feel cared for and connected.

To Dan and Mary Ester: for your strong uninhibited faith, your prayers and your encouragement. Your loving prayers and friendship have made a profound impact on me. The firewood and food that you so lovingly delivered to me were put to great use. Thank you.

To Kim, you are the one that mimics an angel. I simply love you and your son, Trevor!

To Stephanie: my hero, my sister spirit-led soul mate. You get what it means to follow the spirit and do so yourself. Thank you for having my back after the incident on Penland Island. For caring enough about me to let me know when you didn't agree with my choices, but loving me anyway. For all the hours we spent assembling puzzle pieces and for being genuine and real. You totally rock! I love you, girlfriend.

To Jared and Grandfather, Haywood, you made my Christmas Eve extra special when our paths crossed. Jared, you are the only person I knew at the time that didn't think I was the joyful noise when I'm singing. Thank you for that verbal gift. God has a plan for your life, never stop following him. Haywood, you are an amazing man of God. I have so much respect for you and for the love you pour into your grandchildren. You are a blessed man.

To Gerry, God knew what you needed and exactly when you needed it. It touches my heart that you think of me as the Christmas angel. Praise Him. I'm so thankful we met.

To Dr. Rea, Trep, and staff, I learned more about wellness in the two weeks I spent at your Environmental Health Center than at any other point in my life. Thank you for embracing me, listening and hearing, and pointing me in the right direction on my wellness path. I am forever grateful to you all for giving me the tools I needed to move forward.

To Dr. Kordonowy, for respecting my disability even though you had never heard of such a condition. For turning off the lights to shield me from the pain they caused and using your hands the old-fashioned way to perform chiropractic adjustments on me when all of your other patients had graduated to electronic technology. To consulting with your doctor friend, who confided in you that she too had a patient in the next room claiming intense sensitivity to lighting and not knowing what to do with her either. To educating me on EMF Protect—a supplement to curb the effects. Thank you. You are missed.

To Health N Harmony, the visits to your office seemed like I was making a home visit, not going to a doctor's appointment. Thank you all for outpouring of love and prayers into me along with the IV treatments.

To Attorney Leah Broker, thank you for believing in me and seeing me through the process. You helped me keep my dignity.

To the judge who ruled in my favor at my social security hearing. Just hearing the words, "She is disabled from what she is trained to do," took the wind out of my sails. I felt deflated. It's as if a lifetime of working to groom myself for corporate was vanished with one sentence. Without your ruling, I would have lost all hope to support and feed myself. May God bless you abundantly!

To Ian Drobka, at the Pisquah Inn, for exemplary customer service and hope. You displayed God's kindness through your actions. It was my pleasure to meet you.

To the Town of Hayesville for embracing me from the minute I arrived here five years ago. Gratitude starts at the top, I give thanks from the Mayor's office, on down. To Ingles Grocery store, for assigning a shopper to me. To the compassionate people at First Citizens Bank, Walgreen's, Pro Hardware, Tri-County Office Supply, and Prints Plus for diligently coming out to me as soon as I pulled into the parking lot to assist me because it wasn't safe for me to go inside the building. To Harold Parker (and the previous owners) at the Parkers Produce stand on Route 64 for turning off all fluorescent lights, fans, and electrical so I could keep my dignity and shop for myself.

To the stores in Murphy, North Carolina: Wal-Mart, Lowes, and Home Depot for assisting me outside when I could tolerate the parking lot. Your employees went above and beyond to accommodate me. Although I wasn't able to use your services very often; you never questioned my situation for a minute.

To the Hinton Center, Beth, you always went out of your way for me and that didn't go unnoticed. Bill, I still chuckle at our first meeting in the parking lot. Thank you for making a safe place for me.

To Little Joe and Betty, Billy, and Dutch, for being the first people to welcome me to the neighborhood. I love you all. You are the best neighbors and friends anyone could ask for. Thank you for having my back.

To Myrna, a very special lady, thank you for your intimate conversations, your moral support and your assessment of my wellness each time you visit. I know you are always on the run and I lovingly call you my drive-by friend, always in a hurry to get things done. But I'm ever so grateful for the time you are able to stop for a visit and the special prayers you leave behind. I love you.

To James and Robbye, Aaron and Kellsie, Phil, TJ, Dale and Brandon, for having my back in our neighborhood. I'm glad we look out for each other. I appreciate you all.

An extra special *thank you* to Phil, my newest neighbor, and talented musician; thank you for reawakening my senses via your acoustic guitar. It fills my soul to sing with music.

To the Hayesville Presbyterian Church, whose co-pastors Bob and Linda Abel have embraced me. They give so much and humbly never expect anything in return. I prayed for a church family for almost the entire two years out of society. I couldn't have found a more loving and supportive body of believers. Not only do they believe in Jesus, but they believed in me. Both pastors have had a profound effect on so many souls. I'm honored to call you both my Pastors. God is so good.

Margaret, I am grateful for our quality "girl talk" time. I love our uninterrupted moments together. Thanksgiving and Christmas were that much more special because you were with me. You fed "Deborah's Spirit" as you proudly presented me with a fabulous hand-stitched replica of the same. Your endless repairs to my attempt at knitting saved my dignity. I love you. Thank you.

Randy, 007, you totally rock! The endless hours of pleasure you have given to me and my family from the photo shoots we shared still lift me up. Thank you for going along with my shenanigans and encouraging me to dress in drag! You made a fierce Big Bad Wolf. Red adores you and Lady Almina thinks you are scandalous!

To Russ and Shirley, whom I love dearly. Russ, without you, my fire would have extinguished and the soles of my boots would diminish. Shirley, you are the reason my halo appeared, my wings sprouted and I obtained the bread of life, thank you. I couldn't have realized the "angel" without your contributions. I love spending time with the two of you—especially since Russ is always up to something. Happy face!

Vince and Mendy, for giving up your downtime to hook me up to an offline printer so I could realize my dream of writing. It doesn't matter that I can only use in short increments; bottom line is it came together. Thank you.

On occasion Pat (the town barber) or Rhonda (the church pianist, also a hair dresser), would come to my home to trim my hair. Your kindness touched me. Thank you for taking time out of your busy schedules to help me.

To Francine: a loving soul, and her son Ricky. I look forward to each and every moment we have to share. Thank you for letting me take a part in feeding the fish in the river behind your house. It is such a delight to see what appears to be one hundred, ten pound trout, challenged to get to the food first. It's an added bonus when the ducks chime in. I love our visits and I love you. I hope by now you have concluded that I am NOT crazy, just fun loving and playful.

To the Professor, for being the best friend to me that you could, despite the raw grief you were processing after the loss of your wife, the love of your life. We both needed that season of healing to move forward with our own lives. You remain on my prayer list. Despite our lack of communication, you should know that you took a piece of me with you when you left. Time has a way of healing the deepest of wounds. I pray you are well and will be forever grateful that you gave birth to my nickname, Pluck.

To John, Kay, Bill and Nancy, thank you for including me in the most magical cookout on top of the mountain. Your preparation of the site to include a huge campfire, a picnic table, a grill, and—best of all—no power lines, did not go unnoticed. That night is etched in my memory. John and Kay, thank you for providing me with two survival books. They were obviously put to good use because I'm still here. You are all special to me.

To Autumn, I wanted so badly to help you, but I could barely keep my own head above water. I'll pray for you always. Please don't let the past hinder your future. You ARE worthy. God loves you and so do I.

To Cliff and Georgine, Mary's daughter-in-love, thank you for carrying out your mother's wishes by delivering the funds she left for me to have my tooth extracted. I got much needed relief. I can still hear your mother saying, "Be Still." I miss her so much.

To Pastor Steve, thank you for grocery shopping for me with an eye for detail and a passion for quality. You are of the many reasons Ingles holds an exemplary track record for superb customer service. Above and beyond that, thank you for holding worship service in my sanctuary and for your continuous prayers. Where else in the USA can you get someone to pick up your grocery list, shop for you, deliver the goods and pray for you? You are a rarity. I love you, my brother.

To Bill, the customer service manager at Ingles: thank you for ensuring that the tradition of my grocery run remained intact. I appreciate all that you do. God Bless you, my brother.

To Penny and Ralph, for your very special friendships: thank you for going through the trouble of turning off today's modern conveniences so I could participate in the seminar so lovingly held at your home. Thank you to you and the First Free Will Baptist Church for the food ministry. You filled my life with fresh hope and my belly full with produce. I appreciate all that you have done for me.

To the prayer warriors at the Good Shepard Church. Every Tuesday, they immersed me in soaking prayer for about one year. Unfortunately the intensity of the Wi-Fi in the building discouraged me from further soaking prayer time. I've missed you all.

To Ann, Barbara, and Kay: for your endless visits and prayers. I'm still saddened by the way our story ended. I know in my heart you gave your best attempt at trying to help me. Being that my condition is so extraordinary there is simply nothing more you could have done. I trust God will heal me in His timing.

To Edwina: a walking wealth of wisdom. I treasure our paths crossing. Your vision at times stops me in my tracks. No doubt God is using you to heal many people. Thank you for continuing to be a major part of my wellness plan. I simply love you.

To the Bookmobile Coordinators, Debbie and Trudy: for working hard to supply me with books once a month. Your concern, fellowship and support, goes way beyond your jobs. You lovingly tolerated my gift for gab, sometimes being held hostage to hear my camping stories. I appreciate you both. Your hard work does not go unnoticed. Thank you.

To Bob and Rachel: for your attempts to make sense out of my surroundings with your elaborate meters and gadgets. My unusual environmental sensitivities are not easily understood. Your efforts did not go unnoticed or unappreciated. Thank you.

To Bobbie, my dam friend: I still remember the stunned look on your face when Little Red Riding Hood blessed you with a valentine. The joy and laughter that followed will be etched on my heart forever. Thank you for being a joyful friend.

To Josef—my Fabio, Teresa, Julia and Alena: you are all proof that there are no coincidences. I look forward to our new found friendships.

To Wanda, I'm so thankful that you chose the dam beach to sun on, otherwise we may not have met. Your friendship has expanded my knowledge of the world. Thank you for grounding and sharing with me on the shores of Lake Chatuge. Although our lives have gone in different directions you remain in my prayers and on my heart.

To all of the people whose lives have crossed paths with mine. We were each at those crossroads to learn from each other, share encouragement, and grow among ourselves. Although I ask forgiveness that I can't always recall your names; your faces are etched on my heart.

In my mind's eye I send prayer darts, a fireball of love and light to each and every one of you. I recognize we all have different life experiences and needs. We all heal in and on our own timing. I simply want to help move the healing process along if possible by offering an ear, my love and support.

To all of the dogs at the dam that make for a daily dog parade, you fill me with abundant joy.

In memory of Eva, my girlfriend in a dog suit, I miss our quiet time together.

In memory of Klepto: the coolest, funniest, most protective dog that I had the pleasure of loving. I miss you. I will always miss you.

I openly receive and happily embrace all of the blessing that have been poured out onto me. The real joy comes alive in me as I pay those blessings forward. That old saying holds true, "It is better to give than to receive."

God Bless you and yours.

Wellness Resources

Books
Chemical & Electrical Hypersensitivity
A Sufferer's Memoir
By Jerry Evans

Curing Electromagnetic Hypersensitivity
By Steven Magee

Earthing
By Clinton Ober, Stephen T. Sinatra, M.D., Martin Zucker

Jesus Calling
By Sarah Young

Jesus Always
By Sarah Young

Joni
By Joni Eareckson Tada

Less Toxic Alternatives
By Carolyn Gorman

98.6 The Art of Keeping Your Ass Alive!
By Cody Lundin

The Invisible Rainbow
A History of Electricity and Life
By Arthur Firstenberg

The Woman's Study Bible
NKJV New King James Version

When God Weeps
By Joni Eareckson Tada and Steven Estes

Cellular Phone Task Force
P.O. Box 6216   phone: 505-471-0129
Santa Fe, NM 87502   info@cellphonetaskforce.org

Clinic
Environmental Health Center   Phone: 214-368-4132
8345 Walnut Hill Lane   Fax: 214-691-8432
Suite 220
Dallas, Texas 75231   Store: 1-800-428-2343

Lehman's – Non-electric items
289 Kurzen Rd   Phone: 800-438-5346
Dalton, OH 44618

Life Force Therapy
Elaine Muller, RN, HN-BC   ElaineMuellerRN@gmail.com
Holistic Nurse - Board Certified
Practitioner in Jin Shin Jyutsu
Cranial Sacral
Energy Balancing

Photography
R. A. Bond   007Traveler@GMail.com

Products

Less EMF Inc.
The EMF Safety Superstore
776B Watervliet Shaker Road
Latham, New York 12110

Phone: 1-518-608-6479
Fax: 1-309-422-4355
Store: 1-888-LESS-EMF
www.lessemf.com

Sauna

Heavenly Heat
P.O. Box 2892
Crested Butte, Colorado 81224

1-800-697-2862

Wellness Coach

Kathleen A. Rehling
Holistic Health & Wellness
Educator & Practitioner in
Meditation, Yoga
Medical Qigong
Energy Medicine

Phone: 912-222-3996
Kathyrehling1@hotmail.com

I invite you to fill out this form, then pass this book along after you have finished reading it. . . It will be your contribution to bring awareness to EMF. Thank you. God Bless you.

Name	City, State	Country

Please cut out this page once filled and mail to: Pluck, P.O. Box 1062, Hayesville, NC 28904. The author would love to see where the book has traveled.

CPSIA information can be obtained
at www.ICGtesting.com
Printed in the USA
BVHW081501270519
549348BV00014B/729/P

9 781545 649619